A JOURNEY FROM SICILY

TONY MANERA

CONTENTS

INTRODUCTION

"Do what you can, with what you've got, where you are" (Squire Bill Widener; Widener's Valley, Virginia)

Why did I write these memoirs? Obviously, I hope that my life story will be of sufficient interest to justify the reader's investment of time in reading it. But there is more to this work than a simple narrative of the events that have shaped my peripatetic life journey. There are several examples of important lessons learned by just doing what I could, with what I had, wherever I found myself. Perhaps these lessons will be of some value to readers of this work.

I also share my perspective on several important public policy issues. That perspective is framed by my Canadian identity, but hopefully will also resonate with non-Canadian readers, especially Americans and Italians. That's because, as will become evident in the material that follows, Italy is the country of my birth, and I value greatly my Italian heritage. Similarly, the US has played an extremely important role in my life, for which I shall always be grateful. In the end, however, I am Canadian by choice and take great pride in having made what has turned out to be the right path for me and my family.

Many of the issues that I will be addressing are of a general nature, relevant to people of any nationality. Others will be primarily of interest to Canadians. Included in this category are

1

my association with the Canadian Broadcasting Corporation.[1]

While the CBC receives the bulk of its funding from a Parliamentary grant, it is not a state broadcaster. A state broadcaster functions as an arm of the government, which exercises control of the organization and its programming. To insulate it from political interference, the CBC has an arm's length relationship with the government. This independence is what gives credibility to the CBC in key areas such as news and current affairs and remains an essential element of the role it is expected to play. Nevertheless, given that the CBC is dependent on the federal government for the bulk of its budget and for many other decisions that affect the corporation, there is always a risk of political interference. The challenge is how to ensure the CBC's independence while holding it accountable for its use of taxpayer funds.

Another issue of particular interest to Canadians is that of national unity. Other countries, of course, have their own unity problems. Perhaps the Canadian experience, which I address in this work, will be of value to them.

Readers are invited to reflect on the topics I raise and reach their own conclusions. They may or may not agree with my views, all of which are the results of personal experiences, but if my thoughts inspire deeper reflection, then this work will have been worthwhile.

Finally, life would be rather dull if we only thought about serious stuff, hence I have included several anecdotes that readers may find interesting, amusing or both.

Canada and the US are countries built by immigrants and their descendants. Over one hundred years ago, in 1913, when Canada's population was around seven million, 400,000 immigrants were admitted. Today, with a population of 35 million, we admit fewer than 300,000. In fact, without immigration, Canada`s total population would decline, posing significant demographic and economic challenges. One of the myths of our time is that immigrants take jobs away from Canadians (or Americans in the US.) While this may be true in some cases, immigrants also create jobs. In the long run, a country like Canada, with one of the lowest population densities on the planet, could support a much larger population than it does at present.

Of course, today's economy is much different than it was in 1913. A 21st-century immigration policy needs to be tailored to the knowledge-based economy of the future. We also must work harder to eliminate barriers that prevent immigrants from fully employing the skills that they already possess. All of this is doable, if we can muster the political will and leadership.

Having arrived in Canada from my native country of Italy at the age of eleven, I can identify with the challenges that more recently admitted immigrants must face. Leaving one's native land hoping to build a better life for themselves and their families is an experience fraught with uncertainty and sometimes disappointment. Nevertheless, the potential for success is real. It involves hard work, perseverance, willingness to take risks and to seize opportunities as they present themselves. By reading about my experiences, new immigrants may pick up some ideas that will assist them in making the transition to life in the new country.

Of equal importance, those of us who were either born in Canada or the US or have become naturalized citizens, should be sensitive to the difficulties faced by new arrivals. We should welcome them and assist them in every way we can. But this is a two-way street. Immigrants must be prepared to make adjustments of their own.

Recently, there has been much debate about "Canadian values." The debate has often been unnecessarily divisive and could become more so in the future. The key point is that the single most important value that applies to both the US and Canada is respect for the rule of law. Our laws provide a very generous range of freedoms for all. Immigrants can retain as much of their culture and traditions as they want, as long as the law is observed. Once they become citizens, they will have the opportunity to participate in elections and hence influence legislation.

It's been more than sixty-five years since my departure from Italy, my native land. My love of the Italian language, food, music, art and literature has not been dimmed by the passage of time. And, while I identify myself as Canadian, I also owe a great deal to, and have much affection for the American people, whose influence on my professional and personal development has been immensely valuable.

Neither my Italian heritage, nor my American education, living and work experiences, all of which I value very highly, pose any conflict with my Canadian identity, commitment and loyalty. Despite my admiration for the American people, I can think of no country other than Canada in which I would rather live. Canada is the country that enabled my parents and me to escape the poverty of Sicily, giving us the opportunity to build a better life for ourselves. Canada is also the country to which I decided to permanently return after spending several years in the USA.

Despite all the vicissitudes of life, and some tough spots along the way, mine has been and continues to be, a happy life. That is due in large measure to the love and affection of my family and friends, and to the support and encouragement of colleagues throughout my working career.

I wish to acknowledge with great appreciation the important contribution of several individuals who were kind enough to review and critique this work. A brief but incomplete list must include my former CBC colleague Paul Gaffney, the late former CBC board member Bill Neville, former Ottawa Hospital board member Kay Stanley and Professor Andrew Cohen from the School of Journalism at Carleton University.

Tony Manera

Ottawa, Canada - 2017

ANCIENT HISTORY

I have chosen a picture of an obviously tired Sicilian boy taken sometime during the early part of the 20th century to illustrate these memoirs.

Although the boy's identity is unknown to me, this plaintive image conveys a sense of the misery and hopelessness that prevailed throughout Sicily (Italy) in the early 1900's. It could easily have been a picture of my father, who was sent to work picking grapes at the age of nine, shoeless and illiterate. It could also be the picture of a boy getting ready to board a ship that would take him across the Atlantic Ocean to what many believed to be the promised land, America. Indeed, several of my ancestors escaped the poverty of Sicily to build a better life for themselves and their families in the USA throughout the first quarter of the twentieth century. Eventually I would come to know some of these relatives and their descendants, and one of them would play a key role in making it possible for my parents and me to emigrate to Canada, a story that I will tell in the first chapter.

CHAPTER ONE

There was nothing remarkable about Ficarra, a small Sicilian mountain village in the province of Messina, where I was born on May 11, 1940, one month before Italy entered World War II. Like most other villages, its main features were a church, a main square (called "Piazza"), and an unpaved road that led into and out of town. The piazza was home to a monument commemorating the local men who had died during World War I, a water fountain, and some stores. There were also several chairs and tables where men sat to play cards, drink espresso coffee and carry on sometimes heated conversations about soccer, politics and whatever else might be happening elsewhere. Most people earned a living by working on nearby farms, harvesting wheat, picking olives, grapes, various kinds of nuts and fruits, depending on the season.

Aside from being breast-fed by my mother Francesca, I have few if any direct recollections from the first two years of my life. Hence any events from that period that I describe here are based on conversations that I had with my parents when I became older.

My mother and I lived in a small one room house, without any heat, electricity or indoor plumbing. Nearby were my paternal grandparents and other relatives. My grandfather Sebastiano, a short and wiry man, had been injured in World War I, requiring him to walk with a cane. Although illiterate[2], he was very good at basic arithmetic, able to mentally calculate how much people owed him for each kilogram of charcoal that he sold. There were no coal mines in Sicily. Charcoal was produced by burning wood in pits covered with soil to block air from entering. It took several days for the slow burning wood to change into charcoal. My grandfather also repaired broken pots, dishes, chairs, umbrellas and whatever else was brought to the makeshift workshop on the ground floor of his house. Just about everything was recycled in those days, providing a steady stream of useful work for handy people like him.

At some point, I learned about my father Sebastiano[3], whose picture was prominently displayed in our house. He was at war, having been conscripted in preparation for war when I was 17 days old. Initially, my parents were able to communicate by mail, but eventually no more correspondence could be exchanged. My mother did not know whether her husband was dead or alive. For a while she received a small allowance from the government, but eventually that stopped and she managed with help from her family and by doing seasonal farm work.

My mother had several brothers who worked the family farm in the countryside. They supplied her with fruits, vegetables, oil, eggs and flour. She travelled to the farm literally on foot, removing her shoes at the edge of town, hiding them under a bush and picking them up on the way back. This way her shoes did not wear out as fast. Carrying me in her arms (until I was old enough to walk,) she picked up these supplies and brought them to our home. Because food was strictly rationed during the war, there were inspectors along the way who would check what she was carrying. She would have to share some of her provisions with them to get through.

As I became older, I noticed that, whenever she walked in town, my mother kept a pair of large sharp scissors in her purse and never made eye contact with any male passerby who was not a relative. At the time I did not understand her behaviour, but later realized that, with her husband at war, even a fleeting glance at a man could be misunderstood. The scissors were for protection against any would be lothario.

10

During the Allied invasion of Sicily in 1943, German soldiers were retreating towards the mainland and some of them passed through our area. (A picture of me taken about that time is shown at left.) We fled to the countryside, hiding in a barn, but when the Germans came through, they did not harm us. I recall this event very clearly, as well as the sight and smell of burning jeeps. All children were warned against picking up unknown objects found outdoors, as they could be booby-trapped. One of my father's brothers, who was about fifteen years old at the time, picked one these objects, which exploded, resulting in the loss of four of his fingers. I also picked up something I shouldn't have. It was a rusted blade lying in the rubble. I tried to impress my cousin by pretending to shave. I tested the blade on my arm first, resulting in a deep cut. My mother, who was immediately called, cleaned and dressed the wound. It eventually healed, leaving a large scar which remains visible to this day.

My paternal great-grandmother lived nearby. She raised chickens. I would go to see her every morning and she would give me an egg. One day, a bomb fell on her house, completely destroying it. Fortunately, neither she nor I were in the house at the time, and thus escaped unharmed. The shock wave from this bomb was so powerful that it twisted the iron railing on our own balcony! This was my exposure to war, and while I did not fully understand what was going on, it was a very frightening experience for a three year old boy.

My father had been sent to fight in Libya, which was then an Italian colony. At first he and his fellow soldiers were committed to fight, having been brainwashed by Italian dictator Benito Mussolini's propaganda. But the fighting spirit did not last long.

In March 1943 the Italian soldiers in Libya were surrounded by vastly superior Allied forces. Clearly overwhelmed, my father's company surrendered and all Italian soldiers were taken prisoners by the Americans. They travelled by bus to Algeria where they boarded a ship that would take them across the Atlantic Ocean to the USA as prisoners of war (POWs). The ship was in a convoy of 180 other ships, two of which were sunk by German submarines. My father and his fellow prisoners arrived safely in New York and then travelled by train for four days to Phoenix, Arizona.

While in Phoenix, the Italian war prisoners were initially fed American style food, but they soon suggested to their American captors that there were several very good Italian chefs among the prisoners and they would be happy to cook Italian style meals if they were provided with the ingredients. The Americans readily agreed and soon joined the Italian POWs eating Italian food.

During this time my father neither received nor could send mail. He and his compatriots were very worried about their families. Just as my mother didn't know whether her husband was dead or alive, he didn't know anything about our situation in Sicily either. He knew that the Allies had invaded Italy and that heavy bombing and fighting had taken place. We could have been killed or taken prisoners. Given such anxiety, he yearned for a spark of hope, and when one of the other prisoners spoke to him about the Bible and the Evangelical faith, my father found that hope. As he read[4] more of the Bible, he became convinced that Roman Catholicism did not have the answers to his spiritual needs and he accepted the new faith.

This was quite a remarkable event. Nearly all Italians were nominally Roman Catholics, and the Catholic Church exerted a strong influence in their daily lives. However, being Catholic in Italy was a passive condition. People were Catholic not by deliberate choice, but because their parents and ancestors had been Catholic. One observed the rituals of Catholicism, such as baptism, confirmation, attending mass, confession, and participating in the many processions in honour of various saints, because of tradition. Adopting the Evangelical faith, on the other hand, was an active commitment. It was often viewed in the same light as the betrayal of one's country. Hence something very profound, at a spiritual level, had to happen for such a conversion to take place. My father experienced this phenomenon, which I would observe on several other occasions later on.

In May 1944, the Americans tried to convince their Italian prisoners to switch sides and to fight for the Allies. The war was still raging in Europe and the bottom half of Italy had joined the Allies, while the upper half was still controlled by the Fascists under Mussolini. My father and most of the other prisoners refused. For two weeks, the Americans placed them on bread and water rations and forced them to sleep outdoors on the ground with only a blanket as cover. These efforts at coercing the Italian POWs to collaborate failed, and the Americans finally gave up.

Except for the foregoing incident, which pales when compared to the much harsher treatment meted out to POWs held by other countries, the Americans treated their prisoners with dignity and respect. They were well fed and housed and my father put on weight. In 1945 he was sent to Hawaii for the remainder of his detention. He was finally released after the end of the war, and returned to Ficarra in March 1946. I recall seeing him walk up the narrow alley where we lived, flanked by two of his brothers. I was then six years old.

My mother was ecstatic. A large number of people came to our small house to help us welcome my father after an absence of six years. I was very happy to see him for the first time, but also a bit apprehensive, not knowing what to expect from this new person who would now be part of my life. One of my father's brothers (Agostino) was less fortunate. He was killed in Russia, fighting a senseless war of absolutely no value to Italy, just to satisfy the hunger for conquest of two dictators, Adolf Hitler and Benito Mussolini. He was only twenty-two years old when he died, leaving behind a wife and son. His remains were returned fifty years later, so that they could be properly buried in the place of his birth.

My father spoke with my mother about his new faith, and she soon joined him. Given that both of them had been active in the Roman Catholic youth movement before the war, my mother had obviously experienced the same kind of spiritual awakening that my father had. I was too young to understand what was going on. Nevertheless, I became aware of a certain sense of opprobrium, bordering on hostility towards my parents by some of our relatives and the town in general.

Such attitudes and the fact that jobs were very scarce in Ficarra, led to my parents' decision to leave town for Palermo, the capital of Sicily. A businessman in Ficarra had promised my father a job there. The Americans had paid their POWs a small wage for the work they did, hence my father had some money and a very good American winter coat. My mother had some blankets and sheets as well as various pots and pans. Material possessions were much more valuable than money, which had become virtually worthless in the war's aftermath.

We arrived in Palermo by train in August 1946. The job that had been promised to my father failed to materialize. For the first few days we stayed in a hotel near the railroad station. It was very modest and cost very little. My father's money, however, didn't last long. After a few days we had to leave the hotel, but had no other place to stay. At the time there were many abandoned bombed out buildings in Palermo. The owners had probably died or fled. These buildings had no roof and many of the walls had crumbled. They were certainly unsafe. Without any other option, we occupied a room in one of these abandoned buildings and stayed there for a few weeks, effectively becoming squatters. The authorities either didn't know we were there or turned a blind eye, as the only other option would have been to live in the streets.

My father kept looking for work but couldn't find any. My parents were forced to sell some of their limited belongings to buy food. Soon I started going to school and we began to attend a Pentecostal Church.

One day my mother learned that the owners of a nearby pharmacy needed someone to do house cleaning for them. She offered her services and in return we had lodging, free of charge but unfit for human habitation. It consisted of a very small room under a set of stairs, with a barred window at one end. There were a counter and a sink, but no running water, electricity or heat of any kind. There was a drain in one corner of the room, into which we would dump the human waste that we produced, using the common chamber pot. In the middle of one wall there was an opening that led to a series of underground tunnels. I'm not sure about the nature of these tunnels (the building was a few hundred years old) but they were the source of numerous rats that we had to contend with. I was bitten several times during the night when the rats invaded our quarters. We became quite ruthless trapping them and then drowning them. This may appear cruel to some people, but what else could one do with rats?

My father worked off and on in construction as a labourer. He would leave the house every morning at six and look for work all day. Most of the time he would not find any. When he did, he was paid the going rate at the end of the day, which was 1250 Lire, about US$2 at the exchange rate then in effect. Had he worked a full six day week, his wages would have enabled us to live adequately. But, since he worked sporadically, money was always short. I recall a period when our diet consisted mainly of boiled potatoes, in part because they were relatively cheap, but also because they could be bought on credit. Usually, we would eat them with bread, which was a basic staple of Italian meals. On a few occasions, there wasn't enough bread to go around, but my parents always found a way to ensure that I had enough to eat. Sometimes, when we could afford it, we would have some fish, which was delicious and relatively inexpensive. Meat of any kind, however, was served very infrequently, about once a year. A well-off family living nearby had suggested to my parents that they were interested in adopting me. Their pitch was fairly straightforward. I would have plenty of food, comfortable shelter and the opportunity to pursue a good education. Needless to say, my parents would have none of this, and neither would I. No matter how poor we were, the bond between me and my parents was unbreakable. The adoption offer, although well intentioned, was a non-starter.

Meanwhile, we continued to attend the Pentecostal Church and experienced some harassment from the authorities. It seems that they couldn't understand how any Italian could be anything but

Catholic! Fortunately, we weren't prevented from practicing our faith. Other church members, on the other hand, were ostracized by their families and friends. An example of such intolerance was the experience of Elio Madonia, a university student who lived in Palermo across the street from us. His family was well off. I came to know him around 1948 when he gave me some sugar, bread and maps that I needed for my Geography class in school. Madonia had converted to the Pentecostal faith and his family had summarily disowned him. They cut off all financial help and vowed never to speak to him again. He emigrated to Canada in 1949 where he found work initially as a dishwasher in Toronto. Later, he and his family were reconciled. Through sheer hard work and persistence, he became a very successful businessman, community leader and philanthropist. Our paths have crossed on many occasions over the years and we remain good friends. Since his retirement he has used his own funds, supplemented by donations, to build and donate over one thousand houses to poor people in the Dominican Republic.

While in Palermo, I saw many examples of the power of faith to change people's lives. One particular case stands out. Salvatore Rizzo owned a small plant for the manufacture of cardboard boxes. He was a heavy drinker. When drunk he would mercilessly beat up anyone who had displeased him in some way. He was also associated with various shady characters, and feared by his own family and neighbours. Somehow, he came to attend one of our church services and was so moved that he converted to the Pentecostal faith. From then on, he was a different man. The transformation from a violent bully to a caring and devout person was so dramatic that people who had known him before couldn't believe he was the same man.

 Several missionaries from Canada and the USA visited Palermo during the time when we lived there. As soon as they learned of our extreme poverty, they took our name and address and upon their return to Canada or the USA passed the information to members of their church. These brothers and sisters would send us parcels of clothing and food as well as money. Most of them were simple labourers, with limited means, but they were willing to give to someone who had even less. We also received several CARE packages, one of which contained a fruit cake. The picture above shows me picking up one of these packages at the Palermo Post Office. Long after it had been eaten, I could still smell the delicious flavour coming out of the empty can! About fifty years later, CARE Canada used my story to solicit funds, and they raised close to one hundred thousand dollars!

Our main leisure activity in Palermo was to visit friends and other church members. We walked everywhere. In fact, I do not recall ever taking a bus or other form of transportation that required payment. Our walks would frequently take us on a road along the sea shore. On one side there was the sea, on the other long rows of buildings that had been destroyed by bombs dropped by Allied warplanes during the war. The intent was to cripple the harbour, which had strategic military value. In the distance, Mount Pellegrino provided an impressive backdrop to the city below.

During those post war years, many Americans[5] visited Palermo. While walking near the harbour, we would often see them arrive on big ships. Many brought their cars, which would be unloaded from the ships by a huge crane and then driven off. I was fascinated by these English speaking visitors. My big dream was to someday learn English and travel to New York!

Other than walking, I had few opportunities to engage in physical activities, such as sports. Stamp collecting was my hobby. I built up a fairly large collection of Italian stamps, trading with my school friends who had a similar interest. My collection, which I have retained, featured many famous Italians from the world of music, literature, science, the arts and politics. In addition to the pleasure of collecting rare stamps, this hobby provided me with an interesting perspective on Italian history. Stamps issued during Mussolini's time, for example, were used as a propaganda tool to transform Italians into a more war-like people (it didn't work!)

With no radio, or electricity, nor any money to go to movies or the theatre, we were entertained by traditional Sicilian storytellers and buskers. We lived next to a piazza, where these individuals would regale their audiences with fascinating stories of ancient battles, especially those featuring brave Sicilians rebelling against foreign occupiers. Slapstick was very popular and provided a welcome distraction from the daily struggles faced by most people. In our case, we made sure to be on our way home before the hat was passed around at the end of each performance!

We learned about what was happening outside our immediate neighbourhood by word of mouth. One of the most engaging stories making the rounds at the time was that of a notorious Sicilian bandit called Salvatore Giuliano. He had kidnapped and murdered dozens of people under the pretext of taking from the rich in order to give to the poor. Consequently, he became a folk hero. Songs were composed about this latter day Robin Hood. His exploits were rationalized by many Sicilians who could identify with his alleged mistreatment by the authorities. When he was finally killed in a gun battle with the police, all kinds of

19

conspiracy theories were promulgated. One of his closest associates was fingered as the traitor and mysteriously died by poison in jail.

There used to be a publication called "Il Faro" (The Lighthouse) that was produced by the US Italian Pentecostal Churches and sent to Italy. We would receive a copy every month at our church. It contained various articles explaining the Gospel, testimonies from people who had converted to the Pentecostal faith and news from the various missionaries who came to Italy. It also listed the names and amounts contributed by various people to sustain this publication. One month I noticed in the list of contributors a P. Manera, who had sent $5. I didn't know what the P stood for, nor who this person might be. I pointed this out to my parents and they were also curious. We wrote to the editor, enquiring about this P. Manera. It turned out that he was Paolo Manera, my father's uncle who had emigrated to the US in 1910. I'm not sure my father even knew that he had this uncle. Most amazing was the fact that Paolo Manera had also converted to the Pentecostal faith. He was, as most Sicilians of his generation, illiterate, but we managed to establish correspondence through third parties and he was delighted to learn that he had a nephew in Sicily who was also Pentecostal.

This accidental discovery turned out to be the first of many serendipitous events that would change the course of our life. Uncle Paolo sent us money even though he was retired and had been a simple labourer in the railroads. He wanted to sponsor us to emigrate to the US but there was a rigid quota that didn't allow too many Italians into the US at the time. It was much easier to emigrate to Canada, and we thought that it could be a stepping stone to join uncle Paolo in the US at a later time. With assistance from members of the Italian Pentecostal church in Montreal, my father was sponsored and the long process of getting a visa to emigrate to Canada began.

I did rather well at school, skipping grades 2 and 4. I also made several close friends along the way. At the age of 10, I was admitted to the Ginnasio (the academic high school stream). I became class president and earned the highest grades in most subjects, especially Latin. When my father didn't have enough money to buy a Latin dictionary for me, he sold one pair of his shoes to pay for it! I still have that dictionary, because of its strong sentimental value. Although history was included in the curriculum, it was mainly ancient Greek and Roman history, with Italian history limited to its struggle to be united in 1860 and the First World War, when Italy had been on the winning side. There was no mention of World War II, which had recently ended in Italy's defeat.

I also won a prize of 10,000 lire (at the time, this was about what my father could earn for seven days' work) for being the top student in my school. The prize was funded by the US Government. It came with a book about Italy (which I still have) that stressed the important role the US had played in its reconstruction after the War (the Marshall Plan.)

By and large, school was a pleasant experience. Although "Religion" was one of the subjects that all students were required to take, I was exempted without any objection from the Roman Catholic priest who taught the course. I was simply allowed to leave the classroom during the "Religion" period and sit on a chair in the hall outside, where I passed the time doing homework. There was no hostility from the other students, who probably wished that they could have been exempted from the Religion course too!

In October 1950 my father finally received his immigrant visa and left for Canada. My mother and I were to follow later, once my father had saved some of the funds required for our voyage to Canada (uncle Paolo supplied the rest).

By 1951 my father had established himself in Montreal. He worked for the railroad, doing heavy work for 60 hours a week, earning 60 cents an hour. It was a tough life, especially during the harsh winter, but infinitely better than what he had left in Sicily.

It was now time for my mother and me to join my father in Canada. I was eleven years old. We travelled to Rome for a medical examination and an interview for a visa at the Canadian Consulate. There we stayed at the home of the pastor of the local Pentecostal Church.[6]

We were granted an immigrant visa and returned to Palermo, where we got ready to sail for Canada in June 1951. Most of my classmates came to the harbour to see me off. A few brought going away gifts for me, including books and several rare stamps to add to my collection. It was a very moving experience to see them waving at me as the ship pulled away from its dock towards the open sea. I was really looking forward to seeing my father again and to live in Canada, the promised land.

Our time in Palermo was certainly difficult. We lived in poverty, with uncertain prospects for the future. But my parents never gave up hope, even during the darkest days of our lives. And as soon as we knew that we could emigrate, we were very happy. I think that as long as there is hope, one can endure extreme hardship. What sustained us was our faith, and the fellowship of other church members. It was during this period that I first learned the value of persistence and the work ethic. My parents taught me by example.

Their love and concern for my well-being gave me great comfort and were to guide my own actions in the years to come.

.

CHAPTER TWO

After ten days at sea, with a brief stop-over in Lisbon (Portugal), my first glimpse of Canada on June 20, 1951, was of the hills of Nova Scotia. Upon landing in Halifax at Pier 21, where most immigrants arrived, my mother and I were processed and officially admitted to Canada. We then boarded a train for the twenty-four hour trip to Montreal. The train trip was not very pleasant. There were no sleeping berths and the air was very stuffy. At any rate, we arrived in Montreal, where my father welcomed us at the train station. We were tired but happy. At last, our small family was reunited in Canada!

Upon our arrival in Montreal, my father told my mother and me that we had been invited to a reception. We were quite tired, and wanted very badly to rest, and in no mood to spend hours visiting. But my father insisted and so we went to a flat where about fifteen people from the Italian Pentecostal Church were waiting to welcome us to Canada.

The reception was tiring but very pleasant and exciting. The flat in which it took place looked gorgeous to my mother and me. It had a big kitchen, with plenty of cupboards, an electric cooking stove, refrigerator, and an oil furnace. It also had a bedroom, living room and bathroom.

As the evening went on, people began to leave. Pretty soon everyone was gone and we were left alone. My mother couldn't understand what was happening. Who were our hosts who lived in this flat? When would we be leaving for our own place? Finally my father told us that this was our place. We couldn't believe it. By today's standards it was a very modest abode. Compared to

what we had left in Sicily, however, it was a palace! We were overwhelmed.

We quickly settled into our new home. Dad was now working in a chocolate factory. It paid more than the railway job, and involved inside work, where he would be sheltered from the bitter winter cold to which he had been exposed during the previous year. What struck me most in those early days was that people would leave their empty milk bottles with money outside their door and the milkman would leave a full bottle of milk in their place. Also, mailboxes were outside each house's entrance and the mailman would actually put mail in them. In our Palermo neighbourhood, neither the empty milk bottle with money, nor the milk, nor the mail, would last five minutes before they would be stolen! Canadians were a surprisingly trusting people! A picture of my first day in Montreal is shown above.

Our family attended the Fabre Street Italian church and made many friends there. There were several recent immigrants from Italy and they, along with others who had immigrated many years earlier, provided a very valuable support network.

During those early days, the Pentecostal church was more of a grass-roots movement than an organized religion. The fundamental belief was that the Bible was the word of God, and while the Roman Catholic hierarchy discouraged its adherents from reading the Bible (perhaps because it would lead them to question some of the church's doctrines), the Pentecostal faith drew its inspiration from a literal interpretation of the Bible. This inevitably led to some schisms, due to different interpretations of the actual text. Still, the faith was powerful and real. The pastor was a volunteer, who received no compensation (except for a modest rent free apartment and donations from church members). Each service featured the singing of hymns, prayers, testimonies from individuals who wanted to share their experiences with the congregation, and a sermon. The sermon could be delivered by any church member who felt inspired to do so.

Soon after our arrival from Italy, I gave my testimony in church, as did my parents and other recent arrivals. This led to an invitation for me to preach the sermon during one of the regular services. What began as a one-time event was repeated on several other occasions, which was highly unusual for an eleven year old boy. After each service when I preached, members of the church would shake my hand and give me some money. It was generally one or two dollars but sometimes there would be five and even ten dollar bills. I studied the Bible a lot and had a strong and sincere faith that moved many people. Over the next three years (until I was about fourteen), I preached in all the Pentecostal churches in Montreal (Italian, English and French), as well as in Hamilton, Toronto, Rochester and Philadelphia, accompanied either by my father or mother. Meanwhile, I also edited and published a regular Church bulletin, based on research in various used books about the Bible that I bought at the Salvation Army bookstore in Montreal.

It should be pointed out that, neither in Italy, Canada, or the US was the Pentecostal church engaged in any political activities. Individuals, of course, would have political opinions. However, the church stayed completely out of politics, unlike certain Evangelical denominations in the US that have in recent times pursued political agendas, sometimes in direct conflict with the teachings of Jesus Christ.

During our first summer in Montreal, my father's uncle Paolo came to visit us from Toledo, Ohio. He arrived in the middle of the night and we were very happy to get to know such a generous relative. He suffered from diabetes and had gone back to work after retirement to earn additional money so he could help us. During his stay in Montreal he bought for my mother her first washing machine (the old style wringer type) and for me a Royal portable typewriter, which cost him $100, a lot of money in those days. I used this typewriter for over fifty years and eventually gave it to my daughter Deborah, as a family heirloom.

September 1951 was time for me to start school. As I spoke very little English, they slotted me in Grade 5, which was appropriate for my age, but not for the level of schooling that I had already completed back in Italy. There was another student whose parents were Italian, and he was assigned as a "translator" to me, but he spoke a different dialect, and despite his good intentions, I understood very little of what was being said!

My father's uncle Paolo died the following year, shortly before my mother gave birth to a baby girl, to be named Ester. I was very happy to have a sister, even though she kept us awake most nights.

In the Fall of 1952 I was allowed into Grade 8 at the newly built Rosemount High School, after arguing that, having completed the first year of high school in Italy, I should no longer be held back.

Meanwhile, I continued to be active in the church, and made new friends in the Italian community. My closest friend was Vincenzo Bonfà, who came from Italy about a year after my arrival in Montreal. He and I, along with other recently arrived boys from

Italy, spent a lot of time together. When we went out we were often taunted and called names by gang members and would sometimes get beaten up. Our favourite recreational activity was to rent bicycles and ride around town when the weather allowed it. The photo below shows me with two of my close friends.

In the summer of 1953 I landed my first job, in a clothing store. The owner, who was Jewish, hired me because I spoke Italian and this was rapidly becoming an all Italian neighbourhood. I worked long hours and was too timid to ask how much I would be paid. Toward the end of the second week, I finally found the nerve to ask, and was told by the owner that the pay was $9 per (fifty hour) week. I was shocked. It was raw exploitation. Someone told me that he took advantage of people because he was Jewish, and that's  what Jews did. I had never heard this and did not accept that all Jews would behave this way. In fact, in Italy, I had never observed a case of anti-Semitism[7], which doesn't mean that it didn't exist. Later I observed numerous cases of anti-Semitism in Canada and in the US. But my own experiences with Jewish people were entirely positive and I'm glad not to have succumbed to the prejudice that was quite common in certain quarters. Nevertheless, this bad experience taught me to ensure that the issue of salary was settled before undertaking any job in the future.

My next summer job was in a button factory at a salary of $16 per week, a vast improvement over my earlier experience! On the second day, one of the other workers told me that the boss had just fired someone for some minor infraction. Even though my English was improving rapidly, there were still some critical gaps in my grasp of the language, one of which was not knowing what it meant to be fired. I thought it meant that the boss had shot this worker! This really scared me. I never went back to work there, not even to collect my pay. I felt it would be too dangerous! Later someone explained to me that getting fired did not mean getting shot. At any rate, making buttons was not my cup of tea. I mention this true story as an example of the many handicaps that immigrants have to overcome.

A few months after starting Grade 9, I made a key decision that would have significant consequences for the rest of my life. Against my parents' wishes, and the legal requirement to attend school up to the age of fourteen, I stopped going to classes and began to work full time in the office of a construction company. My duties included some bookkeeping, typing letters and filing documents. The pay was $20 per week. In accordance with custom, my pay was turned over to my father, who let me have a small allowance. To overcome my parents' objections, I enrolled in a high school correspondence course, but never completed it.

Conventional wisdom suggested that quitting school at the age of 13 was a bad idea, but not uncommon in the case of immigrant children. I would not advise a young person to follow my example in this regard. There were several factors at play. Bullying by bigger boys at school was certainly one of them. And I was also struggling academically, which was unusual for me, given my superior school performance back in Italy. My still imperfect command of the English language probably contributed to my poor performance. I was also beginning to develop a strong and independent will that, for better or worse, was to become a defining attribute of my personality and character. Whatever my reasoning at the time, the die was cast.

I was very homesick for Italy for several years, and would dream about being back there, only to wake up to the reality that it was just another dream! In fact, a majority of my fellow immigrants planned to save enough money to go back to Italy and live off the interest or open up a small business. The magic number was $10,000 which, given the exchange rate at the time, represented a substantial amount of money in Italy. But few immigrants ever went back. Those who did weren't as happy in Italy as they thought they would be and most returned to Canada. After a few years one only remembers the good things; one has to go back to experience the more unpleasant aspects of life there.

Most Italian immigrants stuck together. This was both good and bad. It was good in the short term because of the support that we gave each other, but bad in the longer term because it delayed their integration into the broader Canadian society. Canada was a wonderful country, but its languages, culture, climate and customs were alien to us, and the adjustment was not easy. It was especially difficult for people like me, who were teenagers. That is the most difficult age to make such a drastic change in one's life. But it was also difficult for adults, who found it harder to learn a new language. Many housewives never learned English or French. Even some men, who worked outside the home, did not learn either language, because they worked and lived in an almost all Italian neighbourhood, and all their coworkers were also Italian. As time went on, there would be local Italian language newspapers, radio and television programs as well. That was not the case with my parents. My father's English certainly wasn't polished, but he could manage quite nicely. Even my mother, who stayed home, learned enough English (and some French) to get by.[8]

After mastering the English language, I held classes in my basement for several of my Italian friends, teaching them basic English. I also completed income tax returns for many recently arrived immigrants, without expecting any payment. The one exception was my Italian barber, whose tax returns were more complicated and time consuming. I suggested to him that some compensation was in order, hoping that he might give me free haircuts. Instead, he offered me access to TV in his home. I accepted and quickly became fascinated with this new contraption, which was absolutely incomprehensible to me. I became a fan of *La Famille Plouffe*, a very popular television program broadcast by Radio-Canada, the French language network of the Canadian Broadcasting Corporation.[9]

Watching television, engaging as it was, nevertheless remained an occasional treat, since we did not own a set. Bicycle riding was my main recreational activity. As soon as I had saved enough money, I bought a beautiful aluminum 10 speed Torpado racing bike, imported from Italy. It cost $125, which was a lot of money in those days, but was amply rewarded by the many pleasant hours spent riding it with my friends.

In 1954 I quit my job at the construction company and began to work as an office boy with the House of Seagram in downtown Montreal. The job paid $90 a month. I usually rode my bike to work, at least in summer. I was pretty reckless, hitting very high speeds on steep slopes, trying to go as fast as the cars! At Seagram's I first worked in the shipping department, sending parcels of various gifts to important customers. One of the gifts that would be sent out was a book commissioned by the House of Seagram called "Canada", by Stephen Leacock[10]. It was my first exposure to Canadian history that I actually found interesting. It paved the way for my subsequent interest in Canadian books, especially those written by Pierre Berton[11], who made Canadian history come alive for me. Unfortunately, Leacock also expressed the opinion that immigration to Canada from Mediterranean countries (such as Italy) should be curtailed in favour of people from the Northern parts of Europe. I took offense at this idea, but I suppose it was a point of view not uncommon at the time.

The pay at Seagram's was not that great but the work was pleasant enough. Eventually I was transferred to the advertising department where I was treated very well by my bosses and colleagues. I would often do errands (get coffee or whatever) for the company founder, Samuel Bronfman, his brother Allan or his sons, Edgar and Edward, who were Jewish. They were all very kind to me, a sharp contrast with my earlier experience working for a Jewish store owner.

While at Seagram's, I got to know Bob Sabloff, an advertising manager who was particularly helpful to me. Although I lost contact with the Seagram people after 1955 when I left the company, I was able to locate Bob Sabloff in 1995 through a mutual friend, Victor Goldbloom (Canada's Official Languages Commissioner at the time) and we had a lovely dinner at Goldbloom's house in Westmount. He and I had worked well together during my time at the CBC and also shared a love of opera. It was really good to see Bob Sabloff again after forty years!

In 1955 I quit Seagram's, and after a short stint as a page boy at the Montreal Stock Exchange, managed to get hired as a check clerk with Canadian Pacific Telegraphs. The pay was $145 per month, a substantial increase from what I had been earning until then. I soon applied for a promotion to a junior clerk position and was successful. This had nothing to do with my performance. Promotions were strictly based on seniority. The new job paid

33

$165 per month, but involved shift work. I would make up runs of telegrams for delivery, mainly by boys on bicycles or using streetcars and, in cases of more distant locations, by adults using cars.

The delivery boys were mostly French Canadian and spoke French among themselves. The supervisors were all anglophones and spoke no French at all. I recall one such supervisor telling the French speaking kids to speak English only in his presence! Such attitudes go a long way towards explaining the resentment by many French speaking Quebeckers against the then dominant anglophone minority. Although many of the people with whom I worked were francophones, they all spoke perfect English. In fact, one could live and build a successful career in Montreal at the time without ever having to speak French. If one spoke only French, however, it was most difficult to advance in business. Most immigrants preferred to learn English, which was portable in the rest of Canada and the US, therefore enhancing their economic prospects. This situation has changed dramatically over the years, and now the French language is widely spoken and is essential to live and work in Québec. In spite of this fact, many francophones in Québec continue to be worried about being assimilated, and resist any measure that would increase the use of the English language.

I had ambitions to become a full clerk, which paid $240 a month, but required many years of seniority to achieve. Auspiciously, an opportunity presented itself. Because we had to operate 24 hours a day, seven days a week, there were various shifts that had to be staffed. One such shift had been cobbled together in such a way that there was not enough time between the end of one shift and the beginning of the next to get enough sleep.[12] For this reason, nobody would bid on the job. I did, and despite my low seniority, was successful. As some of my colleagues remarked, I was the only one crazy enough to work such hours.

My successful bid for a better job is an example of the fact that many opportunities present themselves throughout our lives. The challenge is to recognize such opportunities and to seize them, even if they do not appear that attractive at first. The important thing is to get one's foot in the door, and then to take full advantage of this initial step to move to something better.

In fact, I soon realized that, by trading days off with another clerk[13], this terrible swing shift could be vastly improved to the point where I would be able to get enough sleep. The other clerk was quite willing to go along with my idea, but the CPR bureaucracy was too set in its ways to appreciate such a common sense solution. Then someone suggested that I approach the union. I was not a member, even though we had a collective agreement that covered all employees. Within one day of signing up for membership, the union had succeeded in convincing management to implement my suggested change! This experience taught me the value of unions, even though for most of my professional career, I have held management positions.

In those days I worked a lot of overtime. It was very common to put in sixteen continuous hours. Sometimes I'd work 24 hours straight, even 32! My record was 53 hours, but I must admit that, during those 53 hours, I did catch a few winks at night when nobody else was around. I put in so much overtime that, in 1957, I earned $4700; at the time, for a 17 year old kid, this was real money! My guess is that it would be equivalent to about $50,000 in today's dollars.

Eventually I applied for and was successful in obtaining an all day job in the accounting department. No more evenings or night duty for me. I could finally get enough sleep! The work, which involved organizing routes for bill collection, was quite interesting. A couple of desks away from me, a very nice French Canadian girl drew my attention. I asked her out and soon she became my steady girl-friend. We went to the movies, to parks, to restaurants and so on. Once she had me over to meet her mother, and cooked a steak dinner for me. We spoke French exclusively with each other and this helped me to improve my command of the language. We went out together for several months, but then broke up. I don't think either one of us was ready to make any type of long term commitment.

I made several friends at Canadian Pacific Telegraphs, but also experienced some hostility. A few Canadians resented immigrants like me, who were seen as too ambitious and worked too hard. Such individuals were in the minority, and my tendency to take offence at every slightly negative comment compounded the problem. Eventually I learned to shrug off such remarks and began to enjoy the kind of bantering that goes on in most workplaces.

By the time I was 16, I was drifting away from the church, which had been central to my daily life in Sicily and my early years in Montreal. In addition to the spiritual dimension, the church had provided many fellowship opportunities and shaped my values in a lasting way. It's difficult to explain, even to myself, when and how this change came about. Most teenagers go through a transition that involves challenging authority or beliefs, and I was no exception. Despite my gradual detachment from the church, however, the teachings of Jesus Christ have had and continue to have a profound influence on my life and conduct.

In 1955 I happened to be at Montreal's train station where I noticed that a man who had just arrived from Italy was having difficulty finding anyone who spoke Italian. His name was

Marcello Flammini and there was no one there to meet him. He spoke no English and very little French. I approached him and offered my assistance, for which he was very grateful. I helped him find a room for the night at the nearby Mount Royal Hotel.[14] On the following day I took him around my neighbourhood, where he found a boarding room with an Italian family. This chance encounter was another of those pivotal events that would have an important and long lasting impact on my life.

Over the next several months, Marcello and I became close friends. I helped him find a job and make the adjustment to living in Canada. He was about twelve years older than me, and very talented. He could operate and repair just about anything mechanical or electrical. Within a year of his arrival, he brought over a young woman he had known in Italy (Marcella Marchesini) and they were married in Montreal. I visited them often, along with several other Italian friends, and we spent many pleasant evenings together, eating pasta and drinking wine.

Although Marcello was quite happy and confident when he was with friends, he would often complain about his treatment at work. He felt hostility towards him by his co-workers and bosses. He thought they were trying to get rid of him and that other employees were sabotaging his work. At first I and his other friends thought that this was nothing more than hostility towards immigrants that all of us had experienced at one time or another. But later we sensed that there was more to it than that. Marcello seemed to be paranoid. We all tried to encourage him and boost his spirits. We would spend hours with him trying to make him see the bright side. When he wasn't there, we would share our concern about him but didn't know what else we could do.

Marcella had left her mother, a brother and a sister in Italy. She often spoke about them and one could tell that she missed them. She asked her sister Raffaella Marchesini to write a letter of thanks to my parents for all the help that my family had given her and Marcello in establishing themselves in Canada. Raffaella's letter arrived in December 1956, but she inadvertently addressed it to me. I replied and we soon began to exchange correspondence. Raffaella called herself Lella

for short and at the time I went by the Italian name of Nino, short for Antonino. We quickly established a strong rapport and I would look forward to her letters with great anticipation. Photos of me and Lella taken around 1957 are reproduced on this page.

There was something special about this girl. I was only 16 at the beginning of our correspondence and she was 19. We shared our hopes, our worries, our experiences. There was something magical going on. We soon fell in love with each other through this correspondence. I can't explain how this could happen, but it did. I'm sure it was real love, because it has now lasted for fifty-eight years, and is stronger than ever.

We desperately wanted to meet, but for the time being the best we could manage were a couple of long distance telephone calls. This was somewhat complicated. We had to find a suitable day and time when she could go to a special location in Rome where long distance calls could be received. I would call from the office pay phone, equipped with a large supply of quarters. Long distance calls then were far more expensive than they are now. I loved the sound of her voice and we spoke as long as my supply of quarters lasted!

We exchanged photographs and she also sent me some postcards with views of Italy that had a special coating on which recordings of Italian songs were made and could be played back on a record player. I still have those postcards!

I loved Italian music and songs, which were immensely valued and enjoyed by most immigrants. They were part of our culture, our history, our identity. Italians were prolific composers and there is a folk song for just about any circumstance, be it romantic, melancholic, or relating to the Italian landscape (sun, sea and mountains). Mothers play a central role in the life of Italians, and there are countless songs inspired by that special bond that sons and daughters have with "la mamma". Particularly moving were nostalgic songs that reminded immigrants of their native land. Bit by bit, I assembled a substantial collection of records featuring Italian folk songs, as well as operas, symphonies and concertos by many of the great composers. Although I have enjoyed a broad range of music, my greatest love has been, and continues to be, opera. The first opera record that I acquired was that of Puccini's Madama Butterfly. Since then, my collection of recorded music has vastly expanded.

By the age of 17, it was clear to me that my job at CP Telegraphs, although well paying, offered no opportunity for advancement. Further education was essential to move beyond the clerical level. I had taken some correspondence and night school courses in high school mathematics and was interested in aeronautics. There was a school in California that trained aeronautical engineering technologists. It was named Northrop Aeronautical Institute and was located in Inglewood, one of the communities that made up the Greater Los Angeles area. They accepted foreign students, and as long as one had completed certain high school level courses in mathematics, it was possible to enrol in a 12 week pre-engineering course. Upon successful completion of this course, one could proceed to the regular program.

I made some enquiries, and decided that the best thing to do would be to visit this school and find out for myself what it was all about. I was fascinated by California and the idea of going there was exciting. CP Telegraphs was part of the CP Railway organization, and employees were entitled to a certain amount of free travel each year. After obtaining a free return train ticket, I was able to visit Los Angeles during the summer of 1957. The train ride took several days and did not include a sleeping berth. There were only wooden benches. Sitting all day on those benches and sleeping on them at night was most uncomfortable! But it was a great trip nevertheless. The most interesting part was going through the Far West, which reminded me of the scenery in the many Western movies that I had seen.

Upon my arrival in Los Angeles, I checked into an inexpensive hotel downtown and proceeded to visit Northrop Aeronautical Institute. This school had been established during World War II by the Northrop Aircraft Company to train their engineers and technicians, but was now an independent institute. I was impressed by their facilities, which included several propeller airplanes, metallurgical laboratories, foundries, airframe construction and assembly areas, as well as avionics equipment of various kinds. A meeting had been previously arranged with the Registrar, who filled me in on the curriculum, the fee structure and the types of jobs that recent graduates had been able to secure. He showed me a thick binder that featured many graduates describing how their training at Northrop had enabled them to land their "dream job".

In addition to the typical high school graduate, Northrop enrolled a large number of international students as well as veterans of the Korean War.

This first trip to Los Angeles was most enjoyable. There was no smog at the time. One could see the Santa Monica mountains in the distance and the sky was perfectly blue. The sun was strong and the vegetation lush. I also visited a friend of Marcello, who had recently emigrated from Italy. His name was Giuliano Crescentini. He would later play a very important role in my life, and become one of my closest lifelong friends. Giuliano was an automobile mechanic, specializing in Fiat cars imported from Italy. The Fiat company was establishing a market for its cars in the USA and Canada, and there was a big demand for mechanics who were familiar with these cars.

After my return to Canada, I applied for admission and was accepted by Northrop Aeronautical Institute for the following year. The US Consulate in Montreal granted me a student visa. Technically, students were expected to have sufficient financial resources to support themselves while in the US on a student visa. My savings, however, were limited (about $1,000,) hence I anticipated having to work to supplement those savings.

In May 1958, I sold my car, bicycle and barbells[15]. I resigned my job, packed my belongings, said goodbye to family and friends and flew to Los Angeles. My record collection, books, record player and typewriter had already been shipped in a huge trunk to the LA train station, where I picked them up after my arrival.

My seven years in Montreal were an important period of growing up. I had arrived from Italy as a child of eleven, speaking some French that I had learned in school, but no English. The first few years were difficult, mainly because of the adjustment to a new country. Now, at the age of eighteen, I retained full command of my mother tongue, Italian, was fluent in English, and reasonably proficient in French. Bit by bit, I had overcome many challenges and become not only strong willed and independent minded, but also more self-confident and disciplined. I had learned a lot about life, people and myself.

My decision to study in California involved quitting a job that paid relatively well and was reasonably secure, at least for the foreseeable future. There was no guarantee of success in my studies. In fact, I was not in any way technically inclined and, aside from the obvious desire to improve my economic prospects, I chose to study aeronautical engineering because of the glamour associated with airplanes and rockets. The idea of living in California, with its year round sunshine and mild climate, were other factors that appealed to me.

It's axiomatic that, in life, there is no progress without risk. In my case, I felt the risk associated with the choice I'd made would be justified. My earlier decision to quit school at the age of thirteen had also been risky; and yet, so far, it had not hurt me. In fact, it had allowed me to learn valuable lessons that I might not have learned by staying in school.

CHAPTER THREE

Upon my arrival in Los Angeles in May 1958 I rented a room next to Universal Studios in North Hollywood. It was within walking distance of the Fiat dealership where Giuliano Crescentini had opened up a shop to service the vehicles that were sold there. He had agreed to employ me doing a variety of chores. His English was limited, so I did some interpreting, bookkeeping, customer billing, buying of parts, changing oil and filters, washing and delivering cars, and pretty much anything else that needed to be done. Classes didn't start until July, hence I could work for a couple of months.[16]

During this time I met William Holden and Dana Andrews, two of my favourite actors. William Holden came to pay for service to his daughter's Fiat, which I delivered to his home. He had recently completed filming of "The Bridge on the River Kwai" and was reputed to have been paid $2.5 Million for his role. He was driving a Rolls Royce or Bentley. Dana Andrews also had a car serviced and I drove him back to his home. He invited me in and showed me around his beautiful residence. I had seen the film "The Best Years of Our Lives" in which he had starred and was impressed by his kindness and friendliness.

Giuliano and his wife Pasquina were extremely supportive and generous. Giuliano paid me more than I was worth and Pasquina would often give me food and sauce for the spaghetti that I would cook for myself. My culinary skills were quite limited, and still are!

When the time came for me to obtain a California driver's licence[17], I had no money for insurance. In order to obtain a driver's licence, someone had to sponsor me, assuming financial responsibility in case of an accident. Giuliano, without hesitation, signed for me. It was extremely foolish to drive without insurance in the first place. Giuliano's act was one of great generosity. He could have been financially ruined if I caused an accident that resulted in significant damage. But that's the kind of person he was, and I have never forgotten his many acts of support and encouragement during those years in California. His friendship has endured over the years, and I have visited him on the many occasions when I have travelled to California.

My classes started in July 1958. It was virtually impossible to get around in LA without a car, so I bought a used Studebaker for $125, with payments spread out over several months. Tuition was $75 a month. Rent, food, books and school supplies were on top of that. My savings were nearly exhausted and the money that Giuliano paid me for the one day a week (every Saturday) that I was able to work for him, although very generous, was insufficient to cover all my expenses. I needed a part time job in the evenings, to enable me to go to school during the day. I was referred to the owner of an upscale Italian style coffee shop on Sunset Blvd., in the heart of Beverly Hills. "Caffe' Via Veneto" needed a bus boy. The pay was 95 cents an hour plus a share of the waiters' tips, at their discretion. The hours were 9 p.m. to 3 a.m., six days per week. After cleaning up and bringing outdoor tables in, I would finish work around 3:30 a.m. It was hard to see how I could get enough sleep, given that classes started at 7:45 a.m., but with no other option in sight, I reluctantly agreed to accept this job.

I was to clean tables when customers left and bring water and cloth napkins before new customers arrived. The place was large, and always packed. Even at 2 a.m., there would be a long line of people waiting to get in. It was not unusual to see famous movie stars waiting in line like everybody else. This was the "in place" to see and be seen in Beverly Hills. The menu included Italian espresso coffee, cappuccino, pastries, wine and liquor. There was an inside area and an outside area on the sidewalk with many additional tables. From 9 p.m. until 3 a.m., I worked without ever stopping. The trays were large and heavy. The pressure to clean tables and bring water was relentless. My income depended on the generosity of the waiters and they all expected their tables to be cleared and ready for new customers as quickly as possible. What made my job somewhat bearable was the constant music background that featured many of my favourite Italian songs. For the customers, this provided a more authentic Italian experience; for me it represented a strong emotional connection with my native land.

By closing time, I was unbelievably tired. After cleaning up, around 3:30 a.m., my knees ached so much that pushing down the clutch pedal in my car was extremely painful. Still, I would manage to drive home and get to bed around 4 a.m. Classes started at 7:45 a.m. and ended at 3:15 p.m. I would then rush home, do homework and get some sleep, setting the alarm for 8:30 p.m, just in time to get to work by 9 p.m. Needless to say, there was not enough time to do proper homework and get enough sleep.

I had been skinny throughout my teenage years, but during the time at Caffé Via Veneto I became thinner and was often dizzy. After a couple of months, it was obvious that I couldn't keep this up much longer.

As it happened, fate came to my rescue. One night, when things had been particularly hectic, the owner asked to see me at the end of the shift. When we met, he told me that I had been too slow that night and fired me on the spot.[18] I tried to explain that this had been an unusually busy night, but he would not budge. The following day I began looking for another job.

There were a couple of interesting experiences while working as a bus boy at Caffe' Via Veneto. Once I accidentally spilled some ice and water on Anthony Quinn. He was also one of my favourite actors. Quinn was most understanding and courteous. I apologized profusely, but Quinn told me and the owner that there was no need to apologize; it had been an accident. Another experience with a famous movie star was not as pleasant. One night Zsa Zsa Gabor came in with a bunch of other people. She immediately complained that the glass of water I had put in front of her was dirty. The glass looked clean to me, but one didn't argue with a customer. I apologized and returned with a freshly washed glass. She said this glass was also dirty. Again, it looked clean to me. I went back to the dishwasher and asked him to do a special job of washing another glass and closely inspected it before delivering it to her table. This time she said nothing. Abusing the help seemed to give her pleasure. Many years later, it was reported that she had been fined for abusing a servant. Later still, I read that she had received another heavy fine for slapping a policeman!

Through a mutual friend of Giuliano, I was able to find a job as a waiter at "Nina's Little Italy", an Italian restaurant in Canoga Park. The owners were Vittorio Belvedere, whom everybody called Ricky, and his partner Cathy Salvadore. Recently divorced, they eventually married each other. The pay was $1 per hour plus tips. Ricky, who came from Palermo, asked me whether I spoke good English. After I assured him that I did, he told me to show up the following evening at about quarter to five, so that I could get the required training to start work as a waiter at 5 p.m. Fifteen minutes of training has to be the shortest course I have ever taken!

A waiter could earn more than a bus boy; as it turned out I would average $2 per hour in tips, for a total of $3 per hour, which was not bad in 1958.[19] The hours were somewhat better than at Caffé Via Veneto but the distance from home was greater. Given my bookkeeping experience, I also kept the books for Nina's Little Italy and did their income tax returns. One of my acquaintances who had recently arrived from Italy expressed surprise that I was working as a waiter while studying engineering. He was from the old school, where certain jobs are considered beneath someone who is or aspires to become a professional. I thought it a rather quaint notion. For me, serving customers in a restaurant was nothing to be ashamed of. It was good, honest, hard work and it paid the bills.

Meanwhile, Lella and I continued our correspondence. Her sister Marcella had sponsored her to emigrate to Canada and I planned to meet her in Montreal. I had taken the fall quarter off from my studies in anticipation of her arrival. My flight from LA was a bit late arriving in New York, where I was scheduled to take a connecting flight to Montreal. As soon as the airplane landed, I ran towards the exit, asking the stewardess[20] to please let me off first as I was going to get married and I didn't want to miss my flight to Montreal. All the other passengers heard my plea, and burst into a round of applause!

In Montreal, I stayed with my parents. They and my sister Ester were happy to see me after an absence of six months and so was I to see them. Needless to say, my parents were not too thrilled by the prospect of my marriage. Neither were Lella's mother and sister Marcella. Why would Lella want to marry an eighteen year old Sicilian Protestant (I am not sure which of these two factors was worse in their mind), who had no money nor a steady job? Good question!

At any rate, Lella arrived at Montreal's Dorval airport on October 24, 1958. It had been a long flight, about eighteen hours, including stops in Paris and Gander, Newfoundland, where she was formally admitted as a permanent resident of Canada. Throughout her voyage, she had been sitting next to a fellow who had taken a romantic interest in her, practically proposing to marry her and insisting that she meet him later at some designated place in Montreal. I hope he isn't still waiting!

As Lella and I embraced each other for the first time, I found the sound of her voice, already familiar from our telephone conversations, at once soothing and captivating. It felt as if all those letters we had exchanged had been actual face to face conversations. The following day I took her out for a drive around Montreal. We went up to Mount Royal and Beaver Lake. It was our first opportunity to be alone and to get to know each other. Of course, there was already a base of almost two years' correspondence on which we could build our relationship. Still, Lella was hesitant about marriage. During the next few days, we were able to spend more time together, soon concluding that we were meant for each other. I introduced her to my parents and sister, who were skeptical. In the end, however, the decision on marriage was for Lella and me to make. After a few days of reflection, Lella finally accepted my proposal. A photograph of our first day together is shown in the following page.

Meanwhile, Marcello Flammini, who was married to Lella's sister Marcella, continued to experience problems at work. He could no longer cope and wanted out. He had been sponsored by his friend Giuliano Crescentini for an immigrant visa to the US, where he would work as a mechanic for Giuliano in LA. Marcello was quite eager to quit his job in Montreal and move to California. Together we decided that we would drive to Vancouver, which was closer to California than Montreal. There Marcello and Marcella could wait for their visa from the local US Consulate. So Marcello quit his job, got rid of the apartment and furniture and the four of us drove off in his old Ford. I enquired at the US

Consulate in Montreal about getting Lella a visitor's visa for the US, but I was told that that couldn't happen until she had been in Canada at least six months. This meant that we would have to travel to Vancouver using Canadian roads, rather than the better roads on the US side of the border. The Trans-Canada Highway in 1958 was not complete and for long stretches was not even paved.

Our first stop was in Toronto. There Lella and I were married at City Hall on November 4, 1958, a little over one week after our first face to face encounter. I was 18 and she was 21. Through a mutual friend, an interpreter was found for Lella, since the marriage ceremony would be conducted in English, a language that she didn't yet understand. Lella insisted on rings for both of us, which cost $8 each, further depleting my meagre financial resources.

The decision to marry involved a lifelong commitment whose consequences could not be foreseen at the time. While quitting a good job to undertake an education can be rationally justified, marriage at such a young age, with uncertain career prospects, was not driven by reason or logic. Impulse, instinct, passion, are some of the words that come to mind. Be that as it may, our union speaks to a bond made stronger by the passage of time.

In Toronto, I again enquired at the US Consulate about a visitor's visa for Lella, hoping that the rules would be more flexible now that we were married. Alas, that was not the case. Lella would still have to wait six months before being allowed to cross the US border as a visitor.

So we left Toronto, heading to Vancouver. We stayed at cheap motels and cabins along the way. The Canadian wilderness was truly beautiful. Driving through snow covered roads in Northern Ontario and drinking fresh water from streams near the highway are just some of the unforgettable memories of this voyage.

Across the Prairies, it was rather monotonous. Once we stayed on an Indian reservation, where the sound of wolves howling in the distance kept us awake for much of the night. Crossing the Rocky Mountains was the most adventurous part. The snow packed roads sometimes took us to high altitudes, well above the clouds. There were many hairpin turns. At one point, I came around a tight curve and encountered a very slippery ice covered surface, losing control of the car and skidding left and right. On one side was the upward slope of the mountain, on the other a huge drop of several thousand feet. We could easily have gone over the cliff and been killed. Instead somehow the car came to a stop, facing the wrong way after scraping the upward side of the mountain. We were all scared stiff. It's amazing that Marcella, who was pregnant, didn't have a miscarriage. It's an experience that none of us would ever forget.

It took us about ten days to reach Vancouver. We found a motel whose owners, this being the low season, agreed to charge us a very low rate, in exchange for our helping them out. Marcello dug ditches for new sewers, while Marcella and Lella did some room cleaning. Marcello and I tried to find work, but there was high unemployment at the time and jobs were very scarce. Luckily, I was able to secure a temporary job with Canadian Pacific Telegraphs, the same company that had employed me for three years in Montreal. One of their employees had taken a leave of absence for some reason and they could use an experienced person like me. The only problem was that the job involved making up the routes for delivery of telegrams. I had done this work in Montreal, where I knew all the streets and could make up proper routes. But I wasn't familiar with Vancouver streets. They overlooked this major handicap and hired me anyway. I worked with a map of Vancouver and although that slowed me down somewhat, I managed to do the job. My boss seemed happy with my work and the pay was good.

What I remember most about Vancouver during this brief stay is the never ending fog. It rained most of the time and the vegetation remained green, even though it was December. It was also quite mild, which was pleasant enough, but the fog and lack of sunshine made it somewhat depressing at times. While snow is unusual in Vancouver, it does fall from time to time and it certainly did for Christmas in 1958, which we thoroughly enjoyed.

While Marcello and Marcella were waiting for their visa to the US, Lella and I decided to give the US Consulate in Vancouver another try at getting her a visitor visa. We knew that the rules would be the same as we had been told in Montreal and Toronto, but it couldn't hurt to try. My persistence had no doubt been inspired by the example set by my father, who had gone out every morning to find work back in Sicily, never allowing his failure to land a job to discourage him from trying again the next day. We went to the US Consulate and were told to wait until our name was called. We were there for several hours, and finally I went back to the officer and asked when we could expect to be seen. They had forgotten about us! The officer was obviously embarrassed by our long wait and somehow missed the fact that Lella had not been in Canada the required six months. He gave her a visitor's visa after asking a few routine questions.

By late January 1959, Lella and I were in California, where I went back to work at Nina's Little Italy. When I introduced Lella to Ricky and Cathy, Ricky was pleased but shocked. He told me: "You have no money and you get married!" He was right, of course. Getting married at such a young age, having known each other for such a short period of time and without a steady job, was highly questionable. But I was optimistic that things would work out.

The first night after our arrival in LA, Lella and I stayed in a motel, but the next day we had to find a more permanent place to stay. As usual, I was short of money. One of the cooks who worked at the restaurant, Mario Mastrandrea, realized our predicament and offered to take us in at his house. He didn't know me nor my wife, and didn't even ask his wife. We just showed up after midnight and he told his wife Dolly that we were going to live there for a while, until we had enough money to rent our own place. Dolly was shocked. The photo on the next page shows Lella and me at the restaurant.

Lella spoke no English and how dare her husband bring two strangers to live with them? Soon, however, Lella made herself useful around the house. She and Dolly became close friends. This is just another example of how, when I found myself in a tough spot, someone would unexpectedly appear, ready to help out!

Marcello and Marcella came to LA a bit later, after receiving their immigrant visas and the birth of their son Fredy in Vancouver. Unfortunately, Marcello's mental problems had worsened. My hope had been that, once in Los Angeles, working for his friend Giuliano, he would snap out of his paranoia. Instead,

he got into an argument with Giuliano, threatening to hit him with a hammer and Giuliano had no option but to fire him. I helped Marcello find another job in a factory, but the mental problems just kept getting worse. Eventually he, Marcella and their son Fredy moved back to Italy. It was a very sad situation, ending in divorce. Marcello was in and out of mental institutions for many years, until his death from dementia. He had been a very gifted individual, but his mental problems ruined his own life and caused much damage to Marcella and Fredy.

I developed an arrangement at Nina's Little Italy that enabled me to go to school during the week and work mainly on weekends. I was able to put in 27 hours a week and, with tips, earned a little more than $80 a week, which was adequate to meet our needs. Fridays were particularly tough because I would have to start school at 7:45 a.m. and work from 5 p.m. until 3 a.m. Lella would often come with me to work and help out by serving wine. In California, one had to be 21 to serve wine, and I was just under 19. Most of the time I served wine anyway, but it was safer for Lella to do it since she was over 21.

Nina's Little Italy was about an hour's drive by freeway from my home. When I finished work, I would take some no-doze capsules to keep me awake. I would roll down the windows and have the radio on at maximum volume. The drive was very monotonous at 3 a.m., and it was very difficult to stay awake. When Lella was with me she would constantly prod me to stay awake, but on more than one occasion I dozed off. This was extremely dangerous and I had a couple of close calls. Falling asleep on the freeway while driving at 70 mph is a recipe for disaster. One night when Lella wasn't with me, I realized that I just couldn't drive because I was so sleepy, so I parked the car on the freeway's shoulder and went to sleep. Eventually I woke up and got home after 6 a.m. Lella, who expected me around 4 a.m. was quite worried but relieved to see that I was okay.

I had re-started my studies in March 1959, pursuing the diploma in aeronautical engineering technology, but soon after switched to electronics engineering technology. Although aeronautics continued to interest me, I became quite fascinated with electronics. In part, this was due to the fact that I had no understanding whatsoever of electricity or magnetism. The less I understood something, the more determined I was to unlock its mystery. To paraphrase Albert Einstein, "whatever looks impossible becomes trivial once you understand it." On a more pragmatic level, the space program, with its rockets and satellites, would involve a lot of electronics for guidance and communications, and so I concluded that it made sense to make the switch.

Unfortunately, my academic performance was not that great. There were times when I thought that a different career, such as accounting, would have been more appropriate for me. But I persisted, until one day I asked a question in class that really impressed the professor. He had tagged me as a barely C student, and did not expect me to raise a question that showed such a deep understanding of the subject matter. He made a point of saying to the class that, from now on, he would have to take my questions much more seriously! This event turned things around for me. All of a sudden, I became much more self-confident. Something had clicked, and the pieces of the jigsaw puzzle were falling into place. This was reinforced by some test scores in other traditionally difficult subjects where I was at the top of the class. From then on, I earned mostly A's and B's, and my overall grade point average moved steadily up.

In the summer of 1959, my father came to visit us in California. I took him around the city and we had a great time together. He also spoke to Lella about the Pentecostal faith. Although I had not been attending church services for some time, and Lella was one of those typical Italians who were "nominally" Roman Catholic, I felt an urge to take her to a service at the Italian Pentecostal Church in Los Angeles. There, we were welcomed with open arms by several church members, who invited us to their homes and showed us tremendous hospitality. Most of them had been born in the US but spoke good Italian. Eventually, this initial contact with the Pentecostal church, combined with my father's introduction of the Bible, resulted in Lella's conversion to the Pentecostal faith. One of the many positive outcomes of Lella's conversion was her cessation of smoking, something that I had tried to get her to do for quite a while without any success.

The following year Lella was pregnant. Everything seemed to go well until one day she became quite sick. I took her to see the doctor who concluded that she was having a miscarriage, and that she should be taken immediately to a hospital. She was so sick that I had to carry her in my arms through the emergency entrance of the Northridge Hospital. She was practically unconscious. Before admitting her, the hospital required a deposit of $100. This was clearly a serious emergency and, without verifying that there were sufficient funds in my account, I wrote out a cheque for the required $100. She was admitted, treated and was okay after a brief convalescence. This was my first exposure to an aspect of American life that has troubled me ever since. In the America that I thought I knew, my wife would have received immediate emergency treatment, leaving the matter of payment to be addressed after she was out of danger.

Soon after, I arranged for my parents and sister to join us in California. Like me, they were fed up with Canadian winters and we all felt that it would be good for our family to live closer to each other. My father found work in a candy factory, probably helped by his experience in the chocolate plant in Montreal. This was a good, steady job. One of his co-workers lived nearby, so dad was able to get a ride to work with him.

Throughout the time that we lived in LA, there was a sense that anything was possible. Each day thousands of new residents would arrive from all over the US, Canada, the UK and other countries. New freeways were constantly being added to handle the increasing volume of traffic. The aerospace industry and Hollywood attracted a lot of talent. Many Canadian, British and Italian actors, for example, made their mark in Hollywood. Huge housing developments were sprouting up like mushrooms. At one point, even I considered opening a restaurant with a couple of friends who had cooking experience. As a waiter, I knew how to handle customers and, having kept the books for Nina's Little Italy, knew the business side as well. All we lacked was the money. Even that obstacle did not deter us, having met a retired Italian barber who had just arrived from Chicago and had money to invest in a business of some kind. Fortunately, common sense prevailed and I concluded that my studies were more important than going into business, with all its inherent risks. As my potential partners learned the hard way, it was relatively easy to open a restaurant, and easier still to go bankrupt!

Although, as a foreign student, I did not vote in US elections, I followed politics at both the state and national levels. The four 1960 presidential debates marked a milestone, not only in US history, but also in the coming of age of television. People who watched the debates on television were inspired by Senator John F. Kennedy's confident tone and appearance; for them he was the clear winner. Radio listeners, on the other hand, heard an experienced and knowledgeable Vice President Richard Nixon without any awareness of his lack of make-up or five o'clock shadow. Hence, for the radio audience, Nixon won the debate. Kennedy won the election by a very slim margin of about 100,000 votes. Hence, although there are arguments on both sides, it is fair to suggest that television was the deciding factor. As later research would demonstrate, the visual experience trumps either print or sound.

As events turned out, Kennedy was able to inspire a new generation – not only on social issues, with the launch of the Peace Corps – but also on pursuing great projects, such as putting a man on the moon within a decade. For some time, I had been interested in space travel and fancied myself playing a role in such an undertaking, which had influenced my decision to study aeronautical and electronics engineering technology.

Internationally, Kennedy was just as determined to resist communist expansion as Nixon. His famous speech in Berlin, when he stated "Ich bin ein Berliner" served as prologue for President Ronald Reagan's equally powerful message years later: "Mr. Gorbachev, tear down that wall!" But what resonated most with me was President Kennedy's admonition: "Ask not what your country can do for you; ask what you can do for your country."

I had the pleasure of serving many interesting individuals at Nina's Little Italy, including Hollywood actor Scott Brady. But I also had my share of bad experiences with some customers at the restaurant. Bars closed at 2 am, and we got a lot of drunks showing up for pizza immediately after, since we were open until 3 am on Fridays and Saturdays. A few times, the customers would become threatening and we would call the police. I remember on one occasion when a bunch of guys threatened to break all the furniture, six Los Angeles policemen showed up, all over 6'6" tall, each one carrying a huge billy club. They just stood there, not saying anything. Their mere presence was enough to convince the unruly clients to leave peacefully and quietly.

On another occasion two couples came in. The men were in wheelchairs, obviously paraplegic. Their wives were able bodied and quite attractive. They seemed to get along well with each other and had a good meal with wine. Towards the end, however, something went wrong. One of the men accused the other of trying to fool around with his wife. Strong and loud words were exchanged and soon one of the men was trying to strangle the other. He had unbelievable strength in his arms and three of us, myself and two of the cooks, tried to separate them. Meanwhile, another waiter called the police and they arrived very quickly. By then the two men had quieted down and had left the restaurant after paying their bill. They were in the parking lot in their wheelchairs when they started to fight with each other again. Even the police struggled to separate them. It was quite a spectacle!

Another interesting episode happened one night when a customer paid his bill, left a tip on the table and went outside to his car. I had been standing looking out the window for no particular reason. He must have thought that I was looking at him disapprovingly. He came back in and put more money on the table. Not realizing what was going on, I kept looking out the window. The man came back a third time, putting even more money on the table! He must have thought that I was trying to tell him by my looks that the tip was inadequate! At that point, I walked away from the window and he left. Needless to say, that was one of the best tips I ever got!

I received my Diploma in Electronics Engineering Technology in December 1961. By then, Northrop had changed its name to Northrop University and was granting degrees. Once you had the diploma, you would get full credit towards an engineering degree and required only four full time quarters of additional studies. My plan was to work full time as a technician, so that I could get some experience in electronics, while studying part time towards a degree. Most of the work available in the electronics field at the time was classified as secret and one needed to be a US citizen to obtain a security clearance. As a Canadian citizen, living in the US on a student visa, I would have been unable to obtain such a security clearance. Fortunately, I was able to find a job as an electronics technician with the Hughes Aircraft Company (Electronic Products Division), that did not require a security clearance. Nevertheless, I had to obtain approval from the US

Immigration authorities before I could accept this job offer. Hughes immediately petitioned the US Department of Justice, stating that I was a highly skilled Electronics Technician in a field vitally important to US national defence. This was a somewhat exaggerated description of my role, but it demonstrates how much importance companies engaged in defence related work attached to the recruitment of skilled technicians and engineers. Approval was quickly obtained and I assumed my new duties in January 1962.

The Hughes plant was located in Newport Beach, about 35 miles south of my home in LA and it took over one hour to drive there. The work consisted of aligning and testing complex crystal filters used in military missiles, space and electronic weapon systems. It was not really the best kind of a job for someone who was starting out in the field of electronics because it was so narrowly specialized. A better job would have been one that exposed me to a variety of electronic circuits and systems, but it was still a good job. The only part I didn't like was the pay, $2.10 an hour to start. As a waiter, I was averaging $3 per hour. After three years of college, I would be earning almost $1 an hour less than as a waiter, which required no college education at all. Of course, as a waiter I could not expect any advancement; as a technician and hopefully eventually as an engineer I could expect to advance quite rapidly.

I learned a lot at Hughes. One of the other technicians, Pasquale Siravo, became one of my best friends. We spent a lot of time together, often listening to opera records with friends. He also visited my home several times. He was born in the US but his grandfather had emigrated from Italy. Pasquale had been in the US Air Force and had more experience than I did in electronics. For a while after I returned to Canada we corresponded, but then lost track of each other (both he and I moved around quite a bit!). Through an amazing set of circumstances, we would meet again in 1994 in Florida.

In spite of the full time workload, and limited time to do homework, my academic performance continued to steadily improve. The curriculum consisted not only of electronics engineering courses, but also courses such as Technical Writing, American Literature, American History, Economics, Philosophy, Business Law and Political Science. The other students and I resented having to study these subjects. We were going to work as engineers and did not see the point of taking non-engineering courses. Later in my career I developed a greater appreciation for the humanities, and was glad that I had been forced to pursue them, because they broadened my education and made it possible to advance in my career.

Lella was pregnant again in 1962 and the church gave her a wonderful surprise shower. We received many gifts for the coming baby and there was also a huge cake. It was one of the happiest occasions of our stay in Los Angeles. Because Lella had miscarried once, her doctor took special care of her. The evening of January 20, 1963, Lella went into labour. I took her to the Los Angeles Broadway Hospital and sat in the waiting room all night. It was an unusually cold night for Los Angeles, with temperatures close to the freezing level. Deborah was born the next morning, a healthy and beautiful baby girl. Lella and I were now parents, and my parents were grandparents. It was a wonderful feeling.

Shortly after Deborah's arrival, Hughes lost its contract with the US government and I was laid off. Having just become a father and rented a larger and more costly apartment, being laid off was the last thing I needed. Nevertheless, just as losing my job as a bus boy at Caffe' Via Veneto had enabled me to find a better job as a waiter at Nina's Little Italy, something similar happened this time. Within one week I was hired as an electronics technician by Teledyne Systems. The plant was located much closer to home, significantly reducing my commuting time. The pay was $2.50 per hour, a substantial increase from what I had been earning at Hughes. I was to work the evening shift, which enabled me to continue going to school during the day. The work involved aligning, troubleshooting and repairing US Army radio receivers. Once again, I was lucky to find work that, although connected with the US military, did not require a security clearance. The receivers on which I worked were initially put together by assemblers. Then they would come to the technicians where we would align them and make sure that they met specifications. There were usually some wiring errors made by the assemblers, so most of the time, the receivers required some troubleshooting before they could be aligned. It was generally expected that each technician would complete two receivers per shift. By now I had taken several advanced electronics courses and had close to a year and a half of experience. I quickly mastered the job and within a couple of weeks was producing an average of four receivers per shift, double the expected target. My boss was so impressed with my work that he decided to give me a 50 cent an hour raise. I was now earning $3 per hour, what I had been making as a waiter! It wasn't a lot of money but at least I was headed in the right direction.

There were two problems related to working as a technician at Teledyne. The first was the boredom of working on equipment that I knew inside out. I had worked on so many of these receivers that there was no real challenge any more. If there was something wrong, I would instinctively know where the problem was. My education was far more advanced than the job required and I wanted to put it to better use. The second problem was the environment. Whereas Hughes had been a rather civilized place in which to work, my department at Teledyne was not. Some employees were rather shady characters and there was an open contempt for the blacks[21]. Racial tensions were not far below the surface. At the time, it was not unusual for ads to appear in the Los Angeles Times that specified "whites only" for certain rental accommodations. This became illegal later on, but in the early sixties, discrimination against blacks was quite common. The bathroom walls were covered with obscene graffiti. Several former Navy technicians employed there were quite vulgar. At 8:30 p.m., we all got a half hour lunch break. Most people would have eaten their lunch while working beforehand, so they would get in their cars and head to the nearest bar to drink beer. I went a few times as expected, along with the rest. I didn't enjoy this drinking of jugs of beer and soon stopped going. Following the lunch break, the beer drinkers were even more vulgar and enjoyed making fun of the blacks, who were surprisingly docile. A few years later, after we had left Los Angeles, racial tensions exploded in the infamous Watts riots that killed several people and destroyed many buildings. Years later, we visited our old neighbourhood, which was close to Watts, and were shocked at the extreme degeneration that had taken place. Garbage was strewn everywhere, houses were boarded up, car wrecks were all around.

In June 1963 I received my Bachelor's degree in Electronics Engineering. At Teledyne, I was immediately promoted to engineer and transferred to a different department, where they worked on advanced phase lock receivers used to track satellites for NASA. These receivers were designed to "lock on" a signal from space that would generally be very weak and was often masked by electromagnetic noise. Each receiver would track the signal by continuously adjusting the orientation of the parabolic antennas that were aimed at the signal source. This was a very civilized environment, with highly knowledgeable technicians and engineers working on some of the most advanced transistor circuits then being designed. I learned a lot from several of the more experienced engineers there, including an older chap named Francis Lackey, who did not have an engineering degree but had learned his electronics through experience. Unlike Canada, where you needed a degree and had to be registered to work as an engineer, California had no such requirement. You were an engineer if a company decided to employ you as an engineer.

Lackey and I worked out a mutually advantageous deal. He would teach me all he could about the practical side of electronic circuit design, and I would teach him calculus. I was very good with calculus and, no matter how much practical experience one has, it is very difficult to really understand certain aspects of electronics without a solid mathematical foundation. Lackey taught me another important lesson. When I expressed the view that there wasn't much job security in the aerospace industry that employed us, he told me that the only security that mattered was the knowledge that one had skills to offer that employers needed. In other words, real security can only exist within oneself. These thoughts had a profound and long lasting influence on me. It may explain why, during my professional career, any time I achieved any degree of job security, I would move on to another job![22]

Working as an engineer at Teledyne was a very stimulating and professionally rewarding experience. There were no specific hours of work. We had deadlines to meet and we worked whatever hours we wanted to, as long as we met the deadlines. It was not unusual for some engineers to come in around 4 pm and work all evening and all night. Manufacturers were constantly improving transistor performance and my department led the way in making full use of the latest advances in solid state circuit technology. We were constantly looking for new transistors specifically constructed to optimize their AGC (automatic gain control) characteristics. This was particularly important in our work because the signals we were tracking could vary in strength from the relatively strong to the extremely weak, and hence the degree of amplification they required had to be automatically adjusted over a large dynamic range. Transistors also used much less power than vacuum tubes, generated less heat and took up less space. They made it possible to build electronic equipment ideally suited to applications where low space, weight and power requirements were important considerations. In time, they also resulted in lower costs and the development of integrated circuits, which would revolutionize technology in many far reaching ways.

During our time in LA, we observed many events that would shape American history for years to come. In addition to the racial tensions, we were in the middle of the cold war. The Bay of Pigs attempted invasion of Cuba by American sponsored Cubans had been a disaster. That and the Cuban missile crisis, during which President Kennedy had gone to the brink of war over the issue of Russian missiles aimed at the US from Cuba meant that relations with Russia were not good. There was a palpable sense of apprehension at the prospect of nuclear war. Some people built underground shelters, fully equipped with food, water, sanitation facilities, firearms, ammunition, medical supplies and so on. I did a research project while attending Northrop on how such a shelter could be built. I also recall a humorous event that will illustrate how this climate of fear affected me. One night my wife awakened me by saying, in what seemed to me a very agitated tone: "Russi! Russi! In Italian, "Russi" means "Russians". I immediately got out of bed, trying to figure out where I could get a rifle (I did not own one) in the mistaken belief that the Russians had invaded California. Even though I was not an American, I certainly was prepared to do my share to defend the US against a Russian invasion! Actually "Russi" in Italian also means "you are snoring", which was what my wife was trying to tell me!

Soon after receiving my Bachelor's degree, I applied for admission to the Master's degree program at the University of Southern California. I wanted to specialize in electronic filters, highly sophisticated circuits on which I had worked at Hughes as a technician. These filters, which used quartz crystals, were able to discriminate between wanted and unwanted frequencies with extreme precision, and were therefore very critical in electronic communication between earth based stations and space travelling vehicles. I also felt that the Master's degree would be advantageous in advancing my career. Unfortunately, while I had earned mainly A's and B's in my final two years at Northrop, my grades for the first two years had been poor, which dragged my overall grade point average down. There was also the fact that Northrop had only recently started granting degrees and was not yet accredited by the Engineering Council. I applied anyway and took the required Graduate Record Examination, which all candidates for admission to graduate work in the US were required to take. In spite of top results from the Graduate Record Examination[23], excellent grades in the last two years of my Bachelor's degree program and my industrial experience, the USC admissions department denied my application. I immediately appealed and was interviewed by the assistant dean of engineering, who also turned me down. I then asked to speak with the dean of engineering, who reluctantly agreed to see me. As I entered his office, before I had a chance to speak, he told me flatly that he knew why I wanted to see him, but there was no way that he would overrule the decision already taken by the assistant dean. Undaunted by his pre-emptive rejection, I calmly stated my case and by the time I left his office, he had agreed to admit me on probation. This was not the first time, nor would it be the last, that I would not allow myself to be discouraged by rejection!

In September 1963, I began my graduate studies at USC. Teledyne's very flexible attitude towards working hours made it possible for me to fit in my day and evening classes while still working full time. The company also reimbursed me for my tuition expenses. Graduate studies were much more demanding than undergraduate work. Combining my work experience at Hughes and Teledyne with my academic studies produced valuable synergies, where each part reinforced the other. In a way, I was engaged in what later became known as a cooperative program, one of the most effective learning approaches adopted by many post-secondary institutions in the US and Canada.

While attending USC I experienced for the first time what was to become a lifetime affliction with my lower back. It was diagnosed as muscle spasm, a very painful condition that could be triggered by lifting a heavy weight, making a twisting motion, or simply bending over to pick up something off the floor. I recall having to walk from the parking lot to my classes at USC carrying a heavy load of textbooks in excruciating pain. Each step was a major challenge. The problem has continued to affect me to this day. Sometimes I am okay for several years, then all of a sudden the problem comes back. No physician has been able to find a lasting solution. Rest is the only thing that allows the problem to work itself out. I have learned to live with it.

It was also during this time that, while working at Teledyne in the afternoon of November 22, 1963, my colleagues and I heard the first report that President Kennedy had been shot. Soon, it was confirmed that he had died. A profound sense of shock permeated the entire plant. The earliest reaction that I recall was something to the effect of "Why shoot him when you could just not vote for him in the next election?" While I admired the now fallen president, he was not universally popular. The initial assumption, at least within the immediate circle of my colleagues, was that this had been a politically motivated assassination. It is a sad reality that the US carries the heavy baggage of a violent history. John F. Kennedy was the fourth US president to be assassinated while in office. He had now joined Abraham Lincoln, James A. Garfield and William McKinley in the tragic pantheon of slain American presidents. Two of his successors, Gerald Ford and Ronald Reagan, would be the targets of assassination attempts. And his own brother, Robert Kennedy, as well as civil rights leader Martin Luther King would suffer the same fate in the not too distant future.

In the spring of 1964 I began to think about teaching. As a boy back in Sicily, I had earned high grades in Italian, French and Latin, and fancied myself someday becoming a professor of languages. Now, of course, it wouldn't be languages that I would teach. And so I approached the dean of engineering at Northrop University, enquiring about possible opportunities to teach there. I was the first engineering graduate from Northrop to be admitted to a graduate school. He was impressed with the progress I was making and offered me a teaching job on the spot. After one year as an engineer at Teledyne, I resigned and began teaching as an assistant professor of Electrical Engineering and Mathematics at Northrop University. There was great feedback from my students and the dean complimented me on various occasions. Northrop also paid for my tuition, and arranged a teaching schedule that facilitated my pursuit of graduate studies at USC. Northrop's flexibility and financial support enabled me to successfully complete all the requirements for my Master's degree by January 1965, having earned mostly A's and B's.

During my seven years in LA, working and studying had been my principal and most demanding activities, with barely enough time for sleeping. Lella had also worked for a while in the assembly plant at Mattel (the toy maker) until our first child was born. And while money was always tight, somehow we managed. Our leisure activities, not surprisingly, were limited. For example, we managed to eat out once a year on our wedding anniversary at Mario's, an excellent Italian restaurant in Westwood. We visited with friends from the church, school and work whenever we could find the time. A typical Sunday afternoon involved a long drive along Sunset Blvd. to the ocean and back. The Sunday afternoon drive, in fact, became a tradition in all the places where we lived in later years. One unforgettable event for me[24] was being able to enjoy for the first time a live opera performance. It was Bizet's "Carmen", with the legendary Italian tenor Mario Del Monaco singing the part of Don José.

With my Master's degree in hand, and valuable experience in electronics and teaching, a decision had to be made. Would we remain in California or return to Canada? There were several family considerations. In the end, the decision was unanimous. Our entire family would return to Canada, which would become our permanent home.

One of my colleagues at Northrop had recently arrived from Canada, and he told me that Ryerson Polytechnical Institute in Toronto was expanding and looking for teachers. While Ryerson did not grant degrees at the time, it was highly regarded for its three year diploma programs in various technologies. I wrote a letter of enquiry to Ryerson, outlining my qualifications and asking whether there were any openings for someone like me. A formal offer of employment arrived within days, with space at the bottom of the letter for my signature and a request to return the signed offer immediately. I replied, suggesting that a final decision could be made after my return to Canada. Ryerson wrote right back, saying that they needed a decision immediately to set up class schedules for the fall. They really wanted to sign me up! Few of the instructors at Ryerson had Master's degrees and fewer still had industrial experience with transistor circuits. Most instructors had only worked with vacuum tubes, which were now becoming obsolete. My education and experience were exactly what Ryerson was seeking.[25]

After discussing the whole thing with Lella, I accepted Ryerson's offer and resigned from Northrop. I felt badly about this, since Northrop had paid my tuition at USC and given me a teaching schedule that facilitated my pursuit of graduate studies. But in California at the time tuition reimbursement was a generally accepted practice by most employers, and engineers frequently moved around as some companies lost contracts while others gained them. At any rate, the die was cast. Dad also quit his job, we sold our furniture and prepared to return to Canada.

The seven Los Angeles years marked my transition to adulthood in several important ways. On a personal level, becoming a husband and father brought much joy, along with added responsibilities. The acquisition of important educational and work credentials were the entry point to a more stimulating and rewarding career, although at the time, I had no clear goal other than teaching.

This was also a period during which my philosophical orientation became more clearly defined. It was driven in large part by the work ethic, adopted through the example set by my parents. But I was also greatly influenced by the American ethos of self-reliance and "can do" mindset. These qualities underpinned the belief that individuals, no matter how humble their origins, can become whatever they set out to be. It takes hard work, discipline and perseverance. Most of the people with whom I was associated exhibited these characteristics. I also found Americans in general to be very generous, especially during times when I was facing financial challenges. Certainly, what I was able to achieve in pursuit of my educational goals in the US would not have been possible at the time in Canada. My limited financial resources, my failure to finish high school[26] and the rigid organization of the Canadian school year would have represented insurmountable obstacles. In the US, however, it was possible to work and study. The American system offered a higher level of flexibility, and hence opportunities for anyone who had the desire to succeed. For this, I will always be grateful. Furthermore, my work as a waiter contributed significantly to my learning to deal with a broad range of people.

Hence, my overall experiences during the LA years were overwhelmingly positive and helped to shape my perspectives over the subsequent years.

This was also a turbulent period that foreshadowed the emergence of a troubled American society in the years to come. In addition to the cold war tensions, the Bay of Pigs fiasco and the Cuban missile crisis, the escalation of the Viet Nam hostilities would create deep wounds in the American psyche that have not yet completely healed.

CHAPTER FOUR

Our family arrived in Toronto from California towards the end of June 1965. A few days later, I went to Ryerson and met the new head of the electronics department. His name was Isaac Morgulis, but everybody called him Ike. He had great plans for the electronics department. He welcomed me with great enthusiasm and we began discussing the courses that I would be teaching in the fall semester. I would be expected to take summer courses that year and next to qualify for an Ontario teaching certificate. The pay at Ryerson was slightly less than I had been earning in the US but it was for a nine month academic year. There would be opportunities for summer and evening teaching, for additional remuneration.

The economy in 1965 was doing well in Canada, but it was still hard for dad to find work. He had no trade skills, and initially found work in a hospital doing laundry. The pay was $200 a month. This was well below what one would need to support a family, but in those days, hospitals were not unionized and wages for unskilled workers were quite low.

I attended summer school at the Ontario College of Education in 1965 and 1966 and received my technical institute teaching certificate. Most of the people taking these courses, including myself, resented having to take them. But it was required as a condition of employment, so we put up with it. They included courses such as philosophy of education, measurement and statistics, and so on. We saw little relevance to our teaching duties at the time and would have preferred to spend the summer boning up on our own disciplines. In retrospect, however, the courses did provide a valuable foundation in pedagogy.

In the fall of 1965 I began teaching various electronics courses at Ryerson. I also taught night school. Ryerson had a totally different environment than I had been used to in the US. At Northrop, for example, I went to work in shirt sleeves. Ryerson had a strict dress code. All students and staff had to wear a business suit at all times, including a white shirt and tie. This policy was intended to demonstrate to potential employers that Ryerson was a serious academic institution. It was particularly silly at exam time, when some students would try to sneak in without a tie and instructors were expected to enforce the rule. I once walked from my office to the lab without my jacket, and one of the other instructors warned me that, if the principal saw me, I could lose my annual pay increment for such an infraction of the rules!

Despite the silly dress code[27], I enjoyed my teaching duties. Ike had given me some fairly advanced courses to teach, which upset some of the more senior instructors on staff, but given my education and industrial experience, he felt I was qualified to teach them. I put in a very heavy workload, including night classes.

The commute from my apartment in Scarborough to Ryerson in downtown Toronto was quite an ordeal. I was shocked at the large number of what I considered crazy drivers. Accustomed to the high volume, fast traffic of Los Angeles, a city built for automobiles, where drivers knew how to drive, I found Toronto drivers undisciplined. Traffic was unbelievably congested, with long lines of cars on Eglinton Avenue and the Don Valley parkway. During inclement weather traffic moved even more slowly. It took me some time to get used to Toronto traffic!

Lella and Deborah also had to adjust to their new life in Canada. As winter arrived, it became quite a challenge for Lella to go shopping, having to walk to the supermarket with Deborah in the middle of snowstorms. Deborah did not like the snow at first, but eventually she learned to enjoy it.

Soon after I started teaching at Ryerson, I approached the head of the Plant department and enquired about potential work opportunities for my father. He was soon hired as a janitor, earning $325 a month, a lot more than the $200 a month at the hospital. This was a living wage at the time and dad did very well at Ryerson. He was highly regarded, despite his limited English and skills. He was very proud that he had a son teaching there and boasted of this to his co-workers. Needless to say, my office was the most meticulously cleaned office on the entire campus!

At Ryerson I shared office space with another instructor, Bill Cruden. Bill and I taught the same courses, and we became close friends. We collaborated on lesson planning and laboratory development, and shared questions and knowledge about electronics all the time. This way we challenged one another and learned from each other's insights.

Within a few months of our arrival in Toronto, Lella and I concluded that apartment living was not for us. There were too many constraints on what one could do, which is understandable in a building shared with many other tenants. Lella and I wanted to create our own home, with a backyard where Deborah could play, and a basement, where I could have a workshop. Housing was terribly expensive in Toronto, and we didn't have a lot of money saved up, but we managed to scrape up enough for a down payment on a brand new two storey house in Pickering, almost a ninety minute drive from Ryerson.[28] It cost $19,500; a comparable home in Toronto would probably have cost around $30,000. We moved in during the spring of 1966 and a few months later, were able to have Lella's mother visit us from Italy, giving Deborah the opportunity to get to know her maternal grand-mother.

Bill Cruden had bought a house in the same neighbourhood as I had. This made it possible for us to share commuting. I would drive one week and he would drive the other. Our costs were cut in half and we had company. We spent most of our time discussing technical topics in which we had a common interest. We also managed to get the same night school assignments so we could drive back together on those nights when we taught.

I was now feeling quite optimistic on all fronts. It felt good to be living in Canada. We had a great family life, with my parents nearby, good friends, stimulating work, a nice house, even a brand new car. Deborah and Lella were adjusting to Canadian winters, which were less severe in Toronto than they would have been in Montreal.

The teaching duties for my second year at Ryerson were more challenging than during the first year and also more enjoyable. Ike assigned me the task of completely overhauling the third year course in electronic circuit design. Until now this course had been mainly vacuum tube based. I was to transform it into a transistor based course. This involved not only the lecture portion but the laboratory component as well. I had to order new equipment and supplies. Ike had been successful in obtaining a substantial capital budget, which enabled me to buy some of the most advanced electronic test equipment then on the market. The other instructors at Ryerson had been used to working with the cheapest equipment available. Ike and I, however, thought big. I was used to the latest equipment from my industrial experience in California, and spared no expense in acquiring similar equipment for our labs.

That second year at Ryerson I made another close friend. Like me, Glen Martinson had received his Master's degree in the US, and had also worked at Bell Labs, one of the most prestigious electronic research facilities in the US. Glen was an electronics genius and I learned a lot from him.

The faculty at Ryerson was not unionized, but there was a faculty association that bargained more or less like a union. In 1966 it bargained successfully for a 15% across the board salary increase, unheard of at the time since inflation was quite low. I was no union activist, but somehow word got out that I knew how to type (sort of!) and was quickly elected secretary of the association! Being a member of the executive committee exposed me to a few hard line militants who created unnecessary problems by their uncompromising attitude.

The 1966 Ryerson convocation address was given by the then Minister of Education for Ontario, the Hon. Bill Davis. I was impressed by this visionary and relatively young politician. Our paths would cross several times over the next thirty years, including the time he spent as Premier of Ontario and also after he left politics. That year he introduced legislation to create a network of colleges of applied arts and technology (also known as community colleges) across Ontario, a development that would have major implications for the course of my career. The colleges would offer some three year programs, similar to those at Ryerson, but they would also offer two and one year programs, which would be aimed at the less academically inclined students. The idea was to offer a very broad range of programs in technology, business, applied arts, health sciences and community education. This was a major expansion of Ontario's educational system. It addressed the challenge posed by the large number of high school graduates who would need some form of post-secondary education for the kinds of jobs that an increasingly industrialized economy demanded, but not necessarily at the university level.

Although I enjoyed my work at Ryerson, the prospect of participating in the development of the new college system also appealed to me. These institutions would likely adopt or adapt some of Ryerson's programs and practices, but there would also be opportunities to innovate. It was expected that they would recruit some of their administrative and instructional staff from Ryerson. I had ambitions of becoming a department chairman at some point in the future, but with the rapid expansion of the new college system, this long term goal could be realized much earlier. Hence I decided to keep my eyes open for any interesting opportunities that might come along. An advertisement in the Globe and Mail seeking instructors for Sir Sandford Fleming College[29] in Peterborough caught my attention. I had no idea where Peterborough was and had to look it up on a map. Both the president and dean had been recruited from Ryerson. Dave Sutherland was appointed as the first president. He had been a member of the Council of Regents[30], the body that appointed members of the boards of governors and was responsible for the approval of all programs of instruction. This had given him an excellent understanding of what was expected from the colleges. The dean, George Robertson, had been chairman of the mechanical technology department at Ryerson. I had known him casually.

I decided to apply, hoping to be offered a department head position. The prospect of living in a small city, with its low housing costs and short commuting times also appealed to me. I spoke to Ike about it. He definitely did not want to lose me and tried to get approval to create another assistant department chairman position to which he would appoint me. There was already one such position and he did not succeed in obtaining approval for a second one.

Ike exhibited strong leadership, and was one of my most important mentors. He gave me many opportunities for professional growth and set an example that served as inspiration throughout my professional life. He was also a person of great character and to this day I consider myself very lucky in having had the opportunity to work with him.

Soon I was called for an interview. The drive to Peterborough was most pleasant, taking me through some beautiful countryside. My interview with Dave Sutherland and George Robertson took place over coffee[31] at the cafeteria counter of the Peterborough bus station. The new college consisted of two offices on the top floor of this building, one for the president and the other for the dean. They were quite eager to hire me on the spot. I told them of my interest in a department head position. Robertson indicated that, while that was certainly possible in the future, they would not be appointing department heads the first year. Instead, they offered me a position as engineering technology coordinator, which involved a higher salary than that of an instructor. I would also assume the duties of professional development coordinator, which meant training new teachers, and would be compensated for this added responsibility through a reduced teaching load. The salary was higher than at Ryerson, and the cost of living in Peterborough was definitely lower. After briefly thinking about it, I indicated that I would consider accepting this offer on one condition. As a new college they would need cleaning staff. My father worked as a janitor at Ryerson and they would have to give him an equivalent job. This way our family would be able to live in close proximity to each other. Sutherland immediately agreed and we had a package deal! Father and son. As soon as I returned home, I broke the news of the offer to the family. Lella wasn't particularly happy about the change. We had lived in our new house a little more than one year and to move so soon wasn't that appealing. My parents were happy that we could be close but my sister Ester was very upset. She had been going to school in Toronto and had made several close friends. It is always difficult for a teenager (she was 15 years old) to move and Ester was no exception. "You are ruining my life", she exclaimed. In the end, however, the whole family agreed to the move and I telephoned my acceptance to Robertson in Peterborough. And despite her initial chagrin, Ester eventually adjusted quite well to Peterborough, which has been her home since 1967. In fact, she is the only member of my immediate family who has lived in the same city for such a long time!

CHAPTER FIVE

On July 1, 1967 I began to work at Sir Sandford Fleming, the second instructor to be hired by the new college. My office was squeezed into a small area on the second floor of the bus line building, right next to Dave Sutherland and George Robertson's offices. During July and August I also taught summer school at Ryerson, travelling back and forth between Peterborough and Toronto. Being on the payroll of two employers at the same time enabled me to save enough money to give my father for a down payment on a house that was just a short walk from his job as a janitor at the college.

That summer I worked extremely hard, putting in long hours to get ready for classes in September. There was much to do in curriculum and laboratory development. I hired a technician – Bill Ashby - to install and maintain the lab equipment. He was an amazing individual. With little formal training, he could nevertheless fabricate, install, maintain and repair virtually anything mechanical, electrical or electronic. He built quite an elaborate machine shop and was of great help to all the instructors.

The new college was to operate in a renovated building. The architects did an amazing job in a very short period of time. From May to September they finalized the design, hired contractors and completed all renovations. By early September an old factory had become a functioning college with classrooms, laboratories, offices, cafeteria and all the other required support facilities.

The dean and president hired the instructional, administrative and support staff during the summer. We had many meetings of the new faculty where we participated in creating the academic policies and regulations that would govern the new college. There were many opportunities to innovate. Building something from scratch was challenging but exciting.

During that summer I was sent by Robertson to a professional development conference at Lake Couchiching. The object was to share information on professional development programs being offered by all the community colleges. This was also my first opportunity to rub shoulders with some key people from the Ministry of Education and the other colleges, most much more senior than me. There was Norm Sisco, the chairman of the Council of Regents. He could be considered the architect of the Ontario college system, with a profound influence on how the colleges were shaped from the beginning. He had direct access to Premier Davis and was highly regarded. There was also Herb Jackson, director of the College Affairs branch in the Ministry of Education. He had been chairman of the electronics department at Ryerson a few years back, where he had written a best selling textbook on basic electricity. Herb was a quiet sort of person, but very capable. The electronics department at Ryerson in fact produced several leaders for the new college system. Other senior ministry and college officials also participated in that conference, enabling me to establish several contacts that would be quite helpful in later years.

Building on my previous teaching experience and the many ideas that I had picked up at the Lake Couchiching conference, I developed and conducted several workshops for new teachers, using videotape equipment to help them see themselves in action. This contrasted with the more theoretical approach to which some of my fellow teachers and I had been exposed at the Ontario College of Education.

The long established Forestry school in Dorset (a town about two hours north of Peterborough) was transferred to Sir Sandford Fleming College, to be housed in a new campus in Lindsay. I was dispatched to Dorset to do some training of the forestry instructors, lugging the huge videotape recorder in my car's backseat. The foresters were eager to further develop their teaching skills, and participated with enthusiasm in the various seminars that I organized. At the end of the sessions, they took me out fishing on a tranquil and beautiful lake.

Classes at the new college began in September 1967. I was quite busy teaching several electronics courses and labs, and participating in the many faculty meetings that were taking place. Academic policies were still being developed. People like myself, Sutherland, Robertson and a few others who had come from Ryerson had to learn to avoid saying things like: "At Ryerson we did it this way". While we wanted to create something new and better, it was easy to fall into the habit of just copying what had been the practice at Ryerson.

My teaching duties were most enjoyable and apparently the students appreciated my interest in them. During the winter I was very sick with the flu, but my spirits were lifted upon receiving a giant get well card signed by every student in the class. There was a student who was having great difficulty, especially in the lab. He would get very frustrated when the experiments did not work according to plan. He seemed to lack self-confidence. I spent many hours with him after class, going over each experiment step by step, until he got it right. My patience and interest in him paid off. Soon he was getting very high grades and eventually graduated with distinction. [32]

I developed good working relationships with all my colleagues at Sir Sandford. One English instructor impressed me for his creative approach to teaching. Bob Nielsen taught some of my technology students, who were notoriously reluctant to take courses such as English, because their primary interest was technology. Bob invited me to read some poetry in his English class. I agreed and read Edgar Allan Poe's "The Raven." This was Bob's way of demonstrating to the students that even engineers were interested in poetry! Apparently my brief performance had some positive results.

Peterborough was a very good place to raise a family. With my parents and sister nearby, it was, by most measures, an ideal location. While it did not have the amenities of a large city, Toronto, with its many attractions, was only a ninety minute drive away. I was very busy with my job and, with the exception of an occasional visit to Peterborough's famous "lift locks" and small zoo, didn't have much time for leisure activities. I did, however, take an interest in public affairs and participated in a "community forum" discussing the preliminary Report of the Royal Commission on Bilingualism and Biculturalism. The program was carried on the CBC radio network, in cooperation with the Canadian Institute of Public Affairs. This was my first "on air" CBC experience. It would not be the last!

It was now my fourth year of teaching (one in California, two at Ryerson in Toronto and one at Sir Sandford,) which gave me a great sense of fulfilment. I had learned that a good teacher needed several important qualities: a deep knowledge of the subject matter, the ability to communicate, a genuine interest in students and a commitment to keep on learning. In my view, one ceases to be effective as a teacher when one stops learning. That's because the ability to inspire, the empathy for learners, the excitement of discovery, withers and dies when one is no longer engaged in the learning process. And without these, there can be no effective teaching, only the emptiness of routine. Nothing pleased me more than observing a student's expression when he finally understood some concept that, until then, he had found totally mysterious. Now, because of my explanation, he was finally able to understand it. I should add, however, that a good teacher should also be able to know what questions not to answer. Students should be encouraged to think through some questions in order to develop the capacity to find the answers on their own.

My teaching approach relied heavily on analogies, using examples of everyday phenomena with which students were already familiar to help them understand a particular aspect of physics, electronics or mathematics.[33] To this day, although most of my career has been in senior management positions, I think of myself as a teacher first and foremost.

In the early part of 1968 I began thinking about the next academic year and my ambition to become a department head. The college would certainly grow and more staff would be hired. My relationship with Sutherland and Robertson had been good, but not as informal as in the early days. Robertson indicated that it was unlikely that they would appoint a chairman for the technology department in the near term and, even if they did, there would be other candidates to consider. He did not feel that I was ready to take on broader responsibilities, which was why he had given me opportunities to develop my administrative potential. While a department head position had not been guaranteed to me at the time of hiring, there had been a strong suggestion that such a promotion was likely. Certainly, Robertson and Sutherland had been eager enough to have me that they had also agreed to hire my father. I did not share Robertson's assessment of my readiness to assume broader responsibilities, but it was nevertheless useful to know what my prospects were at Sir Sandford. This led me to conclude that if I were to pursue my career aspirations, it would be wise to look elsewhere.

An opportunity came up when Confederation College advertised for a chairman of the technology department. This college was located in Fort William, in Northwestern Ontario, nearly one thousand miles (Canada had not switched to metric yet) from Peterborough. Lella wasn't exactly thrilled to learn of my interest in applying for this job. But she reluctantly went along with my plan when I explained that, if successful, we would only stay there for three or four years, until a suitable position became available in Southern Ontario. The idea of leaving my parents and Ester in Peterborough after moving them from Toronto did not appeal to me either, but they seemed to be settling in very nicely.

Mitch Anderson, the dean at Confederation College, had taught in the electrical department at Ryerson. He had a reputation as an able and decent person. Before formally expressing my interest in this position, I called him and asked if it would be appropriate for me to become a candidate. It was my way of finding out whether there were internal competitors who might already hold an advantage. Mitch assured me that it would be quite appropriate for me to apply.

A short time after submitting my application, I was invited to an interview with Mitch Anderson and the college president, Air Vice Marshal D.A.R. Bradshaw. He had retired from the air force, where he had served in very senior capacities, including a stint with NATO in Italy. He was a very distinguished man, highly intelligent, courteous and clearly possessing a strong presence. During the interview, Mitch asked a few routine questions about my background and management philosophy. Bradshaw did not ask any questions. Instead he gave a lengthy presentation of the challenges facing Confederation College. He began by pointing out that the college served 250,000 people, in an area of 250,000 square miles, which was larger than France. Most of this territory was inaccessible by road and could be reached only by plane, on skis during the winter, and on floats during the summer. He would then talk about the major industries located in the area served by the college (mining, pulp and paper, manufacturing and tourism), and the special challenges faced by the many aboriginal communities. He went on and on; it was quite fascinating. I noticed that, whenever Mitch wanted to say something to the president, he would address him as Sir. At Sir Sandford Fleming College, everybody called the president by his first name, Dave. But you didn't do that with Air Vice Marshal Bradshaw. In fact, nobody on the staff at Confederation College even knew his first name.

A few days after my interview, I received an offer of employment as chairman of the technology department at Confederation College, effective on June 1, 1968. It came directly from the president, but it would certainly have been based on Mitch's recommendation. There would be a substantial increase in salary. I accepted the offer and immediately wrote my resignation letter to Dave Sutherland, indicating my appreciation for the opportunity he and George Robertson had given me to participate in the starting up of the new college. Despite my disappointment at not having been offered a position as department head at Sir Sandford, it was not my intent to burn any bridges. Dave Sutherland replied, saying that my letter of resignation deserved an A++, for its positive tone and superb writing. As a former English teacher, he appreciated good writing.

During the Easter break, Lella and I drove to Fort William and bought a brand new house in a very nice neighbourhood. We sold our house in Peterborough quite easily, without a real estate agent.

When we had moved to Peterborough, it was my expectation that we would spend the rest of our lives there, with me working as a department head at the college. I had no higher ambition, and Peterborough seemed like a very pleasant place in which to live. Our early exit from Peterborough, however, did turn out to be an entry to a much more promising career.

CHAPTER SIX

June 1, 1968 was my first day as chairman of the technology division with Confederation College. Mitch Anderson would be my immediate boss and I was confident that we would get along quite well. Only three programs were in operation at the time: electronics technician, mechanical drafting technician and engineering technology.

The Lakehead, as the combined cities of Fort William and Port Arthur were known, was a relatively isolated community of about 120,000 people. The nearest large city was Winnipeg, about 450 miles away. Toronto was almost 1000 miles away. Winter came early and stayed late. Snow had been known to fall in June. By mid-August, the leaves on trees would start changing their colour. Winters could be extremely cold, with temperatures as low as 40 degrees below zero, but this was offset by abundant sunshine. Snowfalls would usually be quite heavy. People who enjoyed winter sports loved it. Summers were short but very pleasant. Temperatures never got too hot and there was no humidity. There was certainly no need for air conditioning.

Confederation College had been operating for one year in portable classrooms and rented office space. It was in the process of building a temporary pre-fabricated type of building with classrooms, laboratories and office space on a 100 acre site the college had bought. During that first summer, I worked out of the rented office space in downtown Fort William. Most of my activity was to hire faculty for the coming fall term.

Attracting teachers to the Lakehead was a challenge. We could offer an incentive of $600 per year, called the Northern allowance, to compensate people for the additional cost of living in the area. We usually advertised in the Toronto Globe and Mail, and tried to recruit people who were originally from the Lakehead and wanted to come back to be close to family and friends. However, the bulk of our new recruits had never heard of the area and had no idea what to expect. Mitch Anderson and I did the interviewing, usually in Toronto. Finalists would be flown to the Lakehead to see the place for themselves and to have a final interview with the president, who insisted on meeting every new employee. He rarely asked any questions. Instead he would repeat his monologue about the area served by the college (250,000 square miles, larger than France, with 250,000 people, etc.) I would be expected to attend these so-called interviews and sit through the same speech, time after time. It was a challenge for me to stay awake during each session!

As newly recruited faculty members arrived, usually from southern Ontario, they invariably asked about the purpose of the electric outlets next to each parking space. We took a perverse type of delight in pointing out that, unless they plugged their car into one of those outlets during the winter, it probably wouldn't start at the end of the day. In fact, it was necessary for each car to have a block heater, a battery heater and ideally, an interior air heater. Usually the interior air heater would be on a timer, programmed to turn on about half an hour before the expected use of the vehicle so that it would be warm inside. During the winter my car would be parked at the edge of the driveway, with a long electrical extension cord to plug in the block heater, battery heater and interior car heater in the electrical outlet at the side of the house. This way, it would not be necessary to shovel the whole driveway in case of a heavy snowfall during the night. I could drive off directly into the street in order to get to work on time. Lella would do most of the shovelling during the day.

By September 1968, our temporary, pre-fabricated building was ready on the college campus. It contained classrooms, laboratories, offices, library, audio visual centre and a cafeteria. My faculty and I had ordered quite a bit of equipment and supplies. I had begun the process that would eventually add several new programs in civil engineering technology, architectural engineering technician and technology, radiological technician, aircraft maintenance technician, television broadcasting, industrial electronics and telecommunications. I established advisory committees made up of people from the industry for which we were training students and proceeded to develop my faculty.[34]

In September of that first year, facing the long cold Lakehead winter, several of the senior administrators and I decided to make wine. Mitch Anderson claimed to have some expertise in this kind of activity and since none of the rest of us had any idea how to go about it, we bowed to his leadership. (All we knew was that we needed grapes and somehow we had to squeeze them and allow the juice to ferment). Later, to our great chagrin, we discovered that Mitch had exaggerated his wine making skills.

I offered the use of my basement for this project (without my wife's knowledge). We ordered one ton of grapes from California and a few days later, a huge truck unloaded some 36 cases of grapes at my house. Meanwhile, we had bought several very large oak barrels and glass demijohns. I had also rented a grape crusher and other implements necessary for the task. My wife was quite upset when she learned about this plan, but by then, I had already made the commitment. As soon as the grapes arrived, my colleagues and I proceeded to press the grapes and place the juice in the barrels, along with the required yeast to induce fermentation.

Soon the liquid began fermenting and all seemed to be going well, until one day when I received a frantic call at the office from my wife, telling me that the barrels were leaking. My colleagues and I were involved in a very important meeting at the time. As soon as I shared the news with them, we immediately ran out of the meeting and headed for my house, without telling the bewildered secretaries what was happening. They must have thought we had gone crazy!

Upon arrival at my basement, we found several barrels that were leaking. Over the next few hours, we used every conceivable container we could find in our homes to remove as much fermenting juice from the barrels as possible, in order to relieve the pressure. The basement was full of huge pots and assorted containers of every sort. There was juice all over the floor. We learned, the hard way, that the barrels should have been filled with water for several days, allowing the wood to expand and provide a tight seal for the fermenting juice. None of us had thought about this, so we ended up with the leaky barrels. Eventually things settled down and when the fermentation process ended, we proceeded to distribute the wine among the members of the group.

Mitch had bought a small barrel for his share and we filled it with wine. It's amazing how heavy even a small barrel of wine can be. We wrapped thick ropes around it and four people proceeded to carry it up the wooden stairs from the basement. Unfortunately, they dropped the barrel half-way up. This caused damage to the stairs and the bung also came out of the top. The force of the drop caused wine to shoot up from the opening, spraying the ceiling and walls with wine. What a disaster! Eventually we cleaned up the mess and repaired the steps, but the smell of wine permeated the whole basement for months! The neighbours could also smell the wine, which turned out to be drinkable, which is not to say that it was particularly good. But in the cold Lakehead winter, it wasn't too bad! Needless to say, I have never attempted to make wine again and I'm still married to Lella!

Anderson and Bradshaw were important role models and mentors. Anderson helped me to develop a better understanding of the perspectives of faculty in the other divisions, such as applied arts and business. He and I were both engineers, but he had experience overseeing departments other than technology and, by observing him, I was able to learn many valuable lessons about bridging the gaps between different disciplines.

Bradshaw's strong leadership qualities had been developed over many years in the Royal Canadian Air Force. He would often drop by my office to chat. He had a clear sense of what he wanted the college to accomplish and communicated his vision often and without any ambiguity. He helped me to become much more self-confident and at ease with people more senior than me. He was always focused on the big picture and could see how different individuals could contribute to the achievement of important goals. He was a good listener, an important element of effective leadership. He also taught me about the dangers of stereotyping. We all have a tendency to think of people in the role that we have known them to play and sometimes have difficulty seeing them in a different role. *"Artists are temperamental, accountants are boring, women are emotional, engineers are detail oriented, military people are authoritarian, businessmen are greedy."* These kinds of prejudices, even if not openly articulated, condition many of our judgements, even sub-consciously and hence limit our ability to derive maximum benefit from each individual's potential.

Deborah started school during our first year in the Lakehead (she was a few months shy of her 6th birthday). There were several families in our age bracket living in the neighbourhood, which was ideal for Deborah, who enjoyed playing with the other children. We made several good friends at the college and in our area. We saw some of them on and off after we left, including periods in the 90's when we spent our winters in Florida. The Lakehead was a friendly community and boasted many recreational and cultural activities which would not normally be found in a city of 120,000 people. It was an ideal place for people who enjoyed the outdoors, especially hunting, fishing, camping, skiing and travelling on snowmobiles. Unfortunately, we were not the outdoor type, especially during winter, which took up a large part of the year.

Lella and I tried bowling with our neighbours (with limited success) and we attended several performances of the symphony orchestra, for which I carried out fund raising. There were also college related social functions in which we participated. Given my disastrous experience with wine making, this type of activity was definitely off limits! Instead, I rode my bike when the weather allowed and took swimming lessons. In accordance with established precedent, Sunday afternoons were reserved for a scenic drive, enjoying the area's natural attractions, such as the "Sleeping Giant" (a mountain whose flat top resembled the shape of a giant man lying down) and "Kakabeka Falls", a majestic waterfall about 20 miles from the city. Lella kept house and looked after Deborah and me. She also taught a course in Italian at the college aimed at nurses who looked after older Italian speaking patients. She worked very hard to make the course useful and her students showed their appreciation by presenting her with a beautiful decorative plate.

One interesting experience that I would rather forget involved my getting a speeding ticket while driving along the major road that led from the college to my home. The police officer had clocked me as travelling well over the speed limit and while I didn't doubt that I was driving fast, I didn't think it was that much over the limit. I decided to challenge the speeding ticket and was pleasantly surprised when I appeared in court presided by a judge who taught a part time course in Law at the college. I had met him on several occasions during which we had exchanged pleasantries. But my expectation of a sympathetic hearing was quickly shattered when the judge, who happened to live in the same neighbourhood as I did, dismissed my objection by saying: "I have seen you drive around the neighbourhood, and I don't doubt at all that the officer is right!" And so, I dutifully thanked His Honour and paid my fine.

Meanwhile, the college kept expanding. My position of "chairman" was renamed "director" and then "dean". I was allowed to appoint three department chairmen, one for each of the major program areas reporting to me.

Bradshaw was interested in starting an aircraft maintenance program, to meet the needs for aircraft mechanics for the area's large number of small aircraft operating outfits. He had already found a local company owner who provided valuable advice and donated several used aircraft and engines to the college for the students to work on. I recruited the staff, mainly retired air force personnel who had many years of experience maintaining aircraft. A hangar at the local airport turned out to be an ideal location for the program, which was successfully launched after a brief but rigorous planning process.

Many of the faculty that I recruited turned out to become excellent teachers. Some of them moved on to successful careers in administration. One of my more interesting teachers was a mechanical engineer from Pakistan named P. Ramanathan. Everybody called him Ram. When he first called in response to an ad in the Globe and Mail, I could hardly understand him. His accent was so strong that he would have to repeat himself several times before he could be understood. I had serious reservations about him, but he sounded very enthusiastic. His qualifications were impressive and in spite of my concerns about whether the students would be able to understand him, I hired him. As it turned out, he became an outstanding teacher. His enthusiasm, interest in students and technical competence made up for his speaking difficulties and the students consistently rated him as one of their best teachers.[35]

The rapid expansion of the colleges also resulted in the hiring of some individuals who were not suited to an academic role. Evaluating the potential of an individual to fill a particular job is not a science. You can do all the interviews and reference checks you want and be very impressed with someone, only to discover later that he or she isn't quite the person you thought they were. It would be nice if I could say that my instincts were always right. Alas, I can't. I hired some people, not just at Confederation, but also in my later positions, who didn't work out. Some of them were good people; they just didn't fit in. It pained me to have to tell them that their appointments would not be renewed, especially in those cases where they had left good jobs in other parts of Canada to join the college. It was important to make such decisions, unpleasant as they were, as soon as possible. Giving someone extra time to adapt seldom worked; it just made it that much more difficult when the time of reckoning arrived. In spite of these realities, my annual faculty turn-over was a modest 6%.

Throughout my stay at Confederation College, I taught a course in electronic circuits, to keep in touch with my field of expertise and also with the challenges of teaching. It was somewhat unusual for someone in my position to teach, since the administrative duties were quite onerous and keeping up with a field such as electronics, which was changing quite rapidly, was not easy. But I read a lot of literature on the latest advances and often talked shop with the other electronics teachers. Having a regular teaching schedule also helped me to gain the respect of the faculty, since I could speak from experience about the challenges that they faced. The other benefit, of course, was the ongoing contact with students. This was always pleasant, even though at the beginning of each term, my first message was that, if they were really interested in a career in electronics, they should be prepared to move from Thunder Bay. I had delivered the same message to my students in Peterborough and it was not always popular. Students, after all, had family and friends in their community. But I felt it was my duty to tell them the truth. My views clashed with the official policy of the Ministry of Colleges and Universities, who kept telling us that our job was to prepare students for employment in their geographic area. Although I understood the Ministry's thinking, which was to foster industrial growth in each region, I didn't think that restricting our college programs to serve only the industries located in our college region made much sense. At any rate, graduates made their own choices, with many moving to wherever the jobs were. This enabled us to achieve a 95% job placement rate, which was a success by any standard.

As indicated earlier, the president still insisted on interviewing every faculty member we wanted to hire, repeating his usual speech about the college area being 250,000 square miles, larger than France, etc. One year, he was going to be away on vacation, and I needed a quick decision on hiring a new teacher for an opening that was difficult to fill. It was not possible to arrange a time when both the prospective new teacher and the president could meet, so I asked Bradshaw if this time he would allow me and Mitch to make the final decision, without a presidential interview. He replied: "Of course, go right ahead". I was relieved by his response, not just because I could hire the teacher quickly, but also because I wouldn't have to sit through another rendition of the president's recitation of the challenges faced by the college. My relief, however, was short-lived. He continued by saying: "The only reason I want to interview these new teachers is not because I don't trust your judgement, it's to tell them about our college area, that it's 250,000 square miles, etc." There was no escape from having to listen to the president's speech after all!

In 1970 Lella and I decided that it was time for us to take a vacation in Italy. We had dreamed about visiting our native country for a long time and we looked forward to seeing again our many relatives and friends.

Before we could travel to Italy, however, there was the issue of the military draft to be resolved. Under Italian law, every Italian born male at the age of 18 had to register for the draft and serve two years in the military. This applied even to people like me, who had left Italy at the age of 11 and had been a Canadian citizen for several years. It became necessary for me to complete some bureaucratic paperwork before leaving Canada to avoid being arrested in Italy for evading the draft.

In August 1970, Lella, Deborah and I finally left for Italy. It was quite an emotional experience to return to the land of our birth. In Rome we stayed at Lella's mother's house. We went to the beach and saw many interesting sights, including St. Peter's Cathedral, the catacombs, the Colosseum and so on. I rented a car and quickly began to drive like all the other Italian crazy drivers who seemed oblivious to all the normal rules of the road.

From Rome, we drove to Sicily on the Autostrada del Sole, the freeway that runs through the Italian peninsula. First, we visited Pompei. This was an extraordinary experience. We walked through ancient streets among the ruins of a thriving city, buried beneath the volcanic ashes of Mount Vesuvius for eighteen hundred years.

We then proceeded to Ficarra, the small town where I was born. The main square was much smaller than I remembered. As we walked towards my aunt's house (where my father and all his brothers and sisters had been born), many memories from my early childhood flashed through my mind. It was a deeply moving experience.

The roads in small towns like Ficarra were quite narrow and twisted. We were up in the mountains, and one had to be very careful, especially when another vehicle came from the opposite side. Given the Italians' tendency to drive recklessly, one had to be especially vigilant.

We visited as many relatives as we could. Their hospitality was first class and we were welcomed with great love and affection everywhere we went. I took many pictures and slides on this trip, which was quite memorable.

From Ficarra we drove to Palermo, where I had lived from the age of six (1946) until I was eleven (1951). As we walked about the city, we observed the many once fashionable baroque style palaces, now in decay through neglect and the ravages of time. The traffic was heavy and a strong sense of history permeated everything we saw. This is a place where many different cultures coalesced into a uniquely Sicilian mosaic. We also visited the building where I had lived. The small room had been converted to a storage area for the pharmacy, which was still operating. Seeing where her father had lived as a boy made a strong impression on Deborah, who was seven years old. It also brought back many memories, as I reflected on the much better life that my family and I had been able to make for ourselves in Canada.

It was quite a shock to return to our home in Thunder Bay! We had left the intense August heat of Italy to find that the leaves on the trees had already changed colour and that winter was not far off.

In 1970, the Ontario government directed the two cities of Fort William and Port Arthur to amalgamate. They were side by side, yet had two municipal governments, two police forces, two fire departments, two transit systems and so on. It didn't make sense to have such duplication, but there was much resistance to the amalgamation. The new city was named Thunder Bay but people valued their identity and for many years after amalgamation, they continued to use the old names of Fort William and Port Arthur. (They probably still do).

While at Confederation College, I began to think about writing a textbook on electronic circuits. My knowledge of transistor circuits was quite up-to-date and I was confident of my ability to explain complex circuits better than most textbooks on the market at the time. Because the Canadian market was relatively small, most textbooks of this kind were published in the US. Hence, I approached several of the most likely US publishers, with a description and sample first chapter of my proposed book. Four of the largest US publishers responded favourably, sending me contracts with terms for an advance and royalties. I chose McGraw-Hill Book Company, because of its size, worldwide distribution network, and overall reputation.

Work on this project took up many evenings and weekends over the next four years. My secretary, who was the fastest typist I have ever known, agreed to work after hours (I paid her an hourly rate equivalent to overtime pay) to type the various chapters. It was particularly challenging to incorporate the various mathematical formulas, which included many Greek letters and symbols. In those days, we still used carbon paper and corrections had to be made with white paint on each copy. As soon as each chapter was finished, I would send it to McGraw-Hill in New York, where my editor would distribute copies to several reviewers across the US who would critique the material and send me their comments. I would then make the necessary revisions. It was extremely time consuming work, especially the approximately one thousand illustrations involving circuit diagrams and graphs, which would have to be reproduced photographically for incorporation in the book.

I had promised Lella that we would only stay in Thunder Bay between three and four years; by 1971 the time felt right to leave. Confederation College had treated me very well and both Mitch and the president were very good bosses. Nevertheless, Thunder Bay was so distant from the major population centres and the winters were so long, that we were eager to move on.

In the summer of that year, a job as Dean of Technology was advertised by Algonquin College, in Ottawa. This was the same position I held in Thunder Bay, but Algonquin College was a much larger institution and Ottawa had the advantage of being a major city, close to Peterborough where my parents and sister lived. We could visit them in just a three hour drive rather than the two days it took from Thunder Bay. I was called for an interview and prepared extensively for it, doing considerable research on the college and its offerings. I felt optimistic about my prospects.

101

At about the same time, an advertisement appeared in the Globe and Mail for president of Niagara College in Welland, Ontario. Niagara College had been in the news earlier, as a result of serious problems between the faculty and the administration. The president had resigned and the senior academic dean had accepted a lower level position. Everything pointed to a college facing major challenges. While discussing this with Lella, I expressed the view that only someone with holes in his head would apply for this position!

In my estimation, I wasn't senior enough to be a credible candidate for college president. A dean or vice president of academic studies, with experience overseeing not only technology programs, but also business, applied arts and retraining, would have been a more likely prospect. I was also relatively young, only 31 years old. But despite my misgivings about the troubled college and with the full knowledge that my candidacy would be a long shot, I decided to apply, carefully crafting my resume and letter of application. This involved doing substantial research on the role of college presidents, mainly by reading articles in US publications, where the "junior college" system had been well established for many years. My letter of application incorporated a summary of my educational and management philosophy and how I would handle the sensitive situation at Niagara College.

The interview for the position of Dean of Technology at Algonquin College went very well and I returned home hopeful of getting the job. A few weeks later a letter arrived informing me that someone else had been selected. Lella and I were deeply disappointed. I had been quite optimistic about my chances at Algonquin and felt the rejection very badly.[36]

The following Monday, at the college, there was a phone call from Dave Saunders, a consultant with the firm of Woods Gordon, who was handling the recruitment of a president for Niagara College. They had received eighty applications and I was one of eight candidates who had been selected for an interview. I was pleasantly surprised.

Dave Saunders flew up to Thunder Bay and interviewed me in his hotel room for a couple of hours one morning. By the time the interview was over, he invited me to have lunch with him. We continued to chat about educational philosophy, management style, human relations, financial matters, etc. It was a very satisfying and enjoyable experience. Dave Saunders was thoroughly acquainted with the issues; he knew what questions to ask and he obviously appreciated my answers. I did not, however, build up my hopes, having learned from the Algonquin experience not to be overly optimistic. Besides, with eight candidates being interviewed, it was obvious that seven of them would ultimately be rejected. So it was still a long shot for me.

A few days later, there was another call from Dave Saunders. He told me that the number of candidates had been narrowed down to five or six, and that I was on the short list. He invited me to an interview with the consultant in charge of the search, Larry McAuley, in London, Ontario. This was to be followed by another interview with the Niagara College Search Committee in Welland. At this point, I decided to tell Mitch and the president about my candidacy, to avoid their finding out through a leak of some kind. Mitch, though supportive, felt that it was premature to let the president know. I thought otherwise.

Bradshaw reacted very positively to the news. He knew how not to judge people on the basis of the role that they had been performing and could see their potential in other, more demanding roles. He was genuinely happy to hear that I had been interviewed and was now on the short list. He didn't want to lose me but would do everything in his power to help me get the job. Such a vote of confidence from the college president meant a lot to me.

My interview in London with Larry McAuley was essentially pro-forma. As the partner in charge of this search, he naturally wanted to meet candidates who were scheduled to meet with the search committee. That interview took place on the following day. The committee had about ten members: seven from the board of governors, one faculty representative, one administrator and one student. The interview lasted well over two hours and was quite wide ranging. The chairman of the search committee was a board member named Alex Sharp. He was the area representative for the United Steel Workers Union. Also on the committee was Dick Harwood, who was chairman of the Niagara College board and general manager of Maple Leaf Mills in nearby Port Colborne. Another board member, Margaret Buchanan, who had been a social worker, took a special interest in my early years when we were struggling in poverty in Sicily and seemed impressed by how I had worked my way through university as a waiter. I seemed to have made a positive impression on the faculty member who served on the selection committee. Dave Colussi, an English teacher, very much appreciated my commitment to the academic process. Also important to me was the reaction of the student representative, Rick Smith, who later remarked that "he is the type of man I'd like to negotiate with. He answers your questions in a straightforward manner without hesitation. I was looking for someone who could communicate with students. Manera can do it".

The whole process, in fact, was very stimulating but also exhausting. At any rate, I was satisfied with my performance, believing that I had given it my best possible shot and that no matter how things would eventually turn out, there was nothing that I could or should have done differently. So I treated myself to a Manhattan cocktail and great steak dinner with a robust red wine that evening.

A short time later, back in Thunder Bay, Dave Saunders called again. The field had been narrowed down to two or three candidates. I was one of them, and he asked me to go for yet another interview, this time with the full board of twelve people. I geared myself up for this fourth interview, and discussed the situation with Bradshaw who kept encouraging me. The interview with the full board was quite comprehensive and encouraging. The possibility that I might be successful in getting this job was no longer beyond reach. However, neither Lella nor I wanted to get our hopes up.

I returned to Thunder Bay and waited to hear the news. By now, the fact that I was one of the finalist candidates for the job of president at Niagara College had become common knowledge. My colleagues kept congratulating me on having gotten this far and wishing me well. The next phone call from McAuley was not to inform me of the final decision, but rather to ask me to return for yet another interview with the board!

This fifth interview took place a short time later. Niagara College had obviously experienced difficult times and the board had made many tough decisions. Naturally, they wanted to hire the right person for the job. They couldn't risk appointing a second president who didn't work out. Hence I understood the reasons for their caution, but the extremely lengthy process was causing me a lot of stress. I wanted to get it over with, one way or the other.

Upon my return to Thunder Bay, Larry McAuley called and told me that the board was to meet on Thursday, November 25, 1971, to make a final decision. That evening, after dinner, the phone rang. Lella and I looked at each other, wondering if this could be "the phone call". It was. Dick Harwood, the chairman of the board, was on the line. He told me that the board was offering me the position of president of Niagara College, together with details of salary, benefits and so on. I accepted the offer and agreed to start on January 1, 1972, just a month and a few days later.

Lella and I were delighted. The next day, I informed Mitch and the president. Soon the word spread and congratulations began to pour in from various colleagues. Several members of my faculty lined up outside my office to shake my hand. They would be sorry to see me go but were very happy for me. The head of the English department (who did not report to me) came up to kiss me on both cheeks! Presidents, rightly or wrongly, were often seen as distant from the teaching process. He was delighted that "one of us" had been chosen as president![37]

Later that day I called my parents and sister to tell them the good news. They, too, were happy to learn that we would soon be living closer.

Much needed to be done in a short time. Several projects at Confederation College had to be wound up and there was much reading to do in preparation for my new duties at Niagara. The house had to be put up for sale. Letters of congratulations came from other college presidents, Ministry officials and several former and current colleagues. Herb Jackson, director of college affairs for the Ministry of Colleges and Universities, told me not to be discouraged when I met my fellow presidents, with their grey hair, wrinkles, shaking hands and glasses of milk for their ulcers! At the time I thought he was trying to be funny by exaggerating the challenges faced by my presidential colleagues. Alas, he was not. As the recently appointed president of Mohawk College in Hamilton, Sam Mitminger, pointed out, in a curiously sadistic streak, that the job was much tougher than he had thought. Several messages of commitment and full support arrived from numerous staff members at Niagara College.

The Confederation College experience had been of great value to me. It was the first position where I had exercised authority to hire and fire people. Many new programs had been established, and a strong faculty had been developed, with several outstanding members. New laboratories had been created and important partnerships with local industries were now in place. I had established valuable linkages with all major industries (mining, pulp and paper, transportation) in the college area, from Kenora to Dryden, Atikokan, Terrace Bay, Geraldton, Red Lake etc. My range of technical knowledge had expanded beyond electronics and I had learned a great deal about administration and leadership. Rubbing shoulders with senior people, especially the president, helped me to be at ease with individuals and groups of professionals. I had participated in several workshops organized by community and government groups to attract new industries to the area, in order to boost the local economy. My self-confidence had been growing and I felt a high level of comfort dealing with complex problems, especially those involving people. All of these skills and then some, would be needed to tackle the challenges of my next job.

CHAPTER SEVEN

On January 1, 1972, I became officially the new president of Niagara College and, at 31, the youngest person in Canada to hold such an office. I was confident, but also apprehensive at the immensity of the task at hand. There were many good people at Niagara College, but they weren't all pulling in the same direction. There were also, as there are in all organizations, some poor performers. I knew that things would have to change, but just how this could be accomplished was not clear. It was also my intention to play an active educational role, leading with innovation strategies, improving the quality of learning and expanding the range of programs offered by the college.

On a personal level, our family would be living closer to my parents and sister, and enjoy a milder climate in the Niagara peninsula than we had endured in Thunder Bay. All kinds of tender fruit grew in Niagara's orchards - peaches and pears, grapes, cherries and plums.   Toronto, with its many attractions, was nearby.

While Niagara College's main campus was located in Welland, there were several smaller "satellite" campuses in other parts of the Niagara Peninsula. The college, in fact, served a total population of approximately 350,000 in Welland, St. Catharines, Niagara Falls, Niagara on the Lake, Fort Erie, Port Colborne and a few other smaller communities.

A broad range of programs in applied arts, technology, business, health sciences and retraining were offered by the college. A few specific programs that illustrate the diversity of the college's offerings are electronics, early childhood education, theatre arts, journalism, broadcasting, personnel relations, welding, machine shop, English for new Canadians, and so on. Other programs would be added over the next few years.

It was the college's mission to prepare students for employment, which meant that it had to maintain contacts and collaborative relationships with potential employers. These linkages could not be limited to the college's catchment area, because graduates would often have to move away to find suitable employment. An important vehicle for fulfilling the college's mandate was a system of advisory committees, each made up of people from the various sectors that would hopefully employ its graduates. It was my intention to strengthen these advisory committees, giving them a role in evaluating the degree to which programs were meeting their objectives.

As indicated previously, there had been budget difficulties at the college and the administration had laid off a number of staff members. The faculty association had objected strongly and charged the administration with mismanagement and other misdeeds. They claimed the financial situation had been used as a pretext for firing faculty members the administration didn't like. They had submitted a lengthy brief in which these allegations were made and expanded upon. The brief had gone to the college's board of governors, the Ministry of Education and the Council of Regents. The hostility between the faculty association and the college administration had been fierce.

Niagara College was not unique in having internal difficulties. Many colleges were experiencing similar tensions between their senior administration and their faculty, who were in the process of unionizing. Issues sometimes arose when a president lost the confidence of his board or the staff and, whatever the merits of the case, the president would face pressure to resign. The faculty association at Niagara had passed a motion of no confidence in the previous president and the board had obviously reached the same conclusion. Following my predecessor's departure, the laid off faculty members were reinstated, and each one of them received a letter stating that their lay-off was not due to any performance problem on their part, but caused by budgetary issues.

Against this backdrop, my immediate challenge was to create an environment where faculty, administrators and support staff could work harmoniously in the best interests of students. My strategy was to develop a set of goals and objectives that the entire college community could support, and follow this with appropriate action plans. The goals I had in mind focussed on offering programs that were practical and relevant, not theoretical. There would be no secret agenda with me!

As president, I wanted to be accessible and to communicate with the entire college community as often as possible. I believed in delegating authority so that decisions could be made as close to the level of their implementation as possible. At the same time, I expected accountability and results that would be evaluated. I understood that, like any other human being, I could mess things up all by myself, but if I wanted to achieve positive outcomes, I would need assistance from a lot of people who shared my passion for excellence in education.

It was also important for me to establish positive working relationships with the board of governors, the Ministry of Education, the Council of Regents and the community at large. Many of these people were probably curious as to how I would perform, given my relatively young age and limited senior managerial experience. However, I felt that the board of governors, having selected me, would want me to succeed and therefore, I could count on their support. I also had faculty and student support, given their participation on the selection committee.

After the departure of my predecessor, the dean of the School of Applied Arts, John Giancarlo, had been acting president. He had also been a candidate for the permanent appointment. If he was disappointed at not getting the top job, it certainly did not detract from his professional performance. Given the huge challenges faced by the incoming president, he may actually have felt relieved that someone else had been selected! John turned out to be one of the best leaders and administrators in the Ontario college system at the time. He and his wife Shirley also became close friends with Lella and me, and remain so to this day.

I was most fortunate to inherit a secretary who was exceptionally talented. Mary Hornak was highly efficient, intelligent, discreet, loyal, courteous and respected by everyone. Her first question when I was appointed was whether I smoked cigars. She was quite relieved to learn that I had no such vice! I valued her contribution very highly. She also became a friend to Lella and me and we still stay in touch.

In order to keep administrative costs down, and be as close to the students and to the teaching process as possible, I adopted a flat organizational structure, with no overall dean of faculty or academic vice president. This increased my workload, as I had ten senior people reporting to me, and required me to spend more time coordinating their activities and resolving the various conflicts that arose from time to time. Given the circumstances, I believe this was the best model to avoid the perception of the president as someone who was remote from the academic process.

In addition to the board and senior management, I had to develop a positive working relationship with the faculty association and the student council. Those were the days of student protests all over the world, and "participatory democracy" was the buzzword of the times. I had a very capable director of student affairs, Al Aboud, who communicated well with students, and I also met regularly with the student council. Of course, there were often issues that had to be addressed, but we never had any really serious student problems.

The relationship with the faculty association was more challenging. At the beginning of my term, their executive was in a militant mood, as a result of their battles with the previous administration. I needed to earn their trust, but they also had to understand that I had certain responsibilities and would not shy away from unpopular stands when, in my judgement, these were required.

Some faculty association members held grudges against certain administrators for the role they had played in the implementation of the layoffs. Although I sensed that the previous administration had probably mishandled some decisions, I had no desire to re-open the wounds and wanted to move forward. For example, the faculty association wanted me to dismiss Arnot McIntee, dean of business and continuing education. I found Arnot to be a strong leader. He got things done and was always anticipating issues, so he could stay on top of them. Unfortunately, he had inherited a faculty with more than its fair share of difficult individuals. He wouldn't put up with poor performers, which made him unpopular. But I valued his contribution and retained him in his position throughout my presidency. Sometime after my departure, he retired and was able to pursue his lifelong dedication to the Christian Ministry, which gave him great satisfaction.

I met regularly with the faculty association executive. Most of our meetings started immediately after I finished teaching my class, as this was the most convenient time for all concerned.[38] We would often engage in informal discussion about our classroom experiences before taking up the issues we had agreed to discuss. This type of informal dialogue served as a reminder of our common purpose to ensure that the best interests of our students were always paramount.

I listened to the faculty association's complaints and tried to address them all. Most of the time they were satisfied. On some of their demands, however, I would take a very firm stand, refusing to buckle under pressure. They quickly learned that when I said NO, no amount of pressure would change my mind. On a couple of occasions, one of their members made it clear to me that they had succeeded in getting rid of the previous president and could arrange the same fate for me if I didn't bend to their wishes. I took such comments in stride, sensing that the faculty in general were not unhappy with my leadership. My efforts to give priority to the academic issues over administrative matters was quite evident. I also frequently communicated with the faculty at large and kept them posted on the big issues affecting the college.

One of my earliest confrontations with the faculty association was over my firing of a teacher. The firing was amply justified but the faculty association strongly objected to the idea that one of its members could be fired for any cause. I remember putting the question hypothetically to their executive during one of our meetings. Would they support the firing of one of their members, if they were convinced that the firing was justified? Their answer was clear. They would fight any dismissal, even if they agreed that the teacher deserved to be dismissed.

That position was very difficult for me to understand. After all, they were supposed to be professionals, but the union mentality had taken such a hold that they were unable or unwilling to get past it. When this teacher was fired, the faculty union president stormed into my office yelling and screaming in protest. The fired teacher was one of those who had been laid off by the previous administration, then had been hired back after the faculty protests. Like all other teachers who had been laid off, he had a letter signed by the administration saying there was nothing wrong with his performance and the lay-offs had been entirely due to financial difficulties faced by the college. This made it more difficult for me to justify his firing for cause, but I felt that there were ample grounds for my action. I told the union president that I wouldn't respond to his ranting and raving. The firing was immediately grieved by the union, and the issue went to an arbitration board, which eventually upheld my decision.

This case served two purposes. The first, of course, was getting rid of a poorly qualified person who should not have been hired as a teacher in the first place. The second was the demonstration that I could not be intimidated and that the faculty association was not invincible. Actually, I believe the faculty association president was just putting on a show, to demonstrate to other members of the faculty that he was aggressively pursuing their interests. In private conversations, he was quite tame and conciliatory. Eventually the composition of the faculty association executive changed and, while we still had some disagreements, a genuine atmosphere of mutual respect developed.

One of the realities I had to confront during my early days as president, aside from the sometimes testy relationship with the faculty association, was the enormous amount of time required to deal with non educational issues. Perhaps I had been naïve, expecting to perform as an educational leader, someone who would promote innovation and improve the quality of the learning process of each student. But events beyond my control conspired to limit the time and effort I could devote to these pursuits. Far too much of my energy was consumed by things like building construction issues, budget problems and personnel matters. With the benefit of hindsight, the provincial government should have taken more time to roll out the new college system. While the pressures that led to the "fast track" approach were real and important, a slower development process would have avoided many of the growing pains associated with the early days of the colleges.

An example of the sort of thing that interfered with my educational agenda was a series of anonymous bomb threats.[39] They would usually be called in to the switchboard and I would have to decide whether to evacuate the college. The police would be called in and a thorough search would be undertaken. Evacuating the entire campus, including the day care centre, where many small children were being looked after, was always difficult and represented a serious disruption to our routine. Exams would sometimes have to be rescheduled, for example. Eventually, we developed a protocol that involved the switchboard operator asking a series of pre-determined questions and, based on that information, I would decide whether to evacuate.

Another example of a very time consuming and frustrating problem was the noise level in several lecture halls in one of the buildings that had been constructed before my arrival at Niagara College. The ventilation system was so noisy that students at the back of the class couldn't hear the teacher. After lengthy investigations by various experts, it was determined that the ducts providing ventilation in these spaces were not large enough to deliver an adequate supply of fresh air. This meant that fan speeds had to be increased, resulting in higher than normal noise levels. It was impossible to change the size of the existing ducts, hence several creative solutions had to be found. I hired an expert acoustics consultant who came up with a number of suggestions that ultimately reduced the noise to a more tolerable level. It involved altering the pitch of the fan blades that pushed air into the ducts, and the installation of heavy drapes along the windows that absorbed some of the noise. It was a trial and error approach, but it worked. The college was successful in negotiating compensation from the previous consultants who had designed the ventilation system, but it took a while to get the whole thing sorted out.

At the provincial level, I was now a member of the Committee of Presidents (COP), which was made up of the presidents of the 22 Ontario colleges. The COP met monthly to discuss various issues common to all. I already knew several of the presidents. My former boss at Confederation College, Air Vice Marshal D.A.R. Bradshaw, was chairing the COP that year. I finally got to know, and call him by, his first name. It was Douglas, and we called him Doug.

The presidents were an interesting group of people. Several were very articulate and possessed great wisdom. I learned a lot from them. A few were quite emotional, with one president frequently banging his fist on the table to make his point. There were also some who made me wonder how they ever got to be president! Most of them were considerably older than me. Several were experiencing serious problems either with their board or their faculty or both. They were under intense stress and one could tell that it was affecting their health. A few had serious drinking problems. One committed suicide.

Although the opportunity to discuss common problems with my fellow presidents was valuable, I often left the meetings feeling quite frustrated with the interminable debates that did not resolve various important issues. To some extent, this was due to the different personalities of the presidents, a few of them behaving as prima donnas. But it was also a consequence of the diverse environments in the various communities across the province. The large urban colleges in Toronto, for example, had different pressures than the smaller ones in remote locations such as Thunder Bay or Timmins. Other factors had to do with the history of each college. Some of them had been created by combining previously separate but already functioning institutions; others had been started from scratch.

The most contentious debates were about collective bargaining strategies. Negotiations with the faculty and support staff unions took place at the provincial level. But each college was managed by its own board and president. Certain problems were unique to an institution, yet whatever solutions were proposed, had to apply to all the colleges. Furthermore, the relationship with union and management was awful in some cases, but relatively smooth in others. Hence issues arose that were important at one institution, but trivial elsewhere. Some presidents were prepared to compromise on certain matters, others weren't.[40]

The year 1972 was significant not only because of my assumption of presidential duties at Niagara College, but also because of two happy events in our family life. In Peterborough, my sister Ester married Bill Martin, a good Christian young man. And in St. Catharines, Lella gave birth in November to our second child, Andrew. Because of her previous miscarriages, the doctor had taken special precautions and Lella's pregnancy had been uneventful. Deborah was especially happy to have a baby brother. At the COP, I was congratulated by my colleagues who pointed out that, given the group's average age, this was an unusual and welcome occurrence.

Over the next few years, I was active in the Niagara community and developed many good contacts. For a while, I served as president of the Welland branch of the Red Cross Society. One of the strongest supporters of the college was Alan Pietz, the mayor of Welland. Alan would eventually be elected as a member of Parliament during the time when Brian Mulroney was prime minister.

Although community colleges operated under provincial jurisdiction, the federal government was also involved, through its funding of retraining programs. These were aimed at unemployed people who needed to learn a trade or close some gaps in their education, in order to improve their employment prospects. Hence, it was important for me to establish contacts at the federal level. Fortunately, Dr. S. V. Railton, the local federal MP, was a strong college supporter. He brought the Hon. Jeanne Sauvé for a visit to the college in 1973. At the time, she was federal minister of science and technology and later became Governor General. Lella met her, remarking how fluently Madame Sauvé spoke Italian.

Dr. Railton also assisted me in attracting an excellent convocation speaker, the Hon. Judy Lamarsh, then a Secretary of State in the federal government and a member of Parliament for Niagara Falls. Another impressive convocation speaker was Dr. Bette Stephenson, president of the Canadian Medical Association. Despite a very busy career, Dr. Stephenson had raised a large family and was widely admired, becoming Minister of Education in the Bill Davis government a few years later. I had the pleasure of working with her again in the 90's when she and I served on the province's newly established board for the Office of Educational Quality and Accountability, the agency that administered province-wide tests to all school children.

In 1973, the college was asked by the provincial government to take over the two nursing schools in the Niagara area. The first was the Mack School of Nursing in St. Catharines, the other was the Niagara Falls Nursing school. Both had operated for a long time under their local hospital's control, but with their own boards. I had been a member of the board of the Mack School of Nursing. Each school had a lengthy and distinguished history and tradition. Being absorbed by the college was seen as a loss of identity and was therefore not very popular. We set up a joint committee to work out the details of the amalgamation. Dr. Donald MacDonald (Vice President and Director of Acres Consulting Services Limited), and chair of Niagara College's board of governors, chaired this committee. His capable leadership helped us work out all the details in a collaborative manner, and there were no major hurdles.

In early 1973, a friend helped me find a job for my father as a janitor with the local school board. I felt that it would be good for my parents to be close to us, and enjoy the milder winters in St. Catharines. My father quit his job at Sir Sandford Fleming College, sold his house in Peterborough and he and my mother moved to St. Catharines, where they bought a modest brand new house. It was good to have my parents live just a few blocks away. Ester and her husband Bill visited often and it was always nice to see them. My parents and Lella were also able to attend an Italian Pentecostal Church in nearby Thorold.

Finally, also in 1973, my textbook, "Solid state electronic circuits: for engineering technology", was published by McGraw-Hill Book Company in New York. It had taken me four years to complete this work, which had begun while I was at Confederation College. McGraw-Hill organized a reception in New York where I met my editor, other senior McGraw-Hill officials and several other authors. Later, an international soft cover edition was published by McGraw-Hill Kogakusha in Tokyo; there were two additional printings, in 1981 and 1984.[41]

Throughout my tenure at Niagara College, we experienced financial challenges. I was quite rigorous (some people might use stronger language, such as "ruthless") in conducting budget reviews, paring back wherever I thought we could do so without harming the educational process. Gary Larose, whom I had appointed as Treasurer soon after my arrival, provided first class financial management and advice. He got along well with everybody, had a great sense of humour and made many valuable contributions as a member of my senior management team. I worked hard to avoid layoffs of permanent staff, believing that morale would suffer otherwise. I believe the faculty at large appreciated these efforts.

Not every project I undertook at Niagara was an unqualified success. In September, 1974, I was asked by Al Aboud (my Director of Student Affairs) for permission to participate with the local hospital in the staging of a mock emergency at the college to test their emergency response process. The whole thing had to be kept secret. The rationale for secrecy was based on the notion that it was impossible to evaluate the community's capacity to respond to a real emergency if the participants knew in advance that this was a drill. I gave my approval, without realizing the risk of causing panic among the general population. In retrospect, I should have asked more questions as to what exactly was involved, but I didn't. As things turned out, this was a big mistake.

The hospital had made arrangements with our theatre arts program to use their make-up skills in such a way as to cause a large number of students to appear seriously hurt. They were able to simulate blood, burns and other injuries. Soon ambulances, police and fire vehicles appeared on the scene, unaware that the "emergency" was staged. Nearby students were terrified. Students from the radio and television broadcasting program called local radio stations with the news of what they thought was a real event. Some of those stations, though not all, went on air with the announcement that there had been a major disaster at Niagara College, resulting in a large number of student casualties.[42] So convincing were the simulated injuries that several students and staff transported the "injured" students to hospital, driving at high speeds. There was panic throughout the community. The hospital had insisted on secrecy, and the news media had not been notified. Even Mayor Alan Pietz did not know anything about it.

I was deeply troubled by these events and immediately went into damage control mode. We quickly advised the news media that this was just an exercise in emergency preparedness. I issued a formal statement, as follows:

"I am sincerely sorry for any hardship that may have been created for any of our students, staff or concerned individuals of our community as a result of the college's participation in Wednesday's test of local emergency services. Our participation in this mock test was done as a community service at the request of the disaster committee of the Welland County General Hospital. The college, along with other emergency service agencies – including hospital, ambulance, police and fire department – were requested to maintain secrecy on this test in order to create a realistic emergency situation. We regrettably accepted this request for secrecy and did not inform the local news media that such a test was going to be conducted on this day. I again apologize for any hardship that has resulted from today's events and assure the public that nothing like this will ever happen again at Niagara College."

There was a great deal of harsh criticism by columnists, members of the public and various officials. Ontario Attorney-General Robert Welch was asked to order a public inquiry. But after he was fully briefed on the events that had transpired, he indicated that he saw no need for such an inquiry.

"It's terrible to play with people's emotions like that", said one student. Another student, pale, faint and upset when she spoke to the St. Catharines Standard, said that the exercise reminded her of Orson Wells' "War of the Worlds" – a 1938 radio broadcast which caused wide hysteria by announcing that the world had been invaded by a Martian army. The St. Catharines Standard also carried a statement from a spokesman from the American Labor Party, in which she characterized the exercise as a "low intensity military operation" and a "terrorist act". She claimed that the North Atlantic Treaty Organization and the Central Intelligence Agency (CIA) of the United States used such methods to "gather psychological profiles....to terrorize the population....to get the frame of mind of the average individual to determine how they will react during the real situation".

Everyone agreed that the exercise had not been properly handled and while the responsibility was technically the hospital's, the college had been involved and I accepted my share of criticism. Welland's Evening Tribune carried a balanced editorial that summarized the whole episode as a good idea in theory, but not in practice. Nevertheless, it also spoke about the positive side – that it was a good test of the hospital's ability to cope with a big emergency.

The matter was discussed by the college board, which was satisfied with the damage control I had carried out. Two radio broadcasting instructors resigned, because they believed that they had lost credibility, given that it was their students who had advised radio stations of the event, but eventually, I was able to convince them to withdraw their resignations.[43]

Actually, there was one member of the board who thought that the secrecy surrounding this exercise had been proper and saw nothing wrong with how the process had been carried out. He was Dr. Leo Sturgeon. He had been Chief Medical Officer for the Niagara Region for many years. A tall, heavily built man, he was used to issuing orders and getting his way. His extensive medical knowledge and his position enabled him to speak with authority on medical matters. He could be described as a bit of a curmudgeon and I had clashed with him a couple of times. On one occasion, he tried to "suggest" who I should appoint to an important position. He had a favourite candidate he wanted me to appoint. I asked to meet him alone in my office and, with as much diplomacy as I could muster, reminded him that I was the president and that I would be the one to recommend such an appointment to the board. I noted that, in his previous position as Chief Medical Officer, he would not have tolerated interference in similar decisions, nor would I. He reluctantly agreed with me and, from that time on, became one of my strongest supporters on the board. He respected the fact that I had stood up to him. Lella and I became good friends with him and his wife Martha.

In November 1974, the Student Council decided to invite Xaviera Hollander to give a speech to the student body about her experiences as a high priced prostitute. Hollander had just written a book, The Happy Hooker, that apparently outlined her experiences as what is now called a sex worker. The book had been a best seller and the Student Council had agreed to pay $800 for her appearance. When I learned about this plan, I tried to find a way to block the event. This was difficult, as freedom of speech is a basic value of education and I knew that I would be accused of censorship. Nevertheless, I did not want the kind of publicity that such an event would generate, even though it was the Student Council, not the college, that was sponsoring her visit.

The whole episode became a test of the Student Council's autonomy. At first, I found a way to thwart their plan. Hollander's "lecture" was scheduled at the same time that classes were held. Hence, there would be a conflict between her lecture and attendance at regularly scheduled classes. On these grounds, I blocked her appearance on campus. In hindsight, it was wrong for me to place greater importance on the college's image in the community than on the protection of freedom of speech. And I should have anticipated that the Student Council would find some way to get around my decision.

In fact, the Student Council simply re-scheduled Hollander's visit for a time when no classes were being held. Therefore I could not deny permission without being accused of censorship and interference in the affairs of the Student Council. I relented, and allowed the event to take place. Needless to say, this generated a lot of press. There were many letters to the editor in local newspapers, mostly critical of my decision to allow this person to speak on campus. I defended my decision on the grounds that freedom of speech (within certain limits established by law) was central to the functions of an educational institution, and if the Student Council wanted to waste their money (as in my view they were clearly doing in this case) that was their decision to make. The Welland newspaper wrote an editorial, strongly defending my actions and quoting extensively from my statement that had been issued to the press.

The Board also backed me, as did the administration and faculty. My daughter Deborah, who was only 11 years old, had heard about the controversy and asked me what it was all about. I told her that the students were planning to pay a woman $800 to tell them her life story. I did not go into details about the specifics of Hollander's life story. Deborah replied that she would be very happy to tell my students her life story for a lot less than $800!

Niagara College depended for the bulk of its funding on the Ontario provincial government. It was therefore useful to maintain good relations not only with the bureaucratic arm of the government, but also with key politicians. To this end, I invited several provincial cabinet ministers to visit the college from time to time. The province had imposed a moratorium on capital budgets shortly after I became president, and this had delayed the start of work on new facilities, which were badly needed due to rapid enrolment growth. Several programs operated in sub-standard quarters in various locations, hence there was some urgency to upgrade and expand the college's main campus. Two ministers were particularly helpful in facilitating approval of our building program. One was the Hon. James Auld, Minister of Colleges and Universities, and his successor, the Hon. Dr. Harry Parrott. I had good relations with both of them, as well as other ministers representing local ridings. When they came, I showed them around the college and arranged for them to meet student and faculty leaders. In 1975, the entire provincial cabinet, made up of 24 ministers, and presided by the Hon. William Davis, premier of Ontario, held one of its meetings at the college. At the time, Niagara had the largest enrolment growth of any Ontario college outside Metro Toronto. I made a public presentation to the cabinet on a variety of issues, including a request for some land in Niagara Falls that was surplus to Ontario Hydro's needs, and on which we wanted to build a new campus.[44] A photograph of Mayor Alan Pietz and me welcoming Ontario Premier Bill Davis is shown below.

A rather bizarre event was a lunch meeting of all Ontario community college and university presidents organized by the Minister of Colleges and Universities to foster greater cooperation between these public institutions. It was a fancy affair, held in Toronto. Premier Davis also attended. There was, at the time, a controversy at the University of Toronto over day care, and several students crashed the luncheon protesting the university's policies. One of the protesting students pulled the tablecloth from the table where the president of the University of Toronto was seated and dumped all the food, plates, glasses and silverware on the floor and were proceeding to do the same to the other tables. While most of us looked on, waiting for hotel security or the police to come and evict the protesting students, the president of Brock University, Dr. James Gibson, an elderly and slightly built man, took matters in hand. He physically started to push the students out of the room, leading the way for the rest of us to get involved. I had never experienced this kind of physical confrontation at Niagara College. Eventually security staff arrived and stayed for the rest of the luncheon to ward off further attempts to disrupt the event.

One year, I hosted a meeting of the Council of Regents in the city of Niagara Falls, where we operated a Hotel and Restaurant program, as well as the Nursing program at the local hospital. Norm Sisco, the chairman of the Council, was addressing the group when he, like the rest of us, noticed a constant background noise that made it difficult to hear Norm's words at the back of the room. Norm asked Herb Jackson, who was the director of college affairs, to find the source of this noise and have it turned off. Herb dutifully left the room, looking for a staff member who could turn off whatever piece of machinery was making the noise. He sheepishly returned a few minutes later advising Norm and the rest of us that the staff could not turn off the source of the noise because it was the water roaring over Niagara Falls!

As indicated earlier, I taught a course in electronics throughout my time as president of Niagara College. Due to my heavy administrative load, I arranged the scheduling of my classes for 8 a.m., the earliest time available. This way, there would be less risk of interruption from urgent phone calls or meetings that could occur during the day. Several students commuted from nearby towns and were notoriously late. I dropped many hints about my expectation that they should arrive on time, but the problem persisted. Finally, I told my students that, henceforth, the classroom doors would be locked at 8 a.m. and any student not already in, would not be permitted to enter.

The next time, I arrived promptly at 8 a.m. and noted that no student was present. I was quite upset. Were they defying me? Shortly after, a student showed up and politely informed me that the entire class had been waiting for me since before 8 a.m. in the lecture room across the hall. I had gone to the wrong room! Needless to say, I was thoroughly embarrassed and apologized profusely to my students for "being late". A good laugh was had by all!

In April 1976, the college organized a one day seminar for labour and management people to discuss the wage and price controls that the federal government, under Prime Minister Pierre Trudeau, had recently imposed. These controls were quite controversial, and we felt it appropriate to organize an event where all aspects of these measures could be discussed. The faculty member in charge invited several panel speakers from both management and labour, as well as a representative of the federal government. The labour movement was strongly opposed to these controls. As soon as they heard that we were planning to have a representative of the federal government on the panel, the Canadian Labour Congress sent me a note strongly objecting to the federal government being involved in any way. They threatened to pull out unless the college cancelled the invitation to the federal government representative. They only wanted their members to be exposed to the union party line. My staff and I felt that, as an educational institution, it was important for us to present all sides of a controversial issue and let the people draw their own conclusions. Not to include a representative of the federal government would make a mockery of the process, since it was the federal government that had imposed the controls. I issued a strong statement to the effect that Niagara College would never be a party to one-sided treatment of controversial issues and that, in fact, it was our duty to present different points of view. Several editorials in local newspapers were written backing me 100%. The board of the college also backed me unanimously. The seminar went ahead as planned. I considered the CLC's attempt at interference as an attack on the principle of free speech and balanced treatment of controversial issues. I was happy that this incident gave me the opportunity to clearly spell out the college's fundamental philosophy. The faculty and administration also backed me.

I spent some of my spare time designing and building various electronic circuits. This was in part to keep myself up to date in the field that I was still teaching and also because I enjoyed it as a hobby. One of the first things I designed and built was a digital clock. This was long before these devices became available as consumer items. It required dozens of integrated circuits. It worked very well. Andrew, who was about five years old, became quite fascinated by it. He had learned to read numbers, and one time when he wanted to do something that we wouldn't allow him to do, I told him he could do it when the digital clock read 6:66. Eventually he figured out that this would never happen, and when his mother told him to clean up his toys, he replied: I'll do it when the clock reads 6:66! This kid was too smart for his parents!

A truly memorable and frightening event began to unfold on Friday morning, January 29, 1977, when it started to snow. By noon, snow was falling quite heavily and strong winds had begun to blow. Whenever we had snow storms, Al Aboud, the Director of Student Affairs, would suggest that we close the college and send everyone home to avoid the possibility of people being stranded on the roads. This was a commuter college, with many students driving from St. Catharines, Niagara Falls and other small towns in the Niagara peninsula. I was used to the heavy snowfalls of Thunder Bay and, while Welland did get a lot of snow (much more than St. Catharines), I resisted closing the college unless things got really bad. Usually, if the snow started in the morning, it would taper off in the afternoon and by then the roads would be cleared and students could get back home without much of a problem. So I declined Al Aboud's request to close the college.

As the afternoon arrived, however, the snow and winds did not let up. In fact, they got worse. I still felt we could ride this thing out, but by mid-afternoon, it was obvious that this was no ordinary storm. The Great Blizzard of 77 had arrived. It was the worst storm, in the most severe winter on record. It hit the southern part of the Niagara peninsula with little warning, closing all roads and stranding thousands of students, workers and travellers.

By late afternoon, the storm intensified, with fierce winds whipping up the snow ever higher. Many college students had left, and several were stranded on the relatively uninhabited roads leading out of Welland. A few found refuge in farmhouses; many were stuck in their cars. There were about a dozen pre-schoolers in our day care centre, as well as several supervisors from the Ontario Paper Mill and General Motors who were taking courses at the college. In total, about 700 people remained and it was obvious that we would all be spending the night on campus. I felt a deep sense of responsibility for everyone's safety.

There was no food in the cafeteria, as it was Friday and the college would normally be closed over the weekend, so the kitchen had not stocked up for the next day. There were vending machines around the campus, but they were soon depleted of chocolate bars, potato chips and whatever else they contained. Phone lines were working, so I was able to stay in touch with my wife Lella and with local police and radio stations. The situation in St. Catharines was not as bad as in Welland, but places like Buffalo and nearby towns were hit even harder.

I made it a point of walking around the campus and reassuring students and staff that things were under control. There were several individuals with medical conditions such as diabetes and heart problems. The Ontario Provincial Police (OPP) was very helpful. They delivered insulin and other medications from a local pharmacy to the college via snowmobile, which was the only practical method of transportation. Neighbours from across the street were able to bring a huge supply of soup for the hungry staff and students.

I had one of the teachers look for films to show in the auditorium to keep students busy. Apparently all he could find was a film about baking bread, which was viewed several times over! Some students played volleyball and basketball in the gym. We had radios, but I don't recall whether any television signals could be received. Some wine and beer, however, did make it through!

As I walked between buildings on campus, the intensity of the wind nearly swept me away. These were no ordinary strong winds, well in excess of 70 mph. They whipped the snow to over 30 feet; in some places even the top of telephone poles were covered. Cars were completely buried under the snow. The storm claimed 45 lives in nearby Buffalo but, luckily, none was lost on the Canadian side. We did have a mild case of frostbite with a student who was poorly dressed for the elements.

We all spent the night sleeping as well as we could. I had a couch in my office, which I offered to one of the female clerks. I slept, or tried to sleep, in my chair. Everybody else slept on the floor or arranged chairs in such a way that they could lie down, but it was most uncomfortable.

The news reports that we heard on the radio indicated that many other people were stuck in factories, schools, hospitals and so on. This was a major emergency, unlike any that anyone had ever experienced before.

By Saturday morning, everyone's bones were aching. We were hungry, tired and looking forward to going home. I felt that by now, the storm should be over and soon we would be able to drive home. But I was wrong. I soon concluded that we would be spending a second night stuck at the college. Luckily the heat did not fail and somehow we made it through without major problems.

Finally, on Sunday morning, the sun came out, the winds died down and the snow ploughs were able to clear the roads. I told everyone they could go home but stayed behind until it was certain that everyone had been able to leave. I drove home and collapsed on the bed, too tired to even undress before falling asleep.

A book was written about the Blizzard of 1977. But no one can fully appreciate how fierce this storm was who did not go through it. When nature unleashes its power, we become quite powerless, despite our advanced technology. You just have to cope with it as best as you can, and wait it out.

During the early part of 1977, a college evaluation took place. This was mandated by the provincial government and was carried out by a team of outside people headed by a professor from Queen's University. They conducted surveys and interviews with many people, both inside the college and outside. While the team found areas where we could improve, the report was generally positive. The team reported that I had the highest respect and confidence of the students, faculty and staff. This was nice to hear, but in reality everything that had been accomplished was the result of team work by individuals at all levels of the organization.

Despite serious budget limitations, my six years at Niagara College were marked by a period of major enrolment, program and physical expansion. The college became deeply involved in community activities and a cohesive team of faculty, administration and support staff was able to realize major improvements in the quality of education and student life. Full-time enrolment increased by more than 50% and part-time enrolment by more than 250%. Standards were raised, by requiring a 2.0 grade point average for graduation, instead of the previous 1.7.

An ongoing challenge for the college was the poor preparation of incoming students. Faculty were constantly asking for higher admission standards. I was not unsympathetic to this problem, since I also experienced it through my teaching. But I felt that the whole point of a community college was to give everyone a chance to pursue a higher education. Becoming too selective would deprive many students of the opportunity to demonstrate that they could succeed. Nevertheless, I communicated frequently with local high schools, trying to influence their curriculum to better prepare students for college work. As it turned out, we weren't the only post-secondary institution to face this issue. Brock University in St. Catharines found that many of its students had difficulty expressing themselves in the English language. For a while, Niagara College provided remedial courses in English to Brock students, at the university's request.

Several new programs and educational innovations, including a comprehensive program evaluation process, were now in place. This made better use of advisory committee members[45], because they had the opportunity to meet directly with a committee of the board of governors (on a rotational basis) and provide their candid appraisal of how well a program was performing in terms of meeting employers' expectations. This type of feedback was supplemented by surveys of graduates and their employers. Hence, the college had the benefit of multiple tools to constantly improve its programs of instruction.

During my tenure, several innovative programs were introduced, including independent studies, day release and continuous intake – self paced instruction. The college's involvement with the community was at a very high level. Typical activities included a free income tax service for senior citizens, provided by Financial Management students under faculty supervision; a Centre for Industrial Testing, Consultation and Research, the sponsoring of symphony performances, the carrying out of research for a government commission investigating the effects of violence in the media, and marketing surveys for local businesses.

Administrative costs were cut in half as a percentage of all expenditures. A major building program for business and electrical technology studies was successfully completed. The new space connected with the previously built Simcoe Building, enclosing a large outdoor area where students could relax when the weather allowed it. When I left the college, the board decided to name this area "Manera Court", shown in the picture below.

During the summer of 1977, an ad appeared in the Globe and Mail seeking applicants for principal (chief executive officer) of Vancouver Community College. I thought that moving to the Vancouver area would be a good idea for us and looked into this opportunity. Apparently VCC had experienced serious internal strife between the faculty and administration (it seems that I was destined to seek such situations), and the college principal had been forced to resign by the board. I decided to apply and was soon called for an interview with the selection committee in Vancouver. The committee had the usual mix of board, faculty, student, administrative and support staff representation. I prepared extensively for the interview and it went very well. I was quite candid with them. This interview was followed by another one with the full board. Soon, the board offered me the job, which I accepted.

I looked forward to living in Vancouver, with its mild climate and the opportunity to lead a much larger institution, with greater scope. Neither Lella nor Deborah were happy to leave St. Catharines. Deborah was 15 and that's always a difficult age to make such a drastic change. I felt that they would adjust quite nicely once we got to Vancouver. Andrew was only five and he would have the least difficulty in making the change.

I called Herb Burton, the board chair and told him of my decision to accept this new job. I had mixed feelings about leaving Niagara, where I enjoyed such a good relationship with the board, staff and students. I also didn't like the idea of leaving my parents behind, but felt that, in a couple of years, when dad retired, it might be possible to move them to Vancouver too. Herb and the rest of the board were sad to see me go, but they understood that, at the age of 37, it was only natural that I would want to seek fresh challenges. At any rate, I had told the board when they were interviewing me for the position of president that, if appointed, I would stay for a minimum of five years, but not longer than ten years.

My six years as president of Niagara College were a period of great professional growth. During this time, I learned how to balance my desire to be close to the students and teachers with the need to delegate and get things done through other people. It helped a lot that I had the energy and enthusiasm of a young man, combined with the experience of having had to struggle to obtain an advanced education. I certainly made some mistakes, but learned from them. Perhaps one of the most important lessons taught by my experiences was that, no matter how committed one is to certain goals, unexpected events often interfere with their pursuit, and one must be flexible and willing to compromise. Perseverance pays off, and it's amazing how much one can accomplish by working collaboratively with capable people who share one's objectives.

During our time in the Niagara area, Lella and I were able to build several valuable and lasting friendships. Because we were relatively young, many of those friends, such as members of the college's board of governors, have since died, though the good memories remain.

We enjoyed the many attractions and activities available in the area. I finally learned how to swim, a healthy physical activity that I continued to pursue for many years afterwards. The greatest joy was our family life, given that Lella and I were blessed with two wonderful children, and it was also good to have my parents close by.

There were more than a few pleasant and interesting trips. On some occasions Lella would accompany me to Toronto for college related meetings or functions. For our 15th wedding anniversary we travelled to Ottawa, where we stayed for a few days with some friends who had moved there from from Thunder Bay. This was our first trip away from our children, who were looked after by my mother during our absence.

One voyage involved towing a small trailer to a campground in New York State. There we met for the first time one of my father's cousins who had emigrated to the US when he was a young boy. He and my father remembered each other and were happy to be re-united after so many years. During this trip we reached the conclusion that camping was not our thing! In fact, we left the trailer in the campground, which was rather primitive, drove into New York City and checked into a Holiday Inn, fully equipped with clean showers and air-conditioning! Andrew was only about eight months old, so I stayed with him in the hotel while Lella and Deborah took a guided tour of New York, including the Statue of Liberty. I took advantage of the fact that we were in New York to search for a long lost step-brother of my mother who had emigrated to the US in 1913. All she knew was that he had gone to New York. I called every person in the NY telephone directory with the same last name, but struck out. It would take another twenty-three years and the advent of the Internet before I would finally be able to locate him.

One winter we made our first trip to Florida. The weather was sunny and warm and we all had a great time at the beach and sightseeing. It was on this trip that the idea of eventually owning a condominium in Florida first crossed my mind, a dream that would be realized many years later. Unfortunately, the return trip to Canada was spoiled by a transmission failure that cost a lot of money and time to repair!

The Niagara College staff gave me and Lella a huge going away party on January 31, 1978. John Giancarlo was the chief organizer and, despite some very inclement weather, the event was well attended. John gave me, on behalf of the group, a beautiful oil painting of a Canadian landscape, which still holds a very prominent place in our home. The board also gave us a great going away party and presented me with a chess set that had been made in the college's machine shop by students. John Giancarlo had taught me how to play chess, and I have enjoyed the game ever since.

CHAPTER EIGHT

I assumed my duties as principal[46] and CEO of Vancouver Community College (VCC) on February 21, 1978. I looked forward to my new job, which offered greater scope for achievement and professional growth. With the Niagara experience under my belt, I felt comfortable in just "being myself."

I was also fed up with Ontario's cold winters and looked forward to living in Vancouver, with its mild climate and lush vegetation. A landscape contractor had already planted a broad variety of ornamental plants around our new house, including dozens of rhododendrons and azaleas that would flower sequentially from late February to mid-May.

Soon Deborah and Andrew were enrolled in school. It was mid-way through the academic year, not the best time to change schools. Within days of moving into our new home, however, Andrew made friends with some of the neighbourhood kids and enjoyed playing with them outside. Deborah was fifteen and she found it more difficult to adjust to the new environment.

VCC was the largest community college and the second largest post-secondary institution (after UBC) in British Columbia, with a student population of about 12,000 and a faculty and staff of approximately 1300[47]. Unlike Ontario, collective bargaining in BC was carried out by each college with its own staff. I much preferred this model. VCC was also the oldest college in Canada, having been established in 1965 under the aegis of the Vancouver School Board. According to the Vancouver Sun, VCC "exuded a quality of venerable maternity toward the rest of the college and institute system. Its size, range and tradition made it more of a provincial college than strictly a community one, because people from all over the province were attracted to its programs – some of which weren't available anywhere else in BC."

In 1978 VCC consisted of three major campuses: Langara, Vancouver Vocational Institute (VVI) and King Edward (KEC). Each campus specialized more or less in a particular area of study. Langara offered two year post-secondary career programs, mainly in business, health and arts, as well as the first two years of university level courses. VVI specialized in various vocational programs (auto mechanics, chef training, secretarial, hairdressers, etc). KEC delivered adult basic education courses, such as literacy and English as a second language, as well as a music program. There was also a Continuing Education (CE) division, with responsibility for a broad array of courses in many disciplines, including general interest and hobbies. It operated mainly in the evenings, using space at the three campuses and in numerous other locations throughout the city. Each of these four teaching divisions was headed by a principal, who reported directly to me, along with a Bursar, a Director of College Resources (Libraries, audio visual services, etc) and other administrative personnel.

Head office was located in downtown Vancouver, on the second floor of a bank building. No classes were held there. It was a purely administrative facility where the governing board, CEO, and other central administrators were located. With no classes or students, it was impossible to tell that the people working there had anything to do with education. I was very uncomfortable with this arrangement, which went against my philosophy of being closely identified and associated with the learning process, and planned to rectify this anomaly as rapidly as possible.

There had been tensions at VCC over how much autonomy the campuses should have and what functions should be performed at head office. Apparently my predecessor, Dr. T. J. Gilligan, had centralized too many functions, at least in the opinion of many faculty. Head office was often referred to as "Gilligan's island", an unflattering metaphor that captured the faculty's view of the central administration as a remote organizational unit isolated from the real action, the teaching of students. VCC had also experienced financial problems, resulting in the establishment by the provincial government of a commission of inquiry. At some point, the board lost confidence in Dr. Gilligan and he resigned. Dr. J.J. (Jock) Denholm, principal of the Langara Campus, had been appointed to the position of CEO on an interim basis until my arrival.

The Langara faculty's alienation from the central administration manifested itself in a strong desire to have their campus designated as a separate college. In fact, each of the three VCC campuses was larger than most colleges in BC and could have operated as an independent college. The Langara faculty had petitioned the board and the provincial government to that end.[48] But the board maintained its support for a single integrated college. This way, the college could reap the benefits of shared services, such as financial management, libraries, audio visual equipment, public relations, personnel, computer systems, and so on. Moreover, having a single institution would contribute to the development of a more coherent planning process for the Vancouver area.

VCC operated in a very different environment than was the case at Niagara. For example, while Niagara College received a lot of local publicity, mostly positive, VCC was just one of many organizations operating throughout Vancouver and received media attention only when there was some controversy. Nevertheless, I

143

had a very capable head of public relations, Cam Avery, and he worked hard to ensure that VCC received as much positive media coverage as possible. Also, unlike Ontario, BC colleges handled their own collective bargaining, which was one of the factors that appealed to me. I was fortunate to have as Director of Personnel a seasoned labour negotiator, Dale Jones. The fact that, during my seven years at VCC, we did not experience serious union confrontations is significantly due to his skill in handling difficult labour-management situations. Finally, tuition in Ontario was set by the provincial government, while in BC, each college board had the authority to set its own tuition fees, subject to provincial approval. Hence, in many respects, BC colleges enjoyed more autonomy than Ontario colleges, but they were also exposed to more controversy, particularly on those occasions when tuition fees had to be raised, which was never popular with students.

When I accepted the CEO position at VCC, I assumed that the issue of Langara's designation as a separate college had been settled. Instead, before my arrival at VCC, the deputy minister of education, Dr. Walter Hardwick, was quoted as telling the Langara faculty that the door was still open to such an arrangement. This undermined the college board, resulting in its chair, Dr. James (Jim) Kennedy[49], writing an angry letter to his former colleague and now Minister of Education, the Hon. Pat McGeer[50].

Had Langara been removed from VCC, such action would have represented a material change in the scope of my job, which would no longer have been of interest to me. If the provincial government had seriously contemplated designating Langara as a separate institution, it should have done so before a new CEO was hired. Fortunately, no action on Langara separation was taken at the time, but the issue remained in the background throughout my tenure.[51]

Upon my arrival in BC, I discovered that new educational institutions were being created by the provincial government at a rapid pace. Some of them, like the Justice Institute, were quite small. Two of them (a Marine Institute and an art school) had been relatively small departments operating under the VCC umbrella. I saw no educational or financial rationale for the creation of all these separate entities, each requiring its own board, CEO and administrative overhead. At a public meeting I asked Dr. McGeer how the province could afford to keep creating new institutions without placing at risk the long term financial viability of the existing ones. McGeer replied that he saw no problem. The BC economy, which was heavily dependent on the exports of lumber, natural gas and minerals, was doing extremely well. The colleges had just received an average 17% increase in their annual budgets, which was unprecedented. Housing prices were climbing steadily. McGeer saw nothing but continued growth in the economy, and his government was spending like a drunken sailor. A few years later, the BC economy plunged into one of the worst recessions it had ever experienced. Budgets were slashed, many people lost their jobs, and house prices, which had doubled, now dropped by half. Many people, unable to meet their mortgage payments, lost their homes.

My challenges at VCC were several. I had to decide where to draw the line between centralized functions and decentralized ones. The campuses obviously wanted as much autonomy as possible, and I wanted them to have it in the day to day operations, but there were functions where a centralized approach made more sense, either for economic reasons or for consistency. The threat of further agitation by the Langara faculty for separate designation was always in the background.

The college also had serious space problems. The space available per student was about 70 s.f., compared to 150 s.f. for the typical Canadian college. The most critical space issue was at KEC, which leased an old school on the grounds of the Vancouver General Hospital. The hospital had plans for expansion that required us to move out. But, to date, no other site had been located, nor had approval been granted by the provincial government to either build or lease a suitable building. We were fortunate that the hospital, sensitive to our plight, kept extending our lease at six month intervals.

VVI also needed more space, and that could only be accomplished by building up, since it was located in a narrow lot in downtown Vancouver. So critical was the space problem at VVI that in 1982 its waiting list exceeded 6000 students, delaying admissions to some programs for up to four years. VVI ran four shifts per day in courses like welding and electrical. As reported by the Vancouver Sun, if one were to descend into the bowels of VVI at midnight, one could catch the beginning of the 11:30 p.m. – 6:30 a.m. welding class, masked and ready to spend the night surrounded by flying sparks!

The Langara campus, which had been designed for 3,500 students, was serving 5,890 students and could have enrolled 6700 if there had been room.

VCC was also seriously underfunded. It operated at a cost per student substantially below the provincial average. In 1983, for example, a provincial "report card" showed that VCC had the lowest cost in the province, at $4.94 per student contact hour. The Vancouver Sun reported that VCC had traditionally been the lowest-cost college in the system, a fact rationalized by its huge size. But, as I pointed out, colleges ceased to become more efficient after they reached a certain size and VCC was long past that point. The reality, in fact, was that we operated in so many different locations that economies of scale were difficult to achieve. Still, VCC delivered 23% of all college level instruction in BC, with only 16% of the dollars. Our administrative costs were 45 cents per student contact hour, versus 91 cents for all other provincial colleges and institutes.

In a classic example of the urgent requiring more attention than the important, my initial priorities at VCC were to find a solution to the KEC and VVI space problems and to get much needed financial relief. During my first two years as CEO, over 50% of my time was spent on facilities related issues, not my idea of the best use of a college president's energy.

Even before my arrival in Vancouver, I asked Cam Avery (my director of public relations) to arrange a meeting between me and Education Minister McGeer to discuss the space problems at VCC and other issues. Cam tried, but was having difficulty setting a date, in part because the minister was unusually busy, but also because he was not fond of having meetings with "officials". Shortly after, I gave several press conferences and speeches to various community groups outlining the college's plight and the fact that I had requested a meeting with Minister McGeer. Soon, a very supportive editorial appeared in the Vancouver Sun, the city's major newspaper. I had sent a copy of one of my speeches to the Minister, who had read about my request for a meeting with him in the newspaper. He replied favorably and a convenient time in his schedule was found. In my meeting with Dr. McGeer, I made a strong case for capital funding to build or renovate space for a new KEC campus and more space for both VVI and Langara. He listened politely but there was no immediate commitment.

Meanwhile, I invited all the local members of the provincial legislature to visit the college and to see for themselves how serious our space problems were. Several of them accepted my invitation, including the Hon. Grace McCarthy,[52] Minister of Community and Social Services, who was very gracious and concerned. Final approval to build a new campus for KEC and to make major additions to VVI and a smaller addition to Langara came in January 1980, almost two years after I had begun my lobbying campaign. While the long delay was regrettable, the announcement that our space problems would finally be addressed was welcome news for the staff and students, who felt that VCC had been forgotten by the provincial government. It is noteworthy that not a single square foot of our space request was denied – VCC was the only college in BC that received approval for all the additional space that we asked for.

Creating a new campus for KEC was a major challenge. We looked at several options, including the renovation of an under-used high school owned by the school board. That didn't work out. I looked at some land on False Creek.[53] But that didn't work out either. Vancouver was a densely built city and there simply weren't that many empty sites large enough to build a college campus for several thousand students. So, one of our board members, Barry Sleigh, and I flew over the city in a small airplane, looking for suitable sites. I was quite nauseated by the sudden way the pilot swung the airplane whenever Barry or I thought we had seen a large empty parcel of land!

Eventually we found a promising site at China Creek. It was slightly under 8 acres, on a steep slope on Broadway Avenue. Part of it was owned by an older gentleman named Robert McGregor, who had operated a sawmill there. The rest was owned by the city, and it held a bicycle racing track. The whole site sat on an old garbage dump, which had been filled and covered up years before. The rotting garbage continued to produce methane gas. Building on such a site would be particularly difficult. Normal foundations could not be used. Instead, very long concrete piles would have to be hammered in until they reached solid enough material to support a building.

Before we could build a new campus, however, we had to acquire the land. Max Fleming (the college bursar) and I held several very tough negotiations with Mr. McGregor and the city. They both wanted the highest possible price for their land, in the mistaken belief that the provincial government would easily give its approval. In reality, it was my job and the board's to convince the provincial government that the price we had negotiated was fair and reasonable. Eventually we had deals with both owners and were able to secure the necessary funding from the provincial government.

Once the go ahead was received, we completed the purchase of the land, hired architects and prepared to obtain the rezoning that would be required for VCC to build a campus on this site. This was not an easy process. Whereas in a relatively small place like Welland or Niagara Falls, a decision by the college to build a new campus would have been welcomed with open arms by all concerned, Vancouver was a big city with traffic and parking problems.

There was strong opposition by the neighbourhood residents to the rezoning that would be required for the construction of a college campus at China Creek. The City Council held a public meeting in June 1980 to hear their concerns. A motion approving the rezoning was passed, but several activists on City Council wanted to ensure that the new campus would have a day care centre. To this end, an amendment was proposed that would have made the rezoning conditional on the construction of a day care centre on the new campus. We also wanted a day care centre, but the provincial government had adamantly refused to fund one, insisting that educational dollars could not be used for social services. I pleaded with City Council not to adopt such an amendment, since I couldn't guarantee that we could raise the required funds. There was heated debate among council members and between them and members of the public. I had never seen anything like it. Municipal politics can be very uncivilized. In an unprecedented decision, Mayor Jack Volrich allowed one of my faculty members, Alex Stusiak, who was also the president of the Vocational Instructors Association at VCC, to address the City Council while it was debating the issue. This led to a loud shouting match between the mayor and one of the aldermen. Fortunately, the amendment was defeated by a 5-4 margin. I promised to the City Council that we would continue to work to find funding for a day care centre. But I was relieved that we had been successful in preventing this objective from being included as a condition of the rezoning.

Soon after securing the building permit, I talked Mr. McGregor into donating $20,000 to the college as seed money to help us raise the necessary funds to build a day care centre, and he was pleased when I promised that we would name it after him. I was also able to obtain a further $20,000 from the Vancouver Foundation. But I was still short about $100,000. The obvious source was the Ministry of Community and Social Services, headed by the Hon. Grace McCarthy. The board and I decided to approach her. At the time, we had on the board Nathan Divinsky[54], a professor of mathematics at UBC and former chair of the Vancouver School board. He was a brilliant chess player and had a very colourful personality, never shying away from controversy.

Divinsky offered to accompany me to see Grace McCarthy in Victoria. He didn't know her personally, but was a strong political

150

supporter of the provincial government. As soon as we entered her office, Nathan opened the conversation by saying: "Grace, you've got to find $100,000 to help us build a day care centre, otherwise the NDP[55] will win the next election." We had a very pleasant conversation with Grace McCarthy, and by the time we left her office we had our $100,000!

Having secured funding for the day care centre and provincial approval for the construction, we proceeded with our building program. It was a major undertaking, requiring the services of architects, engineers and a project manager to oversee the entire process.

The VVI building program involved the construction of a nine storey tower as well as extensive renovations to the existing space. It was a very complex undertaking because classes had to continue while building was taking place. The additions at Langara were more modest, since the Langara campus was quite complete, although overcrowded.

These three building projects, with a combined cost in excess of $50 million[56], resulted in vastly improved facilities for students and staff. The Hon. Bill Vander Zalm[57], Minister of Education, officially opened the VVI addition in February 1983.

The new King Edward Campus had to be built, as mentioned earlier, on long piles, sunk deep into the ground. The soil had to be covered with heavy plastic, to contain the methane gas constantly produced by the rotting garbage below and channel it away from the building. Monitoring devices had to be installed inside the building to warn of any accumulated gas. It was a multi-storey structure, cascading down the steep slope of the site. It turned out very well and we had a great opening ceremony, with the Hon. Brian Smith, Minister of Education, cutting the ribbon in

151

May 1983. The building was completed on time, and within budget, even though this was a period of high inflation.[58]

There is a very real risk for any college president to become primarily involved in buildings and finances, to the detriment of the educational process, which is the reason for the existence of the institution. I was very aware of this risk, especially since space and finances were such big problems at VCC. But I took special care to provide leadership in the educational area as well.

Early during my tenure, I launched three task forces, each headed by one of the campus principals. Their mandates were: Market Research (to determine what our program priorities should be); Evaluation (to ensure a high level of quality offerings) and Institutional Research (to provide management with the necessary tools for proper planning). The work of these task forces led to the establishment of an institutional research office, culminating in the development and adoption of the VCC Educational Master Plan.

A program evaluation process was put in place and I insisted that all programs have clearly articulated objectives. In one case, I sent back the proposed list of objectives for a program, stating quite clearly that they were too fuzzy. Faculty members generally do not take kindly to presidents who become too involved in academic matters. In this case, however, there was no pushback and I got a new list of objectives that was much more specific and meaningful. I also made it mandatory for instructors to seek feedback from students on the effectiveness of their teaching. There was some resistance to this idea at first, but in the end it was accepted. I like to think that these measures were successful not just because I had the executive authority to impose them, but because faculty in general agreed that there was a valid educational rationale for their introduction. I also pushed for greater emphasis on communication skills in vocational programs, which was difficult to implement because such programs were relatively short in duration and there wasn't a lot of time to squeeze in additional content. But I felt strongly that communication skills were as relevant in vocational programs as they were in academic programs and modest progress was achieved on this front as well.

Although I enjoyed excellent support from the college board, that doesn't mean there was never a bump in the road. In fact, about a year after I took office, I experienced a serious crisis in our relationship. This was triggered by my decision to ask for the resignation of a senior administrator. I felt that I had ample grounds, because he was making some important decisions without my knowledge or approval. But the individual refused to resign. At the time, only the board had the authority to fire an employee or expel a student. This was a strange and unusual provision spelled out in the legislation. At Niagara I had absolute authority to hire and fire, subject to the normal provisions of collective agreements and contracts. But in BC, a college CEO had to obtain the board's approval before he could fire anybody. Hence I proceeded to make my recommendation to the board. I presented my case and so did the administrator in question. The board was conflicted. The individual was capable and popular. Firing him would have been unpopular with the faculty, but I had been hired to be effective, not necessarily popular. At any rate, the board heard the case, then went in camera, excusing me and all others who were not board members. It was not until 2 am that the board concluded its deliberations. Basically, while acknowledging that I had grounds for my dissatisfaction, the board did not feel that dismissal was in order. All of us were too tired to express any views and the meeting was adjourned.

Over the next few days I contemplated resigning. It was difficult to accept that the CEO could be overruled on such a serious issue, but those were the rules and I had no option but to live by them or resign. In the end, I did not resign. The individual concerned received a stern reprimand from the board and his behaviour improved significantly over the next several months. He eventually left the college. This was a very painful episode for me. It underscored the reality that, no matter what position one holds, one can't always get his way.

During my tenure as president, several new programs were added at all campuses. I was particularly happy to have a coop Data Processing program brought in at Langara. I would have liked to see more programs converted to the coop model, whereby students alternate between academic studies and work, but our enrolment base was too small to make this work. Now, with much larger enrolments, colleges and universities could improve access to post-secondary education and reduce costs to students by developing models whereby students alternate periods of education and periods of paid employment, as I was able to do in California.

A Management Development Centre was also created. The role of advisory committees was strengthened, and I made it a practice to attend some of their meetings. This was the time when several thousand Vietnamese refugees found their way to Canada and KEC played a major role in teaching them basic English language skills and helping them to integrate in the broader Canadian community.

As I had done at Niagara, I taught a course in electronic pulse and digital circuits during my time as president of VCC. This course was based entirely on integrated circuits, rather than individual transistors. I couldn't teach such a course at VCC, because it didn't offer any programs in engineering technology, but the British Columbia Institute of Technology (BCIT) did, and they were happy to hire me. It was a night school course, which included both lecture and laboratory content.[59] At home I built a small workshop in my garage, fully equipped with electronics instruments. Most of my weekends were spent building and testing the circuits for the course I taught, while listening to CBC radio in the background

At VCC I held regular lunch meetings jointly with all three campus student councils to discuss and to resolve whatever issues were of concern. I wanted to stay in touch with students and that meant listening to them. Two significant outcomes of these meetings were the development of student leadership seminars and the introduction of a course on job search skills. Both initiatives addressed real problems faced by students. Student leadership seminars were aimed at students who ran for various positions on the student council. There, they were suddenly faced with having to manage relatively large sums of money and organize various activities involving people, facilities and meeting student expectations. Without any training whatsoever, they were often overwhelmed and their academic performance suffered. The leadership seminars gave them the tools necessary to cope with these increased responsibilities. Job search skills were generally incorporated in the various instructional programs, but some students needed more coaching. Another major issue often discussed at these meetings was tuition, which we had to increase on several occasions. It was always controversial. At my last board meeting, for example, there was a student demonstration opposing a proposed tuition increase. But we had little choice in the matter. Provincial operating funding was always short and we needed the extra money.

In 1981, there was a major recession in Canada. BC was particularly hard hit because of its heavy dependence on the resource sector. Inflation was running at 14%, our enrolment was growing and we had new space that added to our operating expenses. It was obvious that the province was experiencing serious financial difficulties. The Ministry of Education asked each college to tell them what the consequences would be if funding remained flat the following year. Given the level of inflation and the additional operating costs we expected to incur for the growing student body and new space, I estimated that flat funding would be equivalent to a twenty percent cut. I gave an interview to the press making this point and indicated that the consequences would be drastic indeed. Brian Smith, the Minister of Education, told the press that I was overreacting, and that this was just a hypothetical exercise.

I have never been a fan of hypothetical exercises in publicly funded organizations. If they are done in secret, one is deprived of the knowledge that front line employees could offer to achieve cost reductions with minimum impact on services. And there is always the risk of leaks. One does not have to be paranoid to imagine the news headline: "Administration has secret plans to drastically cut jobs and services to the public".[60] If it is done openly, staff and other constituencies mobilize their resources to fight any plan that would negatively affect their interests. Staff and student morale would suffer and it would become impossible to obtain their cooperation in the implementation of any such plans. As CEO, I would be expected to speak out against budget cuts and I did so, not only because I believed that the magnitude of what was being proposed would be damaging, but also because my credibility would suffer otherwise. I told Ministry officials that this was a bad idea, but they insisted.

156

The best way to cut costs is obviously to become more efficient. But VCC was already operating at a per student cost well below the provincial average and therefore efficiency gains were not at all obvious. That left us with two expenditure reduction strategies. One was horizontal and the other vertical. Horizontal cuts would reduce expenditures by a given percentage across all areas. Everyone suffers more or less equally and the end result is that all programs are watered down. Quality is compromised. Vertical cuts involve the dropping of lower priority programs, while retaining funding to the rest. This way quality is maintained, but quantity is reduced. Of course, it is possible to do a mix of both.

My executive committee and I worked on this "hypothetical" scenario and decided to go for vertical cuts, dropping lower priority programs. One of the criteria for deciding what was a lower priority program was whether it was offered at a nearby college. If it was available elsewhere, we felt that an argument could be made for dropping it at VCC. Of course, we had no way of knowing whether the other colleges were making similar assumptions and dropping the same program! When I presented the results to the board, the meeting room was filled with protesters of all types: students, staff and community members. They were not going to accept that their programs might be cut. VCC board member Nathan Divinsky recommended the college openly defy the minister's request. "It's time for the monster to stand up to Frankenstein and say, You can't do this". Divinski's statement was greeted by a roar of applause from the assembled audience. The board, sensitive to the strong opposition and inspired by Divinsky's passionate intervention, decided not to submit anything to the Ministry of Education. They defied the provincial government to fire them. Actually, nothing happened. The whole exercise had been a colossal waste of time and energy, and produced a lot of bad feelings all around.

In 1983, the BC provincial government decided it would have to make further cuts to its expenditures. To enable the various provincially funded institutions to make these additional cuts, the government tabled legislation that substantially restricted unions' power to negotiate job security, overtime rates, scheduling, overtime, etc. It also gave employers major new powers, including the right to fire staff without cause, regardless of seniority. This was an extreme piece of legislation that immediately mobilized the labour movement in BC. The BC Federation of Labour called for a province wide strike (Operation Solidarity) and thousands of union members, including all of the unionized staff at VCC, walked off the job. The entire province was paralyzed for several days. I made it clear to my staff that, even if I were given the power to fire staff without cause, I had no intention of using such power. The polarization between government and business on one side and the labour unions on the other had never been greater. There were frantic attempts to find a face-saving solution and eventually Jack Munro, president of the International Woodworkers of America met with Premier Bill Bennett and a compromise of sorts was agreed upon. The government backed off from some of its most controversial proposals, but a great deal of damage was done in the meantime.

Still, worse was to come. The colleges were told that their budgets would be cut 5% for three years in a row, starting with the current year. This decision was communicated to us in August. Our fiscal year began in April, so we were well into it. Cuts in absolute dollars of this magnitude would be extremely difficult to make in mid-year. They required time to plan and months to implement. Notice had to be given to employees who would lose their jobs, leases had to be cancelled and so on. Nothing like this had ever happened before. I decided to approach the Langara Faculty Association executive, with whom we had recently settled on an 8 percent wage increase, asking them to re-open their collective agreement and agree to a rollback. This request was at once unprecedented and unpopular. But to their credit, the Langara Faculty Association agreed to reopen their contract and we negotiated a rollback that saved the college $300,000. Actually, I found the Langara faculty, despite their campaigns to achieve autonomy, to be quite professional. Once, we had to fire a teacher, and they supported us, because they agreed that such a person did not belong in the classroom. The other unions had not yet settled so we simply held the line on salary increases. The Vocational Instructors Association, for example, accepted a 0% salary increase. We still had to eliminate fifty full time equivalent positions, including several lay-offs, but somehow we managed.

In 1981, Deborah was graduated from high school and began to work, first through an agency and then with Canadian Pacific Telegraphs. This was the same company I had worked for in Montreal when I was a teenager. Deborah also took continuing education courses at VCC and received a certificate in Business Administration. She bought her first car (a white Chevette) and I taught her how to drive. She made several friends, but like Lella, she never really felt at home in Vancouver. Deborah worked downtown, near my office, and we often met for lunch. It was great to see Deborah grow into a fine and bright young woman, and we discussed work related topics as two adults, sharing perspectives on a variety of work related issues.

Andrew quickly developed a strong interest in sports. I took him to a couple of hockey games, even though I had never been a sports enthusiast. I also took him crab fishing at a nearby pier in Port Moody. We would use fish heads or bits of chicken as bait and lower the trap. After a while we would lift the trap and usually there would be one or two crabs. At home, nobody liked to watch me kill the crabs, which I did before cooking them. Andrew had made friends quite quickly, at school and in the neighbourhood and seemed quite happy living in the Vancouver area.

At VCC, I had been lucky to hire a very competent secretary, Jean Elliott. Jean was absolutely fantastic. She was efficient, courteous, vivacious, with a pleasant, outgoing personality. I would put her in the same league as Mary Hornak, my secretary at Niagara College, which is saying a lot. It's difficult to overstate the value of a secretary (or administrative assistant) to a senior executive. They are privy to the most sensitive and confidential information. By their behaviour towards others, they project an image for their boss that can be extremely important. They must not only be efficient, because the workload is unusually heavy, but loyal and discreet. I have been extremely fortunate to have had top notch secretaries in all my senior positions. They made my job much easier and enjoyable than it would otherwise have been.

As time passed, the board composition changed, but I continued to enjoy an excellent relationship with its members, especially when Peter Hebb became chairman. Peter was a senior executive for Guaranty Trust and managed investments for many wealthy clients. He was a no nonsense type of person. You always knew where he stood. I made it a point of keeping him well informed about the important issues of the day and he appreciated this sharing of information.

As stated earlier, it was difficult to get press attention at VCC, except when there was something controversial going on, such as the admission of foreign students. We often enrolled such students, provided that they, or someone on their behalf, paid the full cost, so there would be no subsidy from the taxpayer. In fact, revenues from such programs in excess of expenditures were used to supplement our extremely tight budget, enabling us to offer more courses to BC residents than would otherwise be possible. Some politicians ignored this fact and for their own political ends, accused the college of allowing foreign students while denying admission to BC residents. This was patently untrue. In one case, I had to issue a public statement contradicting the Hon. Jack Davis, a senior minister in the provincial government who had twisted my words to score cheap political points, suggesting that VCC was involved in a "scam".

In fact, we had negotiated a deal for about a dozen students from Libya to take English language classes at the college, subject to board approval. We had made it very clear to the sponsors (The Canadian Association for International Education) that nothing was final until we received board approval. But somehow the communication got mixed up and these students arrived before they should have. There was strong reaction from the public, press and politicians. They portrayed our acceptance of these students as support for Libyan dictator Moammar Khadafy. The board was also upset because they found out about it from the press. I assured the board that an error had occurred and that, until the board approved, these students would not be admitted. The board, in a narrow 6-4 vote, defeated the motion to admit them. They wanted nothing to do with Libya, which was seen as a sponsor of terrorism. I thought that whether to admit students from Libya or not was essentially a foreign policy decision. It was up to the federal government to make such a determination. Having been granted student visas, it was not up to an individual college to second guess the federal government's decision. But my view did not prevail. Board member Jonathan Baker summarized the board's decision by stating that "Khadafy is an advocate of terrorism around the world. We don't want anything to do with him". The following day we sent the students back to Ontario, where other colleges admitted them. Needless to say, we received a lot of unwelcome press coverage on this issue, in print, radio and television. Some people even accused us of training terrorists!

There was at the time a pan-Canadian group called the Association of Canadian Community Colleges (ACCC). I served briefly on its board of directors. Most Canadian colleges were members of the ACCC, which lobbied on behalf of the colleges, primarily at the federal level. They were also heavily involved in promoting international education activities for Canadian colleges, usually funded by CIDA (Canadian International Development Agency). In 1983 I was asked to participate on a team of college and university representatives to travel to Southeast Asia and visit government and educational agencies there to find ways in which Canada might be of assistance with their development programs. There were three college presidents and three senior level university representatives on this team, supported by an ACCC official. We would be gone for a little over three weeks and visit Thailand, the Philippines, Singapore, Malaysia and Indonesia.

The first step in this mission was a three day orientation in Ottawa. We were briefed on the history, culture and current political environment of all the countries we were going to visit.

In my case, the trip to Southeast Asia began in Vancouver, with a flight to Tokyo, then another flight to Hong Kong, followed by a third flight to Bangkok, Thailand. When I boarded my flight in Vancouver, the airplane was stuck on the tarmac for three hours, due to some mechanical problem. Eventually we took off, and eleven hours later, we arrived in Tokyo, which had just experienced its heaviest snowfall in one hundred years. Although we were able to land, we could not leave the airplane because the city was immobilized and the airport was full of stranded passengers lying wall to wall on the floor! We had no choice but to remain aboard the plane for the next twenty-four hours. That meant that we were unable to shave or shower for a total of 38 hours. Food was also running low but there was plenty of booze! I read every magazine that there was to read and tried to get some sleep, without much success.

Eventually the snow was cleared and we were allowed to disembark. Inside the airport we managed to wash and eat some Japanese food (not my favourite). After a further four hour wait, we caught a flight to Hong Kong. By this time we were all very tired and eager to fall into a comfortable bed and go to sleep. Unfortunately, our hotel reservations in Hong Kong had us arriving the previous day and, when we didn't show up as planned, they cancelled our rooms! We had gone without sleep for two days and now we were in a strange city without a room! After a bit of complaining, the hotel staff managed to find us rooms nearby. This was not exactly the most auspicious start to our trip!

Hong Kong was just a convenient place for a stop-over to help us overcome our jet lag. Over the next two days, we had a wonderful time sightseeing and enjoying the fine Chinese cuisine. The city was bustling with activity. I was amazed at how crowded the streets were, with pedestrians and cars covering every space that was available. We saw extremes of poverty and wealth all around us. Close to huge multi-million dollar mansions, with Mercedes and Rolls Royce cars parked in their driveways, were shanty towns, filled with tin roofed shacks surrounded by open sewers. Hong Kong was certainly prosperous, but not everybody shared in the prosperity.

After Hong Kong, we were on our way to Bangkok. As soon as we landed, it was obvious we were in a different world. The first thing that hit us was the extreme heat and humidity. The airport itself was a madhouse. The toilets were filthy and almost unsuitable for human use. We were hounded by locals who wanted to carry our luggage and by taxi drivers who wanted to take us wherever we wanted to go, as well as several places we didn't want to go!

Our ACCC team visited several educational and government institutions in Bangkok. We spoke to educational and government leaders about ways in which the Canadian government could be of help and this information was used upon our return to Canada to develop appropriate programs and exchanges with each country that we visited.

From Bangkok we flew to Kuala Lumpur in Malaysia and from there to the island of Penang. As in Bangkok, we met various educational and government officials, and made extensive notes of their educational development priorities.

Our next stop was Manila, in the Philippines. There we stayed at a very nice hotel. We had access to fine food and accommodations, paying Western rates, while the local help was paid local rates. We participated in several meetings with various individuals, including the Minister of Education. At the time, Ferdinand Marcos was the president. He was, as later events showed, quite corrupt and hated by his people.

The Minister of Education was also a professor at the local university and an avid tennis player. He was a dynamic and progressive individual, very interested in advancing the level of education of his people. He told us that, even as Minister of Education and a university professor, he had difficulty being able to afford to buy milk for his children!

In Manila, we were invited to a reception at the Canadian Ambassador's residence. It was located in an area behind high concrete walls, guarded at its entrance by machine gun toting guards. All around this enclave, the streets were dirty, noisy, crowded and generally typical of Third World countries. Inside the walls of this gated community, we were in a different world. Lush lawns, beautiful vegetation, swimming pools, grand estates and armed guards all around. It was hard to enjoy the sumptuous hospitality at the embassy while being surrounded by such extreme poverty.

From the Philippines we flew to Jakarta, Indonesia. There we saw extreme poverty along with extreme wealth, as we had elsewhere in Southeast Asia.

In addition to the usual meetings with educators, politicians and Canadian Embassy staff, we visited a large museum that contained very graphic portrayals of atrocities committed against Indonesians by the Dutch during the time when they colonized Indonesia. Although the Dutch departed some time ago, memories of their cruelty, such as the 1947 execution of 431[61] Indonesian men and boys, as their families and neighbours looked on, remained.

Throughout this trip, all team members sensed a high degree of respect and admiration towards Canadians. We did not have a history of colonialism, as the British and the Dutch had. And we were not Americans, with the baggage that came from being a military and economic super-power. We made it clear that our goal was not to tell them what we thought they needed by way of development assistance. We were genuinely interested in learning directly from them what their priorities were, and try to find creative ways to assist them. They seemed to appreciate our approach and were quite candid in sharing their points of view with us.

One of the things I learned, for example, was that they didn't need more university graduates. They already had too many who could not be productively employed. Their goal was to reduce poverty levels through economic growth, and to eradicate infectious diseases that were still prevalent, especially among small children. In health care, they needed more and better training for nurses. Basic literacy was the single most urgent requirement pretty well everywhere we went. Also important was training for entrepreneurs who wanted to establish a small business of some kind. Agricultural expertise was in great demand. These were all areas in which Canadian colleges had expertise that could be used to create programs tailored to the specific circumstances of each country. Our thinking was to propose a "train the trainers" approach. This way, although Canadian teachers might at first provide training directly to students, the ultimate goal was to enable locally trained teachers to take over.

We also visited Singapore, a small city state bordering on Malaysia. What a contrast with the other countries on our tour! The airport was spotless and very modern. The toilets were impeccably looked after. The streets were also extremely clean (there was a heavy fine for anyone caught throwing trash on the roads) and traffic moved in a very orderly fashion.

Singapore was a major commercial centre, with a very prosperous economy and a standard of living substantially higher than in any of the nearby countries. It had a British colonial history. The government was somewhat authoritarian, but the citizens didn't seem to mind, given their prosperity. I asked one of the locals about unemployment and he told me that there was none. If someone couldn't find a job, the government would give him one, as there was always work that needed to be done. We followed the usual routine of meeting education and government officials, as well as the Canadian ambassador. Given Singapore's relatively advanced economy, opportunities for Canadian involvement were different from what we identified in other countries. Exchanges between Singapore and Canada that focussed on technology, trade and finance seemed more appropriate and worthy of follow up.

My whole experience in Southeast Asia was quite an eye opener. It made me realize how fortunate we were in Canada, with the many opportunities available to us. I had, of course, experienced poverty myself in Sicily, but what I saw in Asia was much worse.

Once I returned to Vancouver, I gave a full report to the board, staff and to the press, describing what I had learned on this trip. There was a great deal of media interest. Our team's report recommended a substantial development program based on our findings of each country's most urgent educational needs. It became the basis of a memorandum of understanding between the government of Canada and SEAMEO (Southeast Asian Ministers of Education Organization) signed in January 1985. It provided for a Canadian contribution through CIDA of $9.5 million over a period of five years to fund the project. I would have liked to have been a part of the project's implementation, but my subsequent departure from VCC prevented me from participating.

Another area of international education in which VCC played an important role was a program for Japanese students from Takushoku University. These students would come to VCC for two years to take various courses, including English language instruction. They would be billeted with families in the Vancouver area, so that they could practice their English language skills. VCC entered into a contract with Takushoku University, recovering the full costs, plus a modest profit. The program was enormously successful. Strong friendships were made by these students with their host families and, at graduation time, many tears were shed. It was quite an emotional experience for the students. The program was administered by our Continuing

Education Division. Ceremony was very important to the Japanese and there were many occasions for college and Japanese officials to meet, negotiate the annual contract, exchange gifts and share

elaborate dinners.

It was expected that senior officials from the two institutions would visit each other; so I made arrangements to visit Takushoku University in Tokyo in April 1984. There I met the University president and gave the convocation address in English, which was translated into Japanese by an interpreter. We also sent some of our students to study at Takushoku, where they could learn to speak Japanese and become knowledgeable about the business culture of Japan. I met several of these Canadian students and members of their families who were visiting at the time. The above photograph was taken on an occasion when we welcomed Japanese students to VCC. These student exchanges were, of course, quite expensive, and the students ultimately had to pay the cost, so only families with the necessary financial resources were able to take advantage of these opportunities. Exchanges between

British Columbia and Japan were considered very important by both sides, as they fostered trade across the Pacific.

During one of the social functions that I attended in Japan, I met a Chinese delegation that was visiting the university at the same time. The Chinese were very interested in Canada and we spoke at length about various educational programs that we offered and that they might be interested in exploring further. The conversation went rather slowly because it required two sets of translations. The Chinese remarks would be translated by someone into Japanese, then by someone else from Japanese into English. I would then speak in English and someone would translate into Japanese; someone else would translate from Japanese to Chinese. It was very time consuming, but it allowed for many opportunities to drink sake, the powerful alcoholic Japanese drink that is served at these functions. Both the Japanese and Chinese liked to toast often, and of course, I had to join in. Each toast involved emptying a small glass of sake. Needless to say, after a few toasts, the communication, with its double translation, became a bit fuzzy!

The Chinese head of the delegation invited me to visit his institution in Bejing, and being polite, I reciprocated, inviting him and his colleagues to visit VCC. Soon after my return to Vancouver, I received a cable from China, advising me that the Chinese delegation had accepted my invitation and would be arriving in two days. They were interested in visiting my college as well as the "University of Canada", the "University of America", and Niagara Falls! This was during a holiday weekend and, by the time I received the cable, most everyone at the college had left. Nevertheless, Cam Avery (my public relations director) and I quickly worked the phones, reserved rooms for the delegation at a local hotel and made arrangements for them to visit the University of Toronto (that was as close as we could come to identifying the "University of Canada") and the University of Chicago. I also arranged a visit to Niagara Falls, using my Niagara College contacts.

Cam and I went to the airport to meet the delegation and drove them to the hotel. They had their own translator and another chap who never spoke and who we assumed was their "minder", a political person of some sort who kept an eye on everyone. We arranged meetings with our various administrators and faculty and I also invited them to my home for dinner. Lella served lasagna and veal parmigiana, thinking that they might like some Italian food for a change, but most of them only sampled the food. They did not seem to like it or maybe they just weren't hungry. At any rate, we also hosted a reception for them at the college, with many toasts, as usual, and they seemed to be having a good time. Ultimately they flew to Toronto, reminding me of their standing invitation to visit them in Bejing. Unfortunately, I left the college soon after and was not able to take them up on their offer.

In the Summer of 1984, I began to think of looking for another job. Until recently my expectation had been to work at VCC until retirement and to live permanently in Vancouver. Things were going well at the college, where I enjoyed excellent relations with the board, staff and students. Budget cuts were, hopefully, coming to an end and I was feeling quite comfortable with the job. However, I did not feel sufficiently challenged any more. I thought of moving to a field outside education where I could transfer my management skills. After nearly twenty years in education, with thirteen of those years as a college president, I was still relatively young at 43 and the time seemed right to make a change.

As it happened, opportunity soon presented itself. The Canadian Broadcasting Corporation was looking for a vice president of Human Resources. I had a strong interest in human resources, having led in the development of strategies for collective bargaining in Ontario and BC. I also had experience in training, of course, which is an important area of human resources. On balance, I felt that, if I was going to enter a new field, the human resources area would be a good bridge to make the transition. Given that communication was an important element of broadcasting and education, my background as an educator would also be useful at the CBC. Soon I applied and was interviewed, first by a consultant responsible for the search, then by Franklin Delaney (CBC senior vice president) and finally by Pierre Juneau, the CBC's president. They were interested in having me join the CBC, but I was somewhat hesitant at first. Ottawa, in spite of its many attractions, had never been my idea of a desirable place to live. It meant going back to snow shovelling and all the other winter chores from which I had longed to escape. Nevertheless, upon much reflection, Lella and I felt that the positives exceeded the negatives, and I accepted CBC's offer.

Franklin Delaney would be my immediate boss. He reported directly to CBC president Pierre Juneau. The CBC expected a substantial budget cut and a big part of my job would involve downsizing the corporation. There were also difficult negotiations expected with the CBC's 29 unions, as well as other challenges. During one of my interviews, Delaney had asked, in French, about my French language skills. I pointed out, also in French, that it had been over 27 years since I had spoken French at any length and therefore, I would need a period of time to relearn the language.[62] He seemed satisfied with my answer. In fact, a generous description of my French language skills would have been "very rusty". They were well below the level of fluency required to be effective in a bilingual work environment.

I looked forward to the new job, despite the many difficult challenges it presented. Lella and Deborah were happy to leave the Vancouver area and return to Ontario, where they had felt more at home. We would also be closer to my parents, sister and her family. Regrettably, I had not taken into account the effect it would have on Andrew. He was 12 years old, a very difficult age to move. I casually announced one evening at the dinner table that we would be moving to Ottawa, and Andrew was completely shocked. I could tell that he was not happy. He would be leaving behind many friends, and I had been very insensitive breaking the news the way I did. I regret very much my lack of appreciation at the time of the short term impact such a move would have on Andrew. Eventually, he adjusted quite nicely to living in Ottawa.

I met VCC board chairman Peter Hebb and told him of my decision to leave. I was giving six months' notice, so there would be plenty of time to find a replacement. Peter asked me if there was anything the board could do that would convince me to stay. I was touched by this gesture, but my decision had been made and there was no turning back.

In the weeks leading to my departure several going away events were organized by the Langara Faculty Association, the Vocational Instructors Association, the administrators and the board. They all presented me with something unique to show their appreciation for my service. There were some critics as well. They resented my role as someone who had implemented the provincial government's budget cuts. It's hard to know what they expected of me. I had frequently spoken against budget cuts, publicly and privately, with officials and ministers in the provincial government. Several faculty leaders had expressed their admiration of my efforts to make the case for VCC in a forthright manner. But, when governments make decisions, you either implement them or resign. Had I resigned, which had never been suggested by faculty, students or any other group, someone else would have been appointed to carry out the budget cuts, perhaps someone not as committed to the quality of education as I was.[63]

The Vancouver years had been difficult and challenging, but my board, staff and I had weathered the storms with mutual respect. I had done my best to provide educational leadership while dealing with major financial and space problems. Some innovative instructional programs had been developed and two major and one minor building project had been successfully completed. I had also led a provincial task force in the development of a new funding formula for the colleges, which promised to improve VCC's financial situation. And, of course, VCC was now an important player on the international educational stage.

While the challenges at VCC had been more formidable than I had anticipated, I was fortunate to work with some very capable people who shared my passion for learning and commitment to students. As my former colleague and continuing good friend Jock Denholm[64] put it: "Education is a people kind of business. Some people understand this; others do not."

CHAPTER NINE

The years 1985 to 1995 cover the longest time I have worked for a single organization, the Canadian Broadcasting Corporation. During that time I experienced the highest highs and the lowest lows of my professional career. But, before getting into what I actually did during those ten years, it may be useful to offer some historical context about the CBC.

During its early days, Canadian broadcasting was dominated by American radio stations transmitting near the border with Canada. The impetus towards the establishment of a Canadian broadcasting system came from the desire to provide a Canadian counter balance to that predominantly US programming presence. As far back as 1932, then Prime Minister R.B Bennett vowed that "We will show the States that Canada is no appendage." He went on to add that "properly employed, the radio can be made a most effective instrument in nation building." Under his leadership, The Canadian Radio Broadcasting Commission was established in 1932.

This was followed by the creation of the CBC in 1936, with support from all political parties in the House of Commons. It took great political courage to launch this enterprise in the middle of the Great Depression. MacKenzie King was Prime Minister at the time.

The vision articulated by both prime ministers resonated with Canadians who did not want to be culturally assimilated by the US. This was especially important to anglophones, who enjoyed access to a vast quantity of American radio programming in their own language. In a similar vein, francophone Canadians wanted to be able to pursue their distinctive French language cultural aspirations.

But there was more to the idea of Canadian broadcasting than a mere desire to avoid American cultural domination. Fierce battles were fought over whether the air waves should be reserved for public service or become a vehicle to generate profits through advertising. The most articulate Canadian spokesman against the latter option was Graham Spry, who pointed out that, in the world of commercial broadcasting, "The primary consideration of the broadcaster, indeed, is not the listener who hears, but the advertiser who pays." This concern was echoed in 1932, when a Parliamentary Committee recommended that advertising should take up no more than 5% of program time.

Commercial broadcasters were interested in radio because of its profit making potential. And it wasn't just the Canadian Graham Spry who decried the exploitation of the medium for profit. The American radio pioneer Dr. Lee de Forest, in a written statement to the Parliamentary Committee, said that radio was being debased by advertising, adding "We look to you in Canada to lead radio in North America out of the morass in which it has pitiably sunk. May Canada fulfil my early dream."

So, controversy about broadcasting policy is nothing new. Opposition to the CBC as a publicly subsidized broadcaster has been ongoing from its inception. It comes in part from individuals who genuinely believe that "government does best that which governs least," an idea often attributed to US president Thomas Jefferson. Advocates of this philosophy oppose any government role in cultural matters.

But there is a different perspective that should also be considered. Funding support of culture is the foundation of great civilizations, and cultural development cannot be left entirely to market forces. This view was articulated by Max Frankel, former executive director of the New York Times, when he pointed out that "without government subsidy and tax supported philanthropy, there would be no great universities, no great libraries, no great museums, no grand opera or basic science."

Historically, antagonism to the CBC has come from some, though not all, private broadcasters. The motivation is obvious. Less CBC, more profits for the commercial sector. The arguments have been specious, self-serving, but nevertheless enduring.

When I joined the CBC in 1985, it consisted of two television networks (one in the English language, with headquarters in Toronto, and the other in the French language, with headquarters in Montreal), as well as regional broadcasting stations in most provinces, four domestic radio networks, a Northern radio and television service broadcasting in seven different aboriginal languages and an international radio unit (Radio Canada International). The regional stations carried, in addition to network programs, local news shows and a fair amount of locally produced entertainment programming, which sometimes would be carried by the network. The CBC was also affiliated with a number of privately owned television stations that carried CBC network shows as well as their own locally produced programming. The AM radio networks featured music, news and current affairs programs, while the FM radio networks concentrated mainly on classical music. The international short wave network, Radio Canada International, broadcast in many foreign languages throughout the world.

The domestic radio services were unique in that they carried no commercials (with a few rare exceptions), and had very loyal audiences. They aimed to provide thoughtful programming, similar in many respects to the National Public Radio in the US. Because they carried no advertising (as a condition of their licences), they were entirely dependent on the government's annual grant to the CBC. Compared to television, radio was and remains relatively inexpensive.

The Broadcasting Act required the CBC to provide a wide range of programming that informed, enlightened and entertained, while reflecting the different regions of Canada, a costly proposition because audiences in some regions were relatively small. There were also certain responsibilities assigned to the CBC that did not apply to the private networks. Chief among these were a much higher level of Canadian content, the promotion of Canadian talent and coverage of important national events (the Throne speech and budget speech in Parliament, Veteran's day commemoration, Canada day festivities, visits by the Queen, etc). This coverage might not be profitable, but could contribute to nation building.

The CBC also carried a substantial dose of imported American entertainment programming, which could be purchased at a relatively low cost, while bringing in substantial advertising revenue. Canadian entertainment programming, on the other hand, was expensive to produce, and did not usually generate sufficient advertising revenue to cover its cost. American shows were also expensive to produce, but their initial cost could be amortized over the huge American market (in English it was about 12 times the size of the Canadian market). Hence, any additional revenue they earned from the relatively small Canadian market was gravy for the American producers.

Furthermore, the CBC operated several French language radio and television stations outside Québec, where French speaking populations were rather small and no private commercial broadcaster would provide such a service. Yet it was a matter of national public policy to foster Francophone culture throughout Canada. These expectations and the small amount of advertising revenue generated by purely Canadian shows, meant that the CBC had to be subsidized.

The CBC traditionally produced and broadcast professional sports programming, such as hockey. It also carried summer and winter Olympics, as well as Commonwealth games. Hockey and the Olympics were usually money makers. This enabled the CBC to cover local amateur sports, which was not profitable, but provided exposure to promising athletes. It also allowed the CBC to develop the creative, technical and logistical expertise to do a first class job of covering the Olympics.

Given the sheer volume of CBC information programming, it should not be surprising that governments of all political stripes would be unhappy at times with CBC coverage of certain events.

For example, for quite a while, there has been a secessionist movement in the province of Québec. There are several historic reasons for this, which go beyond the scope of these memoirs. Suffice it to say that, while I was living in Montreal as a teenager, I personally observed instances of anglophone arrogance and discrimination towards the francophone majority. Conditions have changed dramatically since those days. Now French is the official language in Québec and, to the extent that there is any discrimination, it is felt more by the English speaking minority.

Nevertheless, over time, many politicians have felt (with some justification) that there were many sovereigntists in the French language networks of the CBC. With sovereignty in Québec supported by more or less 40% of the population, it would be naïve to think that people holding such views would not be found within Radio-Canada, the French language arm of the CBC. The real issue, of course, is whether these sovereigntists abused their positions to advance their political agenda. Needless to say, this is a matter of perception, with some people detecting a sovereignty bias in every news report, while others believing that, on balance, information programming did not lean in one direction or the other.

Other politicians were more concerned about leftist bias. In fact, all of us, not only journalists, have some kind of bias. What counts is whether personal bias is allowed to influence news and current affairs programs. And then there is such a thing as "confirmation bias", where if one expects bias, one will tend to see it, whether it's there or not.

An example of how perception of bias can occur is a somewhat unflattering account by former Prime Minister Brian Mulroney of a 1986 CBC report of his attendance at Canada's first G-7 summit in Tokyo, as described by him during a taped interview with author Peter Newman. A careful reading of what was actually broadcast by the CBC (source: CBC Archives,) reveals a much more balanced report. In all fairness to the former prime minister, when I brought this discrepancy to his attention, he did not recall the event and acknowledged that, while he did have some issues with CBC reporters, he had a high regard for David Halton. He indicated that if he could, he would try to rectify the matter.

Through various opinion polls taken over the years, the vast majority of Canadians have given the CBC consistently high credibility ratings. This does not mean that bias of some kind doesn't creep in from time to time, but there are procedures for dealing with such cases. Several years ago, for example, an ombudsman reporting directly to the president was added for each of the English and French language news and current affairs services in order to further enhance the CBC's journalistic accountability.

Finally, some politicians would like the CBC to behave as a cheerleader of sorts, by providing favourable exposure to whatever policies, programs or activities are carried out by the government. The CBC, just like any other reputable news organization, will not do that. Reporters are trained to be suspicious and, while there may be occasions when they go too far in challenging the government's message, the public is better served by journalists who ask too many questions than by journalists who ask too few questions. One thing can be said for sure. No Canadian prime minister or provincial premier should expect a "Dear Leader" kind of treatment from the press. The fact is that politicians need the media and work hard to ensure the best possible coverage for themselves. As the late British politician Enoch Powell once said: "a politician complaining about the media is like a sailor complaining about the sea!"

Of course, many legitimate criticisms can be levelled against the press in general (both public and private). When reporting the news, journalists should not be editorializing, yet at times they do. Criticism, on such occasions, is perfectly justified. Still, I believe that any prescription to deal with the occasional abuses would be worse than the disease. The best policy, in my judgement, is to ensure vigorous competition, so that a broadly diverse range of opinion is available to the public.

Clearly, when I arrived on the scene, the CBC faced major problems. Externally, there was a hostile government and a strong lobby of private broadcasters who wanted the CBC to be emasculated. Internally, there were even bigger problems, some financial and others organizational. Financial problems were due mainly to government cutbacks, but also to the inefficiencies of out-dated labour practices. There were obviously cleavages between management and labour over this. The jurisdictional barriers between different unions made it impossible to organize staff in the most efficient manner. This problem became more serious as technology evolved, making the production of programming less labour intensive. But there were other sources of conflict. The media divisions, which were responsible for programming, were resistant to any head office involvement in their operations. This is not uncommon in large, decentralized corporations. Head office is always seen as remote by the operating divisions, who want as much autonomy as possible. In a creative organization, the problem is often exacerbated by the conviction on the part of the producing arms that the head office bureaucrats have no clue about the challenges faced by the people charged with making the product. A consequence of this mindset made it often difficult for head office to get information from the field. There was also conflict between the regions and the networks. The regions always felt short-changed by the networks.

A further cleavage existed between English and French sectors, which mirrored the political divisions in the country. There was a different way of doing things in the French sector than in the English sector. The audiences were also different. English language speakers watched a lot of American TV; French language speakers preferred home grown French language shows. Costs on the English side were a lot higher than on the French side. This reflected the market situation. An English speaking performer, for example, could be lured to the US where really big money could be made. The cost of rights to events such as sports was much higher on the English side (because of larger audiences) than on the French side. So budgets within the CBC reflected these realities, but this did not alleviate the feeling of being second class citizens by the French side, who always complained that they were being short-changed in comparison with their English language counterparts. The debate was endless and a source of constant strain. It is remarkable that some joint English-French productions actually took place from time to time, given the uneasy relationship between the two.

There was also a radio-TV cleavage. Radio was a much less costly medium than TV and, of course, had a much lower budget. It also generated no advertising revenue, so it was at the mercy of head office for all its resources. But Radio had a much more loyal audience than TV and could mobilize public support against budget cuts much more effectively.

These divisions within the CBC must be understood if one is to cope successfully. They can't ever be completely resolved, however. They can only be managed. In addition to the organizational challenges, there were, of course, personality issues. Some of the people did not get along with others. This happens in all organizations and the CBC was no exception.

Given all of the external and internal challenges faced by the CBC, it was obvious to me that the organization that I had just joined needed more allies. It had to build bridges linking it to the many constituencies that had a stake in its future. That objective was pursued, with varying degrees of success, by the two CBC presidents with whom I worked (Pierre Juneau and Gerard Veilleux.) It also became one of the highest priorities of my own presidency.

CHAPTER TEN

March 1, 1985 was my first working day at the CBC's head office in Ottawa. I had arrived the previous evening from Vancouver, where spring was definitely in the air. Ottawa, instead, was still in the grip of winter, with deep snow on the ground and very cold temperatures.

During my first few days on the job, I was taken around to meet all the other vice presidents and several senior managers in Ottawa, Montreal and Toronto. During one of these "get acquainted" tours, I met Trina McQueen, then in charge of news and current affairs for English TV. McQueen's first question to me was: "Why on earth do you want this job?" As I would soon learn, the human resources portfolio at the CBC was far more challenging than I had imagined.

The answer to McQueen's pointed question was that I had wanted to transfer my management skills to a new field outside education, and the vice-presidency of human resources at the CBC seemed to offer a viable route for such a transition. As an educator, I was also attracted to a core element of the CBC's mandate: to inform and enlighten. While the means of service delivery were different, I saw education and public broadcasting as having much in common. Both were "people" based enterprises, engaged in the business of communication. This perception was reinforced many years later by Knowlton Nash, the CBC's iconic national news anchor, when he said: "The media is, I think, essentially a teacher in the broadest sense of that word. Although it may sound excessively flattering, I think we're really in the educating business."[65]

Whatever the merits of the common ground between public broadcasting and education, I found that my strongest asset was the art of listening, developed over many years by trying to understand what people were really saying. Reading between the lines is not a discipline that can be taught; it is an art shaped by a desire to understand what motivates people to behave in a certain way.

Shortly after my appointment, but before I assumed my new duties at the CBC, the federal government announced an $85 million cut to the corporation's annual parliamentary appropriation, which was slightly in excess of $900 million.[66] Most of the CBC revenue came from this appropriation; the rest from advertising revenue. This cut would have a major impact on the CBC, which had to slash 1150 positions. Extensive use was made of early retirement incentives, but about 350 layoffs were required to achieve the reduced staff levels. Several programs in drama and current affairs were cut, and more commercials were added to increase advertising revenue.

The problem with early retirement incentives is that some of the people who take them up are also the people that one would like to retain. Hence there is a net loss of talent. There are also some people who were planning to leave anyway, but once the incentives became available, they simply adjusted their plans to take advantage of such incentives. This meant that the overall cost of achieving staff reductions was higher than it would otherwise have been. The trade-off, of course, was that involuntary departures were minimized. This was good for staff morale, an important consideration in any organization.

186

In 1985, the CBC had about 12,000 permanent employees and several thousand more on contracts of various durations. These ranged from a three minute commentary to a few hours performing on a show, to several years in other instances.

The CBC employed a very broad range of people. There were actors, singers, dancers, writers, researchers, producers, directors, carpenters, electricians, technicians, camera operators, engineers, lawyers, accountants, computer specialists, journalists, secretaries, clerks and so on. There were also a president, thirteen vice presidents, several directors and mid-level managers.

Except for managers and confidential secretaries, all these people were unionized. There were 29 unions in all, each fiercely protective of its jurisdiction. Relations with most unions were awful. There had been several strikes in recent years, with vandalism, intimidation and occasional violence. There was a great deal of mistrust between management and unions. At any one time, there would be hundreds of grievances. Many ended up in arbitration, which often lasted several months. Even arbitrators' decisions, which were supposed to be final, were often appealed to the courts, either by the unions or by management. These appeals could drag on for years and cost thousands of dollars in legal fees.

My immediate challenge as vice president of human resources was to prepare for the coming negotiations with the unions. Most of the downsizing had already been completed when I arrived, although there remained many issues that had to be resolved. In addition, there were the usual responsibilities associated with any HR department. These included processing the payroll, staffing, benefits, training, job evaluation, compensation policies, discipline, and administering the pension plan.

Many reports had been written about the CBC and I read several of the most recent. However, I was under no illusion about my knowledge of broadcasting in general and the CBC in particular. This contrasted with my previous jobs where, as an educator, I had risen through the ranks, from professor to department chairman, to dean and president, and knew how everything worked. Now, in spite of my belief that education and broadcasting had much in common, the devil, as the saying goes, is in the details. There was much for me to learn in a relatively short period of time. I also had to adjust to the fact that I was no longer the top person in the organization, and this meant that I had little control over how I organized my time. But nobody had forced me to change jobs. If I found this new job overwhelming at times, I had only myself to blame!

There was a perception in government and other circles that the CBC had been poorly managed. To the extent that there was merit to this view, one could reasonably ask: "Who appointed the board of directors and the CEO"? As long as the government is the sole decision maker, it has to accept responsibility for any management shortcomings. The fact that, as of 2016, no woman has ever been appointed chief executive of the CBC, despite the availability of many highly qualified women, speaks volumes about the inadequacy of the current process. For example, the Hon. Michel Dupuy, Minister of Canadian Heritage, met with the CBC board on January 11, 1994. When asked by the board about the government's progress towards naming a new president, he spoke about the need to find "the best man for the job." Could this have been a Freudian slip? I don't know, but I do feel that a better governance model would be one in which the board of directors is given authority to select the president.

The CBC was a publicly funded broadcaster, receiving most of its budget from the federal government. So it was expected to operate like a public service. However, the CBC was also in show business, where the rules and culture were vastly different from the public service. I was used to frugal management of taxpayer funds in my previous role as a college president and found some of the spending practices at the CBC excessive for a tax supported institution. CBC president Pierre Juneau tried to curtail those excesses that came to his attention and he set the example with very modest and defensible expenditures in his own office. So did his successors.

As I tried to learn about the various human resources issues I would be confronting, I met all the vice presidents and each one of them had a long list of problems they wanted me to resolve. It was obvious that several vice presidents wanted to use the downsizing as an opportunity to get rid of people who were either poor performers or had bad relations with their colleagues or bosses. I knew the dangers of this approach from the Niagara College experience and had to explain that there were collective agreements and legal restrictions that set boundaries on what we could actually do.

I also met with the leaders of every union representing CBC employees at the CBC. Rather than asking them to come to my office, I went to their offices, which were spread out in various locations (Toronto, Ottawa and Montreal.) I wanted to know what issues they considered important and to understand their different perspectives. There were mixed reactions to my "bridge-building" efforts. Some union leaders were open to a constructive dialogue, others were suspicious, while a few were openly hostile. Nevertheless, I found such meetings useful in achieving a better understanding of the issues and the personalities involved.

During those first few months after I joined the CBC I was very lonely without my wife and children, who remained in Vancouver until the end of the school year in June. I also had to deal with the reality that my French was quite limited. I made an effort to speak French with all my francophone colleagues and the French language unions, but I had a long way to go to develop the necessary fluency. Still, I could tell that the francophones with whom I spoke appreciated my efforts. I embarked on a very serious program to improve my French language skills. I had been relatively fluent in French during my teenage years in Montreal, and having Italian as my mother tongue eventually enabled me to achieve a sufficient level of fluency to work effectively in French and English.

One of my first recommendations to Pierre Juneau was that he should meet with all the union leaders, not to talk about collective bargaining issues, but to share with them his vision for the corporation and the challenges that we faced. I believed that this kind of "bridge-building" would facilitate the collective bargaining process. Despite strong objections from some other advisers, Juneau accepted my advice, and as expected, there were angry comments and a lot of cynicism expressed by the unions. But I felt that you had to start somewhere. It was my intention that such meetings should continue, but Juneau did not follow up and the only time after that he met with unions was when we were on the edge of a strike.

A great deal of my time was spent in the development of strategies for the coming round of negotiations with the CBC's various unions. I had a very capable director of industrial relations, Pierre Racicot, on whom I relied for advice and guidance. He knew the history of collective bargaining at the CBC better than anybody else, and had a good sense of what might work and what wouldn't. Juneau had also set up a committee of external advisers to assist us in these preparations. The recently elected Progressive Conservative government was skeptical about the CBC's capacity to take on the unions. For example, there were provisions in place that guaranteed a minimum number of employees in the technician category, which prevented the CBC from reducing its staff even through attrition. To counter the government's perception of a weak management team at the CBC, Juneau was very politically astute in picking advisers who were close to the government. Several of these individuals were later named to the Senate and to other senior positions in government, in which case they could no longer serve as advisers to the CBC. Nevertheless, most of them added substantial value to our strategic thinking. Juneau also made it a practice of meeting with the Minister of Communications, the Hon. Marcel Masse, to brief him and his senior staff on the progress of our union negotiations. I accompanied him on these meetings, where I was expected to help convince the minister that we had our act together in terms of negotiating strategy. These meetings were conducted exclusively in French, which was an additional challenge for me, because my French was still "rusty". Hence I spent a lot of time, not only trying to anticipate the questions that might be put to me, but also to ensure that I knew the appropriate French language terms.

CHAPTER ELEVEN

The year 1986 was a time of transition for the CBC. A new computerized system was introduced to handle the corporation's finances. Unfortunately, the new system failed and the auditor general was unable to give the corporation a clean audit opinion. This generated a lot of bad press for the CBC and reinforced the perception among many people that the CBC could not manage itself. Fortunately, many managers had kept their own records and the auditor general was able to reconcile most of the money, except for $57 million. There was no question of fraud, or lost money, but the headlines suggested that the CBC was so poorly managed that it had lost track of $57 million. Parliamentary hearings were held, and Juneau moved quickly into damage control mode. A new vice president of finance was named, and external consultants were retained. Eventually the system's problems were rectified and the CBC was able to satisfy its audit requirements.

Thankfully, the challenges I faced at the CBC were balanced by the fact that my family life was proceeding happily. Lella was glad to be back in Ontario. Deborah enrolled at Algonquin College where she earned a three year diploma in Business Administration (with a human resource specialization). She worked during the summers. Andrew continued his school studies and soon made many friends, became heavily involved in sports and got a part time job in a grocery store. I helped both our children financially with the costs of their education, despite their reluctance to accept such help. I recall that it took me over six months to get Andrew to tell me how much his tuition cost, so that

I could give him the fifty percent that I had intended to contribute. In fact, both Deborah and Andrew valued their independence and self reliance and never asked either for financial assistance or help in finding work. What I offered was advice whenever I was asked, but they made their own decisions. As things turned out, they were very wise decisions indeed.

My sister Ester, her husband Bill, and their children Tanya and Joshua came to see us from Peterborough from time to time, and we visited my parents in St. Catharines every few months. We enjoyed our big house in Nepean (then an Ottawa suburb) and made many improvements to it over the years. I had planted trees in every house that we had lived in and, with Andrew's help, planted a Norway Maple and a Colorado Blue Spruce in our backyard. Over the years, I added many other plants and took great pride in my garden. I also continued the daily swimming routine that I had established in Vancouver. I swam 20 laps at the Carleton University 50 metre Olympic pool early every morning, and was at my desk by 8 a.m.

In late summer, 1986, the vice president of French Television left and Juneau appointed Franklin Delaney, my immediate boss, as his successor. With Delaney's departure for Montreal, Juneau had to find a replacement for him as senior vice president at head office.

Although at the time of my being hired at the CBC I could neither plan nor foresee how my career would develop, I envisioned the possibility that at some point I might assume broader responsibilities than human resources. After eighteen months at the CBC, I had learned a lot about its operations. And, as a college president, I had held broader responsibilities, hence I felt that I was on the right track for the job of CBC senior vice president. I discussed my potential candidacy with Juneau, who

194

was receptive. Hence, I decided to apply and was interviewed by the search committee. There were, of course, other candidates to be considered. The process was carried out very professionally by an outside consultant, who interviewed several candidates, both internal and external. Juneau never interviewed me. I found out, quite by accident, that he was recommending my appointment to the board of directors at their meeting in Halifax, which I was also attending. I suppose Juneau saw no need to interview me since he already knew me and wanted the matter to be discussed by the board in camera, to avoid leaks. Whatever the rationale, he came out of the board meeting to advise me that the board had approved my nomination, but that I should not tell anyone until other candidates had been notified. I was pleased and assumed my new duties in early November 1986.

It would be nice if I could claim that, after twenty months as vice president of human resources, all the major issues for which I was responsible had been resolved. But the reality is that those issues would require ongoing attention. What I tried to do, with modest success, was to build a higher level of cooperation with the unions and the other vice presidents, and to provide leadership on collective bargaining strategies. Broadcasting, like education, is a labour intensive enterprise, and that means that one cannot lead unless one is able and prepared to listen. As already indicated, I always tried to see things from the other person's point of view. Sometimes this worked, other times it didn't. But it was always worth a try.

For me, listening to what other people had to say was an instinctive process. It was like walking, riding a bike, or swimming. I did it without being consciously aware of it. But other people noticed. One of them was Patrick Watson. Several years later, when I was appointed president of the CBC and

Watson was board chair, he made it a point of stressing in a closed circuit televised address to all CBC staff that I was a good listener!

One of my most important responsibilities as senior vice president was the chairmanship of the Planning and Allocation Committee (PAC). PAC was made up of the president, executive vice president, vice president of finance and vice president of planning and corporate affairs. While the Board of Directors was responsible for approving the overall budget, PAC decided on the detailed operating and capital budget allocations, and because of that authority, was the most important and influential decision making committee at the CBC. Every major decision that had financial implications had to go through this committee and while, as chair, I was not the sole decision maker, I could expect to exert considerable leadership and influence in that role. It also meant that, whenever vice presidents did not receive the full budget that they had requested, I would get blamed. As time went on and budgets became tighter, the role of PAC attained greater importance. A perception developed, that as chair of PAC, I was the most powerful executive at the CBC. This was, of course, completely inaccurate. PAC was an advisory committee to the president. But the fact that neither Juneau nor Veilleux had ever rejected advice received from PAC reinforced the above mentioned perception.

As senior vice president I was also responsible for human resources, finance, supply and services, management information systems, engineering, the law department and, critically, the building of a new broadcasting centre in Toronto for the English TV and radio networks. All of the vice presidents and executive directors responsible for these functions reported directly to me.

At the time, the two most senior positions reporting directly to the president were the executive vice president (Bill Armstrong) and the senior vice president (me). The executive vice president was responsible for all programming and was considered as second in command. The media (TV and Radio) vice presidents reported to him. As senior vice president, I was third in command. Juneau, Armstrong and I operated as a troika that discussed the most sensitive issues and performed the annual performance evaluation of all other vice presidents.

Of the many areas that reported to me, human resources was the one with which I was most familiar and I continued to be involved in the many issues that were active at the time. I recommended that Pierre Racicot be named as my successor. Juneau and the board accepted my recommendation. Pierre was an excellent person to fill this role. He had led the industrial relations department for many years, and had in-depth knowledge of the major collective bargaining issues and key players. Later on, he moved to another position as regional director of the National Capital region. This gave him the opportunity to manage a media operation engaged in the production of television and radio programs. Although disappointed at losing Racicot, I understood his desire to broaden his experience.

The CBC had built its Montreal TV and radio network headquarters in the early '70s, but the English networks in Toronto remained without a suitable home. They operated from various buildings scattered throughout the city. Fortunately, several years earlier, the CBC had acquired 20 acres of prime land in downtown Toronto. It was envisioned that this land could be used to build a proper headquarters for the English language networks.

Although no capital funds were forthcoming from the federal government, the CBC building would only need to occupy part of the site, making the rest available for office and/or residential development. Revenues from such development could be used to pay for part of the construction costs of the new CBC building. The rest could be funded from savings realized by moving out of the many owned and leased buildings then occupied by the CBC throughout the city of Toronto. Franklin Delaney had set up a project office to develop this idea and to enable it to become a reality.

The Canadian Broadcast Centre (the name finally adopted for the Toronto CBC headquarters) would cost several hundred million dollars. Approvals were needed from the federal government's Treasury Board and the City of Toronto. A developer had to be selected, not only for our building, but also for the rest of the site, so that the building could be properly financed. Contracts would have to be awarded for the development, construction and equipping of the facility with the latest state of the art broadcast and computer technology. The project would take several years to complete and, as it turned out, would encounter several major hurdles along the way.

While I held overall responsibility for the construction of the new broadcast centre, the key people who did most of the planning were engineering vice president Guy Gougeon and his successor Brian Baldry, as well as Janet Day, who had been recruited from the city of Toronto's planning department. All three, supported by many others, made extraordinary contributions to the eventual success of the project.

To ensure the best possible return on the value of our property, we invited proposals from a wide range of reputable and well established real estate developers. The biggest names in Canadian real estate development submitted proposals. Our site on Front Street in the heart of downtown Toronto was highly desirable and the timing was perfect for reaping maximum advantage from this piece of prime territory. The real estate market in Toronto, both commercial and residential, was very hot, and prices were climbing wildly. The best proposal for the entire site came from Bramalea, a major developer with a long history of successful real estate development throughout North America.

We celebrated our agreement with Bramalea on September 6, 1990 at a dinner attended by CBC and Bramalea executives, including their board chair, the Hon. Bill Davis. I sat at his table when shortly after dinner, we were advised that the provincial election results were in and, for the first time in history, an NDP government, led by the Hon. Bob Rae, had been elected in Ontario. There was great consternation among the business people in the room, since the NDP was not perceived as a business friendly party. But Bill Davis, who had served as the Progressive Conservative Premier of the province from 1971 to 1985, remained calm and assured all around him that there was no reason to panic. He thought that the NDP would probably place a higher priority on the environment, which he felt was not a bad thing.

We also selected Cadillac Fairview, another prominent real estate company, to develop the CBC's own building. We held a competition for architects and finally chose a consortium led by the well known American architect Philip Johnson, who would work with a team of Canadian architects, mechanical, structural and other engineering firms. The actual equipping of the building and studio design would be done or closely overseen by our own engineering department, because of its highly specialized technical requirements. The choice of Philip Johnson generated some controversy, because he was not Canadian, but I argued that if Canadian architects (such as the renowned Arthur Erickson) could be chosen to design prestigious buildings around the world, we had to be open to foreign architects for a world class building such as the new CBC broadcasting centre. We eventually won this battle.

Given the impossibility of planning for every contingency, any individual who occupies a position of responsibility must be able to deal effectively with all kinds of unexpected events. A wrong move may have long lasting negative consequences for the individual and the organization. The following anecdote is an example of such an event.

Whenever Juneau was away on vacation or on a trip, the executive vice president automatically acted as president. If both were absent, I was designated to act as president. On one such occasion, it was late Friday afternoon and I was getting ready to leave the office when an urgent phone call came from an RCMP (Royal Canadian Mounted Police) officer in Halifax. According to this officer, the CBC's Halifax TV station had got wind of an RCMP drug bust that was to take place that night and they were planning to announce this on the evening newscast. The RCMP were very upset about this because it would jeopardize their plans and tip off the drug dealers. They had asked the station to hold the story until after the bust. Apparently, they had not received assurance from the local CBC news editor that they would comply with the RCMP's request. To hold back a news story is a major issue for journalists, whose job, after all, is to tell the news as quickly as possible.

I called Bill Donovan, the regional director, explaining that I was calling him in my capacity as acting president, and asked him to fill me in on what was going on. He was somewhat reluctant to get into details. The news departments, both in the print and electronic media, pride themselves on their independence, and

200

interference by management (real or perceived) is frowned upon. He told me that they had not yet decided whether to carry the story, although the newscast was to go to air in less than half an hour. Then he asked me pointedly whether I was ordering him to kill the story. Although I had the authority to do just that, it would have been unwise for me to exercise such authority before exhausting all other options and carefully evaluating all of its potential consequences.

I decided to involve Bill Morgan, the network's director of news and current affairs in Toronto. He was a senior and experienced journalist and knew exactly how to handle such a sticky issue. He immediately got in touch with the Halifax news people and they worked out a deal with the RCMP to hold the story in exchange for exclusive rights once the bust had taken place. This episode brought home to me very forcefully how careful one must be in the management of news operations.

In my position as senior vice president, my three most important and challenging priorities were: a) overseeing the distribution of the always insufficient financial resources; b) the development and execution of collective bargaining strategies and: c) the successful completion of the broadcast centre in Toronto. These three portfolios were what kept me awake on many nights. That doesn't mean that there weren't other important issues in key departments that also reported to me. Whether it was computer systems, finance, legal issues, purchasing decisions of equipment or engineering related matters, I had to deal with a host of decisions with significant long term ramifications. Fortunately, I could rely on advisers with experience and knowledge. They never failed me.

The stress level was unprecedented and for a while it made me physically sick. My wife and I would often go for long walks along the Rideau Canal in the evenings. She was a great source of moral support to me. Kim Campbell, then a minister in the Mulroney government, also had a habit of taking walks with her companion along the same route and we sometimes met and chatted about old times from our Vancouver days. My daily swimming routine, reading a variety of books, gardening, playing chess and listening to my favourite music were some of the activities that took my mind off work. For a while I continued to putter around my fully equipped electronics work bench. I recall designing and building a random number generator for a friend who believed that it would prove advantageous when playing the lottery. This was not true, of course, but I did it because it was a fun thing to do[67]. All of these extra-curricular activities helped, but still I felt the pressure of work. Sometimes I thought that mine was an impossible job, but in retrospect, I'm glad that I persevered.

Juneau's term as president came to an end in August 1989. Although he and I were not close, our relationship was one of mutual respect. I was grateful for the opportunity he had given me to assume broader responsibilities as senior vice president. He was also supportive when conflicts arose between me and other vice presidents, usually involving budget matters. On one occasion, when we were dealing with some difficult collective bargaining issues, Juneau paid me what I considered an important compliment, by remarking how calm I remained throughout the fierce debates raging within our own management team. A cynic might say that, if someone remained calm in such circumstances, it was because he didn't fully understand the seriousness of the situation; I prefer to think that better decisions are made when people do not become too emotionally involved. Juneau was a man of impeccable integrity, but he carried political baggage from his brief stint as a minister in the cabinet of Liberal Prime Minister Pierre Trudeau.[68]

CHAPTER TWELVE

The Broadcasting Act had been amended in 1989. One of the changes involved separating the role of president and CEO from that of board chair. This did not affect Juneau, who had filled both roles, but it would affect whoever would be named to succeed him. Soon Prime Minister Brian Mulroney announced that the new president and CEO of the CBC would be Gérard Veilleux. At the same time, Patrick Watson was appointed to the CBC board and designated as the new chair. But he could not actually serve as chair until the new legislation was proclaimed, and this did not happen for several months. The delay was understandably frustrating for Watson.

Watson was a well known journalist, writer, producer and interviewer. His appointment won a lot of praise from the cultural community. His fame could be traced back to the sixties for his role as host/producer of the TV current affairs program "This Hour Has Seven Days". There had been much controversy about this program, pitting Watson and his fellow producers against politicians and CBC management. Nevertheless, he went on to develop a distinguished broadcasting career. Of the many public affairs programs that he produced, the "Struggle for Democracy," I found most compelling.

Veilleux, on the other hand, had no broadcasting experience at all. But he had served as a senior officer in several provincial and federal departments, including the position of Secretary of Treasury Board. When he first joined the federal government, his grasp of the English language was poor. But he perfected it by listening to CBC radio. Given the perception by the government and others that the CBC was poorly managed, Mulroney must have felt that he should appoint someone with a strong management background, and that Veilleux and Watson would bring complementary skills to the CBC. As soon as their appointments were announced, Watson and Veilleux met for several hours and discussed how they would work together. By all accounts, they got along remarkably well and publicly expressed great confidence that they could work quite effectively together.

Veilleux described his management style as one of implementing "constructive damage to the status quo." All who worked closely with him, including myself, understood this to mean that he wanted change, provided it was constructive. And few disagreed with the proposition that change was needed if the CBC was to survive. The only question that remained was what kind of change and how to bring it about.

Watson had been previously approached by the Mulroney government about his possible appointment as CBC president. This took place while Juneau held the office, so the only way for Watson to be named president was for Juneau to go. Watson, despite some reservations about the removal of a sitting CBC president before the end of his mandate, seriously considered such an opportunity and discussed it with the prime minister and other individuals, including some senior CBC executives. But attempts by Mulroney to get rid of Juneau failed, leaving Watson in the lurch. Meanwhile, Mulroney was being told by several individuals, including one of his close advisers and CBC board member Bill Neville, that appointing Watson as CBC president wasn't a good idea. In the words of Bill Neville: "There was no evidence to make one believe that Patrick could manage the place."[69] Perhaps the chairmanship of the CBC board was a consolation prize of sorts.

One of the few bulwarks protecting the CBC's independence is that directors, including the president, are appointed "during good behaviour" for a specific term. In other words, they can only be removed from office for "just cause." How Watson could rationalize his role in facilitating what amounted to a breach of the CBC's independence is a puzzle for which I have never found a satisfactory explanation.

I had organized a number of thick briefing books for the new president, outlining the various issues and decisions that would have to be made in the next few months. Shortly after the prime minister's announcement, Veilleux came around to the CBC head office and met the various vice presidents. He seemed quite open and approachable, but showed little interest in the briefing books that I had assembled.

Soon Veilleux named Michael McEwen as executive vice president, responsible for all television and radio programming. McEwen was very capable and knew the corporation well, having risen through the ranks to the position of vice president for English Radio, but he did not speak French. This was definitely a handicap.

The appointment of unilingual individuals to senior positions in federal institutions is a subject of much controversy. The Canadian political reality places great value on bilingualism, which is of course highly desirable. On the other hand, requiring fluency in both official languages means that many otherwise capable persons are excluded from consideration, thus reducing the available pool of qualified candidates for many important jobs. A common practice to get around this dilemma is to appoint strong bilingual deputies to senior officials who are unable to communicate in both official languages. This arrangement is not ideal but it works. It is superior to another common practice, which is to appoint unilingual candidates who commit themselves to become functionally bilingual within a certain period of time. This seldom works, because after a certain age, most people, no matter how diligent, are simply unable to learn a second language. I have known and worked closely with dozens of unilingual anglophones who took French language lessons for months or even years. Unless they already had a base of knowledge in the French language, or worked and lived in a predominantly French language environment, they never developed the ability to actually work in French. This approach, therefore, represents a waste of money and talent, since time spent trying to learn a new language is time not spent performing their regular duties. Another practice, which I do not condone, is to advertise senior jobs stating that candidates must be bilingual, then appointing a unilingual candidate. Such appointments are rationalized by stating that the successful candidate has committed to become functionally bilingual as quickly as possible, which of course is unlikely to happen. Furthermore, no one knows whether, language proficiency aside, such an individual was the best qualified person for the position. By prescribing bilingualism in a job description, it is reasonable to conclude that many highly qualified unilingual (French or English) Canadians, recognizing their own language limitations, rule themselves out and never apply or allow their name to go forward. The end result is that the merit principle is compromised.

Veilleux quickly made a very positive impression on most people at the CBC. He had a very open style of management, was obviously a quick learner and knew the country well. He also had many important contacts in the federal government and knew who to call to get things done. He had been appointed by Prime Minister Mulroney, so he obviously had the confidence of the Conservative government, which was a major difference from

Juneau, who had been appointed by Liberal Prime Minister Trudeau.

In the initial weeks following his arrival at the CBC, Veilleux spent a lot of time with the media vice presidents in Montreal and Toronto. This was to be expected, since major programming decisions were made in the network centres. The media vice presidents were quite impressed with him, particularly on the English side, and he seemed to be quite impressed with them.

An incident during Veilleux's initial weeks at the CBC caused me some concern. We were discussing our proposed union negotiating strategies. Veilleux had been in charge of negotiating with all the federal government unions during his time as Secretary of the Treasury Board. He made a comment about an approach to negotiations based on his government experience. In response, I pointed out that negotiating with CBC unions was a lot different than negotiating with public service unions. CBC unions behaved more like industrial unions, and we negotiated under different legislation than the federal government. My sense, which was shared by most of my colleagues, was that it was a lot more challenging to negotiate with CBC unions. Veilleux angrily snapped back telling me not to talk about things that I knew nothing about, namely federal government union negotiations. He gave me a real dressing down, right in front of several of my colleagues. I realized that I had made an error and just took the verbal lashing. After the meeting, I went back to my office, convinced that my relationship with Veilleux was not off to a good start. Minutes later, Veilleux came into my office and apologized for his outburst. I replied that I had been wrong in making the statement I did, the way I did, and appreciated very much his coming to see me to clear the air. He realized that he had overreacted and was very gracious in acknowledging this fact.

Soon after Veilleux's arrival, I discussed with him the budget process and our assumptions for the coming year. I also made a couple of specific recommendations. The VP of Finance, Stephen Cotsman, and I had discussed how much of a cut we could handle at head office and concluded that we could manage a 10% reduction over three or four years. After some further reflection, I felt that we could do it in one year and so recommended to Veilleux. This would be a much larger (in percentage terms) cut than would be expected from the media divisions, but I knew we had to set the example. Cotsman was a bit distressed at my decision, because he felt it would be too much to handle in one year, but he went along with it. Another recommendation I made to Veilleux was to decentralize authority for support services in the field to the media heads. This had been demanded by the media for many years but I had resisted it because of all the problems we had maintaining common standards and getting information from the field. But now I felt that Veilleux's experience as one of the most senior managers in the federal government would enable us to maintain the necessary controls without the need for direct line authority over the field offices of the various support services. Veilleux agreed with both of my recommendations and we implemented them. The appropriate changes were reflected in the budget.

Throughout this period I experienced many episodes of my long standing back problem. There was often much pain and discomfort. In fact, during several meetings, I would either stand up against a wall or lie down on the floor carpet, which was quite funny, except for the pain that I endured. Veilleux showed a lot of interest in and concern for my back problem and our working relationship became very open.

The new president included me in a broad range of discussions and decisions. He had a real appreciation of the fact that all aspects of CBC operations had to be integrated. He also valued getting advice from two independent streams (one headed by the executive vice president and the other from the senior vice president). He quickly realized that if he were to concentrate all authority in the executive vice president (which was what the media vice presidents wanted) he would become a prisoner of just one way of thinking. That, of course, was the reason why Juneau had created the position of senior vice president, and Veilleux immediately understood the value of that arrangement.

Over the next few months, my professional relationship with Veilleux kept getting better. I also enjoyed a good working relationship with Michael McEwen, although we did have the odd disagreement. On one occasion, the media vice presidents were dragging their feet on a position I was recommending for our labour negotiations. Since they reported directly to Michael McEwen, I angrily snapped, telling him: "Michael, it's your job to tell the media vice presidents to shape up and start working as a team!" It was out of character for me to lose my cool. Veilleux, who was present during my outburst, said nothing. Michael got the message and the media vice presidents became much more cooperative.

By now, everyone acknowledged that Veilleux was a remarkable leader and that he expected me to play an important role. In fact, Veilleux would often just walk in my office and spend an hour or two discussing the major issues of the day, asking for my opinion and testing his many ideas with me. I found that we could be quite open with each other. It was obvious that he trusted my judgement, and he also trusted my ability to keep our discussions confidential. The CBC was notoriously leaky and Veilleux needed a sounding board he could trust. I also found it a lot easier to raise any concerns I had with him, something that I had not always felt comfortable doing with Juneau.

In 1991 it became necessary for the CBC to make further budget cuts. Advertising revenue had suffered a big drop, and parliamentary appropriations were insufficient to bridge the gap. A decision had to be made where to cut. While, as I have already stated, we did make deep cuts at head office (10% in one year), these were mostly symbolic in the context of the overall CBC budget. A rigorous analysis of head office costs had revealed that they represented only about 3% of the entire corporation's budget. Further head office cuts, as advocated by some people, would have simply shifted those costs to the networks and regions. That would have resulted in duplication of effort, and hence been counterproductive.

The real money, and hence the bulk of the cuts, was in television, especially English TV. A strategic decision had to be made between cuts at the network and cuts in the regions. John Shewbridge (the vice president of planning) developed various options for consideration. Veilleux restricted the number of people who were involved in the decision making process, to avoid leaks. This proved to be quite controversial, but it was well known that, the more people were involved, the greater would be the risk of leaks. Veilleux made his recommendations to the board, which approved the cuts, although everyone knew that they would generate a great deal of opposition throughout the country.[70]

The day before Veilleux was set to announce the cuts (all regional stations would be closed except for one in each province, and for two in Ontario and Québec,) the CBC's own English language news department got wind of these plans and broadcast the news. Where the leak occurred was never determined, but

212

Veilleux was furious. His own people had disclosed highly confidential information and he was very angry with them. From a journalistic perspective, however, significant cuts to the national public broadcaster's service constituted news – and that fact takes precedence over considerations of company solidarity. In this case, the leak prevented Veilleux from announcing the cuts in the appropriate context and explaining the rationale underlying them. The announcement alienated many of the CBC's regional directors, who felt that broader consultation should have been undertaken before such drastic cuts were announced. Also upset were a large percentage of the public and many politicians at the local, provincial and federal level. Hundreds of angry letters were received and special hearings were called by the CRTC and Parliamentary committees.

Veilleux, McEwen and I had to appear before a Parliamentary committee to answer many questions about the cuts. We also met with the caucuses of the Liberal Party, the Progressive Conservative Party and the New Democratic Party (NDP). The Progressive Conservative caucus, including Prime Minister Brian Mulroney, showered praise on Veilleux for being able to make tough decisions and there were no hostile questions or comments that I recall.

The Liberal and NDP caucuses, however, were a different story. Both were vicious. They verbally attacked Veilleux for implementing these cuts and, of course, they also attacked the government at every opportunity in the House of Commons and in the media. The attacks from the Liberals were particularly ironic, because five years later, when they came to power, they slashed the CBC's budget by more than three times the dollar amount that had been cut by the Mulroney government.

The cuts went ahead, despite the protests. They generated a lot of press and were condemned by many people within the CBC and outside. Patrick Watson took some very strong criticism by several of his former colleagues who had seen him as the man who would "save" the CBC. (Perhaps they should have considered that to qualify as a "saviour", one has to be crucified first!) But now Watson had gone along with the cuts, and defended them publicly. Even the iconic Canadian writer Peter C. Newman was critical of Watson, whom he had characterized as "the embodiment of broadcasting integrity" for his failure to exhibit any courage in standing up for his principles during his three years as CBC's chairman.[71]

As stated earlier, there were three major priorities on which I focussed in my role as senior vice president: budgets, union negotiations and the construction of the broadcasting centre in Toronto. Budget cuts, of course, had major impacts on our collective bargaining strategies, which were now being developed by the vice president of human resources, Marie Poulin[72]. She had served as associate vice president for Regional Broadcasting (looking after the French language services) and as Secretary General for the board of directors. She was also quite active in the Francophone community. I had selected her because of her "people" skills. But she could also be tough when circumstances required it. A couple of years after her appointment, she accepted a position as a communications official in the Prime Minister's office and eventually was named a Senator. This meant that the vice presidency of human resources suffered through lack of continuity over an extended period of time, as several vice presidents moved on for various reasons. This factor contributed to the delay in consolidating the large number of different unions at the CBC into a more manageable and workable framework. I had initiated the process, but it took much longer than I had anticipated for it to be realized, in part because of opposition by some unions and some CBC vice presidents from the French language side. Marie Poulin's successor, Charles Gendron, was a tragic case of another short lived vice president. He was a very good man who had held a similar position in the private sector. Unfortunately, soon after his appointment he was stricken by cancer and, although it looked like he had beaten it, there was a relapse and he died at the age of 53.

Meanwhile, on the family front, my parents were still living in St. Catharines, but were getting on in years. In 1990 dad was 75 and mom was 78. It was getting difficult for them to look after the house. If they were to move to the Ottawa area, we could support them and spend more time with them in their declining years. When I called and asked my parents what they thought of the idea, my father said he would like it, but he didn't think that mom would want to move; mom said that she would like it, but dad would never agree! So, with a little back and forth dialogue, it was settled. They would move to Ottawa. Not only would they be closer to us, but it would make it easier for my sister Ester and her family in Peterborough to visit all of us. Within a few weeks, my parents sold their house in St. Catharines, I bought them a condominium in Ottawa, and moved them with their furniture here. It all happened so fast!

Moving my parents so that they could be closer to us was a pleasant distraction from the unrelenting pressures of work, where controversial issues kept coming up. For example, in 1991 there was considerable debate about the best way to fund the CBC. Patrick Watson had publicly raised the idea of adopting a system of licence fees that is common in Great Britain and other European countries. Under this system, everyone is charged an annual fee based on the number of radio and TV sets that they have in their house. I was asked to comment on this by the press and replied as follows: "My own view is that it is not a realistic option, although it would be improper for me to rule out something in any final way". Michael McCabe, president of the Canadian Association of Broadcasters, was more blunt in dismissing the licence fee idea as a non-starter. "I find it difficult to believe that it would work in Canada", he said, adding that the notion summoned up memories of "the radio police". The Globe and Mail[73] pointed out that "A licence fee would be a move back to the future for the CBC." When the charge was abolished in 1953, the year after the launch of CBC Television, licence fees paid by Canadian owners of radio receivers represented almost half of CBC revenues. The headline in another newspaper was: "CBC senior vice president Tony Manera rejects board chairman designate Watson's plan to introduce licence fees". Actually, I don't think that Watson had such a plan. He had simply raised the idea as an option that, in his view, should be considered. No one in a position of authority took Watson's idea seriously, and it is safe to say that my public disagreement didn't please him at all!

Watson and I would experience further clashes in the years to come. This doesn't diminish my admiration of his extraordinary talents. I knew him as a quintessential Canadian, with knowledge in a broad range of subjects and a capacity to communicate in a thoughtful and compelling way.

Despite the brouhaha over licence fees, by now I felt quite confident in my job. The CBC faced many challenges, but my working relationship with Veilleux and my colleagues in general was excellent. Having weathered the stormy fall-out of the regional service cuts, I looked forward to the future with some degree of optimism.

216

In 1990 I decided to buy and erect a greenhouse in my backyard. Ottawa has very cold winters, which makes operating a hobby greenhouse a challenging and costly undertaking. This project would bring me much pleasure, and some grief, over the next several years. I had always loved gardening. The greenhouse environment reminded me of my native Sicily, home to many of the plants that I would now be able to grow.

The first year I planted seeds in the fall for tomatoes, eggplants, green peppers and beans. The first tomatoes were harvested in mid-winter and they were delicious. I added fig plants, banana plants (started from seed), jade plants (started from cuttings), aloe vera plants, various types of cactuses, prickly pears, hibiscus, loquat, and bougainvillea. I also brought in several containers of annuals from outside (begonias, geraniums, etc) that continued to grow throughout the winter, requiring me to constantly cut them back because they were getting too big!

Although growing tomatoes, eggplants, green peppers and beans during the winter was lots of fun, there were problems with a variety of insects that found the greenhouse environment an attractive place to breed. It was too time consuming to keep the insect population under control and I stopped growing vegetables after a couple of seasons. This way, I could concentrate on the rest of my plants.

Not all of my attempts to grow semi-tropical fruits were successful. But I did rather well with figs. I had about ten fig plants in various containers, which produced excellent fruit. Later on, I planted some fig plants directly in the ground, where the roots had unlimited space to grow. This resulted in much greater fruit production. Of course, I had to keep pruning the plant branches because there was only so much space in the greenhouse. One year I harvested almost 500 figs! The nice thing was that they would ripen throughout the summer, from late May until well into November, so that there was always a supply of fresh figs during that period.[74]

In 1991 the time felt right to take a family vacation in Italy. This gave Andrew, who had never been to Italy, an opportunity to see the places from where his parents and grandparents had come and to be exposed to the many natural and cultural attractions that Italy has to offer. While inside St. Peter's Cathedral, which I consider one of the greatest architectural and artistic masterpieces of all time, Andrew exclaimed: "I'm impressed". There we also saw Michelangelo's magnificent sculpture Pietà, protected by a Plexiglas cover (a madman had previously attacked it causing some damage, which had since been repaired). The genius of Michelangelo, including the paintings in the Sistine Chapel, has fascinated countless generations over the last five centuries. It is something that everyone who can should see at some time in their life.

Andrew was now attending Carleton University, while holding a part time job in a grocery store. He was also quite active in sports and had several friends. Deborah had made substantial progress in her career with the Regional Municipality of Ottawa-Carleton. She was also doing part time teaching at Algonquin College and was writing many articles on human resources issues and on religious topics which were widely published. Lella looked after all of us, including my parents, who had become quite close to her. Lella's role as wife, mother and daughter-in-law was quite demanding, and she fulfilled it with love, patience and tremendous strength. I don't know how I could have ever managed without her support.

At the CBC, I had the unenviable task of negotiating the departure of several senior people. This was a role that I played during Juneau's presidency as well as under Veilleux. Each case was different. Sometimes there were policy differences; at other times, personality conflicts. Invariably, there would be strong feelings. I often dealt with lawyers representing the departing individuals. These events were stressful for everyone concerned. Several long-time friendships were destroyed. There were also numerous marriage breakdowns. Veilleux carried the heaviest burden, and while supremely stoic in public, he was certainly feeling the stress internally.

For several years, John Shewbridge, the vice president of planning, had been working on a proposal to create a television service aimed at the US market. This would provide another outlet for CBC programming and, given the size of the US market, could be quite profitable. During Juneau's term, John had been assigned exclusively to this project for a couple of years. He developed the concept and the business plan, with assistance from others, especially Paul Gaffney, a seasoned television producer/director and strategic planner, who would later become the executive director of my office when I became president.

Juneau had also retained outside advisers to help us sell the idea to the government of the day, since its approval would be required. Among these advisers was Bill Davis, former Premier of Ontario. As I have already indicated, I knew him from my time as president of Niagara College and saw him on many occasions when he came to CBC head office in Ottawa. Davis was, of course, very well connected with the Progressive Conservative government of Brian Mulroney and it made sense to have him on board. But the project never got off the ground during Juneau's presidency. It was during Veilleux's term that the project finally came to fruition. Veilleux found a private sector partner, Power Corporation, to share in the investment and risks, and a deal was made. The CBC invested US $6 million and Power Corporation invested the same amount. Later this investment was increased to approximately US $10 million each. John Shewbridge and his counterpart at Power Corporation negotiated a very favourable contract with the US based Direct TV, a major direct-to-home satellite broadcasting service. Although the ultimate goal was to get carriage on cable, where the real money was, a satellite service was a good start.

The project development was led by Shewbridge and the deal with Power Corporation was finalized by Veilleux, but the actual launch of the service took place during my time as president. It involved two separate services; an entertainment channel called Trio and a news channel named Newsworld International. A few years after I left the CBC, the channels were sold to Vivendi International for US $155 million, quite a handsome profit for an initial investment of about US $20 million. The profit was split 50/50 between Power Corporation and the CBC.

The Canadian Broadcasting Centre in Toronto was successfully completed during Veilleux's presidency. There were, however, serious problems, because the real estate market in Toronto had virtually collapsed. The developer, Bramalea, owed CBC $100 million plus a share of the rental income from the office building they were planning; but they had miscalculated the real estate market by a very large factor and were on the verge of bankruptcy.

We had relied on the funds from Bramalea to finance our building. If we forced the issue, however, they would have simply declared bankruptcy. I had no luck finding a mutually acceptable solution with Bramalea's president (who had been brought in from Texas). I also met with Bill Davis, who was still chairman of their board. I trusted Bill Davis without any reservation. After a long private conversation with him in a hotel room at Toronto's airport, he convinced me that the best we could do was to retain the $20 million we had already received[75], while Bramalea gave up all its rights. They were left with nothing, but the CBC had to find another developer to replace them. Given the sorry condition of the real estate market in Toronto at the time, this was not easy. Eventually we were able to work out a deal with the provincial Worker's Compensation Board to build an office building for their needs.

Another financial problem arose with the City of Toronto. As part of the process to obtain zoning approval for our building, we had agreed that the City of Toronto would buy several buildings we owned and which we would no longer require once our building was completed. The price agreed upon reflected market values at the time plus an inflation escalator clause. But, with the collapse of the local real estate market, the buildings were no longer worth anywhere near what the City had promised to pay us. The deal we had signed made no provision for such a contingency. A deal is a deal, we insisted, and the City had to pay. After all, we had also contracted to build for a certain price, and nothing changed the price we had to pay our various contractors. But the City absolutely refused to pay the amount they owed us. I had a meeting with the Mayor, who confirmed the refusal to pay. However, we had an ironclad agreement and, unlike Bramalea, the City of Toronto could not declare bankruptcy. They had the power to tax. They were simply trying to intimidate us so we would settle for a lower price. In a not so subtle way, they threatened that if we persisted, they could always cut off our water and garbage collection! I did not expect responsible elected officials to employ such tactics. We had the law on our side and I authorized the launch of legal action. The issue was finally settled in CBC's favour in 2000, five years after I had left the CBC. The amount involved was about $15 million, which the City of Toronto paid through a combination of cash, rezoning and waiver

221

of grants in lieu of property taxes that the CBC would otherwise have paid to the City.

Although not directly involved in the day to day activities of the CBC's engineering department, I maintained a professional interest in the technical aspects of production and transmission. In the early 90's, for example, there were promising developments in the field of high definition television. I was able to observe a demonstration at the Massachusetts Institute of Technology (MIT) Media Lab, which was quite impressive. However, that project was based on analog technology, with all of its inherent limitations. Meanwhile, great progress was taking place with digital technology, which promised not only sharper images, but also more efficient use of frequency spectrum,[76] with the potential to dramatically increase the number of broadcasting channels. In order to keep abreast of these emerging developments, I attended several engineering conferences in Europe on digital broadcasting. Eventually the digital revolution would have a profound impact not only on the technical means of production and distribution of audio and video signals, but also on the business models of broadcasting. The CBC, like all other broadcasters, needed to anticipate the challenges and opportunities presented by the rapidly changing technology. But, at the same time, we had to walk a fine line between moving too quickly, before a particular technology was sufficiently mature, or waiting too long, and finding ourselves behind the times.

As indicated earlier, the 1991 Broadcasting Act separated the role of board chair from that of the president and CEO. This was in line with best governance practices, but it also opened the door to potential problems if the board chair and CEO held different points of view on important issues. The new act also made no mention of an "executive vice president"[77]. This meant that the

CBC president and board had full freedom to organize the top level of CBC management in whatever way they thought best. Although at first Veilleux retained the executive vice president position (to which he had previously appointed Michael McEwen), he later decided to eliminate it. In its place, there would be two senior vice presidents, one for radio and one for television. My own position was renamed as "Senior Vice president – Resources and Administration". The CBC by-laws were amended to provide that, in the absence of the president, whoever occupied my post would act as president. This effectively meant that I was now second in command. I could sense Michael's disappointment at this change, which also came as a complete surprise to me.

Early in 1993, I decided to retire from the CBC on December 31st of that year. Things were going very well for me. I enjoyed my job and my relationship with Veilleux and my colleagues. I had considerable input and influence on the CBC's operations and planning, and was very well rewarded. But I also felt that the CBC could benefit from a fresh perspective that a new person would bring to the job. At any rate, it had always been my intention to retire as soon as my financial situation made it possible, and to become a self-employed consultant afterwards.

Coincidentally, in early August of the same year, Gérard Veilleux announced his own intention to leave the CBC on October 31. He felt he had spent a long time in public service and wanted to do something in the private sector. He had been at the CBC for four years, with a year left to the end of his mandate.

On August 7, 1993 the Ottawa Citizen published an editorial which was critical of Gèrard Veilleux, who had just resigned as CBC president and Patrick Watson, who was still board chair. The editorial stated that the two men had "sat quietly watching the CBC die the death of a thousand cuts". It went on to say that a career bureaucrat (Veilleux) could perhaps be forgiven, but that it was much harder to forgive Watson, one of the country's best known broadcast journalists, calling on him to also resign. I wrote a letter to the editor, which the Ottawa Citizen published the next day, pointing out the unfairness of its criticism, including the gratuitous call for Watson's resignation. A column by Jamie Portman published by the Montreal Gazette on August 20, 1993, heaped further criticism on Veilleux and Watson, and to top things off, lambasted me personally for having come to their defence!

CHAPTER THIRTEEN

As we entered October 1993, it was not clear whether the recently elected prime minister, the Rt. Hon. Jean Chretien, would be announcing the appointment of a new president for the CBC in time for the November 1 date when Veilleux would be gone. The CBC by-laws provided that, in the absence of the president, the senior vice president – resources and administration, which was me, would be empowered to act as president. But it's one thing to act as president for relatively brief absences when the president is on holidays or sick. During such occasions, the acting president simply carries on the day to day management but avoids making major decisions with any long term impact. With the position of president vacant, and without knowing when the prime minister would announce an appointment, the person filling the position of president would have a much heavier burden to carry. The CBC board had the authority to name someone to fill the job of president for up to sixty days. I was prepared to serve and would have felt disappointed if the board had chosen someone else; but, frankly, it wouldn't have bothered me terribly. After all, I was planning to retire in a little over two months.

During the October 28, 1993 board meeting, the matter of naming a president was addressed.[78] I was called in by the board to ask me if I was prepared to serve. One of the board members suggested that someone else could be the official public spokesperson for the corporation. I do not believe that the board as a whole supported this idea, which struck me as rather bizarre. Nevertheless the question had been put and, without any hesitation, I replied that I wasn't prepared to go along with such a proposal as it would dilute the authority of the CEO. The board member then asked me point blank: "Are you telling me that you are not prepared to serve as president if this proposal (to transfer authority for speaking on behalf of the corporation to someone else) is adopted?" My reply: "That's exactly what I am saying". Although I wanted to serve as president, even for a short time (it would have been a nice way to cap my career at the CBC,) I was not prepared to set the precedent that would reduce the powers of the president. The board excused me and continued to meet in camera. After a short while, I was called back in and was advised that the board accepted my position and that I would be named president for a period of sixty days (which was the limit of the board's authority under the Broadcasting Act). The board's decision was unanimous.

I was pleased to accept this vote of confidence by the board and, on November 1, 1993, was driven to the Privy Council office in the Langevin Building in the shadow of Parliament Hill and sworn in as president of the CBC. Cabinet approval of this first 60 day appointment was not required. Back at the office, Michael McEwen had organized a brief reception where all the other vice presidents congratulated me and offered their support. It was a very courteous gesture and one that I appreciated very much. My expectation at the time was that I would serve for sixty days and leave the CBC on December 31, 1993, as I had originally planned.

A few days after assuming my new duties as CBC president, the Hon. Michel Dupuy, Minister of Canadian Heritage[79], called me and we arranged our first meeting, during which I briefed him on the major issues facing the CBC. This was followed by further meetings over the next few weeks. A former diplomat, Dupuy was a quick learner, and seemed genuinely interested in, and supportive of, the work of the CBC. We covered the full range of topics involving programming, finances and the looming multi-channel universe, which would revolutionize the world of broadcasting.

As Christmas approached, and with no word as to when a new president would be named by the prime minister, the CBC board asked me to serve as president for a further 60 days and I agreed; but this second appointment required approval by the federal cabinet. We barely made it in time before the Christmas break to obtain the required order-in-council.

Under the circumstances, the CBC board was hesitant to make any major decisions that would have long term consequences, in order not to tie the hands of the incoming president. But I quickly came to the conclusion that we should not delay the naming of vice presidents to fill important vacancies.[80] We also needed to prepare for appearances before the CRTC for the renewal of our TV licences and for several applications to launch new cable channels. Furthermore, there were important negotiations for hockey coverage and Olympics broadcasting rights. The CBC could not afford to drift. It needed a firm sense of direction. Hence I decided that, during whatever time I would be serving as president, I would not postpone making key decisions normally within the purview of the chief executive officer. At first the board demurred and during one of our meetings, I lost my temper, which was uncharacteristic of me. I apologized, and the board finally concurred with my view.

On January 14, 1994 I was asked to meet with Prime Minister Jean Chretien at his official residence on Sussex Drive in Ottawa. I surmised that the invitation had something to do with the appointment of a new CBC president. I had neither applied for, nor indicated any interest in this job. My plans were to leave the CBC as soon as a new president was named, but now I had to

227

consider the possibility that I might be asked to take on this job for a longer term. After careful reflection, I concluded that, if this were the case, I might be able to secure a better financial framework for the CBC.

Moreover, my knowledge of the CBC and of the rapidly changing broadcasting environment, coupled with my thirteen years' experience as college president, gave me the confidence that I could make a worthwhile contribution as president of this uniquely Canadian institution. My meeting with the prime minister was quite pleasant, and when he asked me whether I would accept the position of CBC president if it were offered, I had already given the matter a great deal of thought, and my reply was affirmative. Naturally, there would have to be further discussions, but these could take place with the Minister of Canadian Heritage and possibly officials at the Privy Council. In fact, I had several follow-up meetings with Heritage Minister Dupuy, during which we worked on a financial arrangement that would be consistent with the Liberal Party's election platform promise of stable funding for the CBC.

Given my earlier meeting with the prime minister, it was obvious that I was being seriously considered for the permanent[81] appointment as CBC president. This meant that I had a certain amount of leverage that I could use to obtain the best possible financial commitment for the CBC. My preferred option was for the new government to cancel the two $50 million budget cuts that had been announced by the previous government, but I had to be careful not to overreach. I understood that Dupuy had to clear whatever commitments he made with the Minister of Finance, the Hon. Paul Martin, so it was very critical that I play my hand astutely. In the end, I was successful in having the two $50 million cuts spread over five years (rather than two as originally envisaged). Furthermore, the government agreed not to impose any further budget cuts to the CBC over the next five years and to provide us with a limited borrowing power for certain investments that would have a positive financial return. There was also an undertaking to identify other funding sources for the CBC. All of these measures were confirmed in writing by the minister.

Could I have gotten a better deal? I don't think so, but it's impossible to say for sure. There is a point in any negotiation when, if one pushes too hard, there is no deal to be had at all. As later events would demonstrate, it's not only the details of a deal that matter, but also the parties' ability and willingness to abide by its terms. For example, the CBC had negotiated a very good legally binding agreement with the Bramalea Corporation for the development of its site in Toronto, but when Bramalea was on the edge of bankruptcy, all that we could realistically expect was retention of the money already in our hands. The government of Canada, of course, was a more secure partner than a private corporation, but it could face circumstances that would prevent it from honouring its commitments to the CBC. That I failed to anticipate that possibility haunts me to this day.

On February 2, 1994, I was advised that my appointment as president and CEO of the CBC for a full five year term would be announced by the prime minister on the following day.[82] There had been no discussion with anyone about my salary or benefits package. I placed a call to the Privy Council officer in charge of this detail and he told me that he was about to draft the order in council that would be submitted for the approval of cabinet that afternoon. Having learned a long time ago how important it was to know the salary and terms of employment before starting a new job, I was able to settle this matter in a few minutes. It was relatively straightforward, as the parameters for the compensation of order-in-council appointments were well known to me.

Later that afternoon, Patrick Watson was invited to meet with the minister so that he could be advised of who the next president of the CBC would be. We drove together to the minister's office, but I waited in the car while Patrick was being briefed. Upon his return, he shook my hand and asked me if I was happy with the deal that I had negotiated for the CBC. I told Patrick that I was and he smiled with obvious satisfaction.

My appointment as CBC president was historic in three important respects. As a native of Italy, I was the first person of neither English nor French extraction to serve as head of the CBC, arguably Canada's most important cultural institution. Symbolically, this demonstrated Canada's acceptance of immigrants as full participants at all levels of Canadian society. I was also an "insider". It was quite rare for CBC presidents to be appointed from within the corporation.[83] Finally, to the best of my knowledge, I was the first CBC president to have negotiated important financial commitments for the CBC by the federal government prior to acceptance of the position. A photograph of me taken during the early days of my presidency is shown below.

A whole book could be written about my time as CBC president. Eventually, that is exactly what I did.[84] Some of the material in this section has been extracted from this earlier book, and expanded where appropriate.

The news of my appointment as CBC president generated mixed reactions. Some pundits lamented my lack of programming experience, which was fair comment. Others thought that, given the tremendous challenges faced by the CBC, it made sense to have someone leading it who was already familiar with the organization. Two individuals, Trina McQueen and Ivan Fecan, with whom I had worked closely for several years while they held senior positions at the CBC, issued statements that were carried by the Canadian Press. Their comments demonstrated a knowledge of my character and personality that I had not anticipated. In other words, they knew me better than I thought they did, perhaps even better than I knew myself! Trina McQueen, for example, who was now heading up the Discovery Channel, said that I "didn't flinch from tough decisions", but that I was "vulnerable to appeal on the grounds of compassion or decency." Ivan Fecan, who had left for greener pastures in the private sector (in spite of my best efforts to talk him into staying at the CBC) pointed out that I loved Canada and was in fact Canadian by choice, all of which was true. He went on to make several other generous remarks, but what really made an impression on me was his statement that "If some politician tried to make it difficult for him, he would walk. He would not compromise his own integrity." It was easy to understand that tough decisions would be required, as McQueen had pointed out, but Fecan's observation that I would "walk" rather than compromise my integrity proved prescient. In fact, at the time of my appointment as CBC president, I do not recall the thought that I might find myself in such a position crossing my mind at all. Perhaps it should have.

In various speeches that I gave after my appointment as CBC president, I would pose and answer the rhetorical question: "What's an engineer doing running the CBC?" by saying: "Building bridges!" In fact, this metaphor very clearly described what had to be done. The CBC needed to build better bridges between itself and its public, between its management and employees, between its supporters and adversaries. It had to avoid becoming insulated from the broader society in order to remain relevant.

Early on in my tenure, I began to articulate publicly a vision of where I hoped to lead the CBC, conditioned by financial realities as I saw them.

My vision was driven by several fundamental principles, the first of which was that most Canadians should find some programming on the CBC that would be of interest to them. If only the elites listened to or watched the CBC, it would not be a truly public broadcaster. This did not mean that the CBC should try to be all things to all people, but that its schedule should include, for example, coverage of amateur sports, French language programming outside Québec, children's programs, events of national significance, programs aimed at Canada's aboriginal people, ballet, opera and other performing arts. Such content might not always attract huge audiences, but it could contribute to nation building. Of course, the CBC should also feature popular programs that appeal to a large number of citizens, but audience share should not be the only criterion by which programming success is judged.

Implementing such a vision would mean – as it always had – that commercial revenue would never be sufficient to cover the costs of producing and delivering CBC programming. Hence the need for an adequate and stable level of public subsidy. This principle had been recognized from the time of the CBC's inception, and continued to be valid.

I also wanted the CBC to reflect the different communities in which Canadians lived. Canada was not a monolithic country. In addition to the English, French and aboriginal cultures, there were strong ethnic communities and regional differences that needed to be recognized and celebrated. A CBC anchored entirely in Toronto and Montreal could not perform its role with any legitimacy or credibility. Its demise would be inevitable.

With regard to news and current affairs programming, I wanted to strengthen accountability mechanisms without sacrificing aggressiveness. Accountability could be enhanced through on-air programs that examined current journalistic issues, more training and development opportunities for journalists, properly supported ombudsman offices and direct feedback from audiences. Context was the key to provoking thoughtful dialogue on the major issues of the day. It was also crucial for journalists to feel that, as long as they observed the CBC's journalistic standards, they would be supported and defended no matter whose feet they stepped on. I delivered this message directly to the two most senior heads of news and current affairs, on both the English side and on the French side.

Canada was changing. The CBC had to reflect that reality to a greater extent than it had until then. I thought it important to have more diversity in both on-air staff and behind-the-scenes personnel. As an immigrant myself, I felt a particular duty to make the CBC more reflective of contemporary Canadian society.

I was philosophically in favour of reducing CBC's dependence on advertising, because of the steering effect that advertising had on programming choices and scheduling, influences that were incompatible with the ideals of public broadcasting. But it was also necessary to balance the books. Hence I was cautious not to make unrealistic promises. Reducing dependence on advertising, for example, was tied to the realization of alternative revenue sources. Furthermore, the CBC needed to develop new specialty channels, not only to tap new revenue sources, but to moderate the effects of audience fragmentation in an increasingly competitive broadcasting environment.

Looking back on the vision articulated soon after I became CBC president, it remains relevant in today's environment. What has changed, of course, are the means to pursue that mission, and the resources available to the CBC. We now live in an environment where traditional broadcasting is being challenged by the various media platforms available through the Internet. CBC is adapting to these changes by increasing its on-line presence and therefore connecting with its audiences in a multitude of ways. But that wasn't the case in 1994 when I was beginning to translate this vision into practical action plans.

My strength was in human resource management and my strategy was to surround myself with strong programmers and managers. My role was to set the overall direction for the CBC and to generate a climate in which creativity could thrive. I wanted to give all the people who worked for the CBC, in whatever capacity, a sense of shared purpose and hope. I was confident that they could and would do the rest.

I proceeded by addressing employees in all of the major centres throughout Canada where the CBC had a presence. My message was that, no matter what we did, at the end of my five year mandate, there would be about one thousand fewer employees. This was the inescapable reality imposed on us by the two $50 million cuts that we would have to absorb. I was very candid, pointing out that such an outcome had already been set. The key question was whether we would achieve the contraction the dumb way or the smart way. The dumb way was to cut all budgets by a more or less equal percentage and do the best we could with whatever resources were left. The smart, but harder way, was to rethink how we did our jobs. If we maximized the use of technology and re-engineered (there's the engineer in me again!) our operating practices, we could cope with the cuts without reducing or watering down our services to the public. In fact, I was confident we could actually improve the quality and quantity of our programming.

It was also possible to achieve most, if not all staff reductions, by attrition, so that involuntary departures would be minimized. This would require a paradigm shift by employees and their unions. My reason for optimism was based on the government's commitment not to impose any further budget reductions, and the fact that we would have five years to implement the previously announced $100 million cuts.

While there was certainly some scepticism, I believe that my openness and frank delivery of the available information was a key factor in getting CBC unions on side. I just told them the truth, uncomfortable as that may have been. In retrospect, however, I realize that my strategy had been too closely tied to the government's funding pledge, which left me with no escape route when that promise was broken.

The first test of unions and management working towards a common goal came with what came to be known as "The Windsor Enterprise". In 1990 the CBC had shut down its TV supper-hour news programs in several Canadian cities, including Windsor, Ontario. Windsor was a special case, because of its proximity to the US border and lack of local Canadian broadcasters other than the CBC. That meant that an exception for Windsor could be justified, and for some time the CBC had been working on a plan to reinstate the Windsor supper-hour newscast. The key question was not whether, but how this objective could be accomplished.

In 1993 a potential solution had begun to emerge. Digital technology had made possible small-format video cameras that enabled one person to act as both reporter and camera operator. Digital editing and on-air playback, using disk-based systems instead of videotape, also promised better quality and improved efficiency. The technology was promising, but it had yet to be tested in the real world of newsgathering and news production.

CBC management in Windsor and in Toronto wanted to try using the new technology to restart the Windsor service with fewer staff and hence, less funding. We could treat the Windsor project as an experiment to assess the new technology. The community, the board, management and the staff of the CBC all wanted the same thing; what could possibly stand in the way?

There was, in fact, a major obstacle: "union jurisdiction". Journalistic and technical functions at the CBC were handled by different unions. The multi-skilling needed to take full advantage of the new technology required new work methods that crossed traditional jurisdictional boundaries. Union jurisdiction is a legitimate tool for protecting jobs. Rapid technological change, however, can make existing jurisdictional rules obsolete and illogical – just when unions are focussed on the preservation of jobs in the face of technological development. This conundrum placed unions and management in a potential lose-lose situation where a stalemate could be avoided only with goodwill and leadership on both sides.

Negotiations to beat the odds and find a mutually acceptable solution began in 1993 and intensified by early 1994. The unions wanted to find a compromise, but they did not want to give up their traditional rights. They also saw an opportunity to promote the concept of some form of co-management whereby they could play a more influential role in implementing the changes in work methods. To reach a deal, they would have to make uncomfortable concessions on jurisdiction and convince their members that such changes were in their best interest – not an easy sell when more budget cuts were looming ahead.

Management was in its own bind. In addition to the multi-skilling in television, we wanted more flexibility in radio, to introduce new digital workstations that would eliminate the need for tape editing and greatly simplify radio production. Some members of television management were ready to drop this demand in order to gain on the television front. It was an unfortunate characteristic of the CBC that when one sector wanted something very badly, it often showed an unseemly willingness to sacrifice the interests of other sectors of the corporation. Balancing the often competing interests of all the different parts of the CBC is the natural role of senior management; that is why Pierre Juneau, Gérard Veilleux and I, during our respective terms, insisted that union negotiations be centralized under control of head office.

Negotiations were concluded on February 7, 1994, after a tough seven-hour negotiating session. Both the management group and the union leadership found a way to rise above their narrow, short-term interests and see things from a longer and broader perspective. Unions and management would share the decision-making as the new work models were implemented, and we would treat this collaboration as an experiment, to be jointly evaluated. The arrangement would give the unions more power than they had ever enjoyed; in fact, several members of management and the board were legitimately concerned about giving up too many management rights. The unions wanted this arrangement to become part of their collective agreement, which meant it would be subject to grievance and ultimately, to external arbitration. I felt that grievance and external arbitration were incompatible with the concept of joint management and held firm. Eventually, a compromise was reached. The arrangement would be included in the collective agreement, but there would be no recourse to grievance or arbitration. Both management and unions wanted the experiment to succeed; therefore I had good reasons to be optimistic.

In the rapidly evolving broadcasting environment, new technological developments meant that, while over the air broadcasting would continue to be important, a much larger number of channels could be made available by cable or satellite. The net result of this new and exciting multi-channel universe would be greater audience choice but also significant audience fragmentation. This phenomenon would affect all broadcasters, including the CBC.

The only logical strategy for dealing with audience fragmentation was to develop a series of specialty channels. The CBC had already taken the first step in 1989, by launching Newsworld, a 24 hour news channel on cable. We also wanted to launch a similar news channel in French, but the economics were more of a challenge because of the smaller population. Work was also underway on plans for headline news, performing arts and entertainment channels.[85]

Launching new specialty channels meant they would have to generate sufficient income (from advertising and/or subscription fees) to cover their costs, and obtain a licence from the regulatory authority, the Canadian Radio-television and Telecommunications Commission – the CRTC. Given the money at stake, there was considerable competition for these licences. The CBC faced strong opposition from private interests and for this reason, we formed several partnerships with the private sector. In the case of the French language news channel RDI (Réseau de l'Information), we were successful. In the case of the performing arts channel, we were partnering with Bell Canada, but the National Arts Centre had submitted a competing application. Unfortunately, despite our best efforts to join forces with the NAC, we were unable to find common ground and the licence was awarded to another private sector entity. The failure of these two prominent cultural organizations (the CBC and NAC) to create together an exciting performing arts service was a sad loss to Canadian culture that could and should have been avoided.

The CRTC continued to demonstrate a lack of appreciation of the fact that new channels were important to the CBC's survival in the multi-channel universe. Through strategic alliances and by building on our existing infrastructure, we were confident of our ability to offer attractive new services without placing undue pressure on the corporation's finances. Basically, the CRTC saw new channels for the CBC as cost centres, while we saw them as profit centres. At any rate, the CRTC did grant a licence for "Showcase", an entertainment channel featuring Canadian productions, in which the CBC had a minority interest, in partnership with Alliance Communications.

As I have already stated, federal governments often perceived a sovereigntist bias in the CBC's French language information programming. Bias, of course, is somewhat subjective. Its perception depends in part on the audience's own bias. For example, in 1994 Prime Minister Jean Chretien stated in the

House of Commons that "the CBC should inform people on the advantages of Canada". As an immigrant who greatly appreciated the many opportunities that Canada had given me, I was personally quite sympathetic and in harmony with the idea that, as Canadians, we should certainly be aware of the many advantages that we enjoy. But, as the head of Canada's public broadcaster, I saw real danger in expecting the CBC to "inform people of the advantages of Canada" in the context of a looming referendum on Québec independence. The CBC's credibility, as an objective and credible news organization, would have suffered a serious blow.

In fact, had I agreed without qualification with the prime minister's comments, I would have been accused of allowing the CBC to be used as a political propaganda tool. Henceforth anytime someone perceived our news coverage to favour the "federalist option", the sovereigntists could be expected to claim that Manera was directing his journalists to promote the federal government's view. On the other hand, if I had dismissed the prime minister's statement out of hand, federalists' fears that the CBC's French-language news was biased against Canadian unity would have been strengthened.

I was in the kind of lose-lose situation that clever people try to avoid. But I couldn't really duck the question, since it was bound to arise sooner or later, so I decided to comment publicly. My position was that bringing out the advantages of Canada would be a consequence of providing objective reporting. By giving all Canadians reliable information about all parts of Canada, as the CBC did, we would enable them to better understand each other and this ultimately could contribute to greater national unity. My comments were reported on the CBC's French Television network under the headline "CBC president Tony Manera contradicts the Prime Minister". This was not the headline I had sought, but upon reflection, I felt it was as good as any to distinguish the CBC, as a public broadcaster, from a state broadcaster.

In any event, Québec sovereigntists were pursuing their objective through a democratic process. The people of Québec had elected sovereigntist governments on more than one occasion and at the time, the sovereigntist Bloc Québecois, led by Lucien Bouchard, formed the official opposition in the Canadian Parliament.

The CBC's arm's length relationship with the federal government was further tested on other occasions when attempts were made to influence a senior appointment as well as the journalistic coverage of the ongoing debate involving Québec sovereignty. The candidate I was planning to name to a senior position was viewed as politically biased in favour of Québec sovereignty, an opinion not supported by any evidence. The individual in question, with whom I had worked closely for a number of years, was a professional of the highest integrity whose behaviour had never been tainted by political partisanship.

With regard to the appointment, I was told that, if I went ahead with my plan, every door to the government would be closed to me from then on. I was shocked by the tone of this threat. I did not want to antagonize the cabinet, given that the CBC was dependent on the government for the bulk of its funding. But I also had a responsibility to shield the CBC from any type of political interference in its operations.

I never asked anyone that I was considering for an appointment about their political views. To do so would have amounted to a form of McCarthyism, where people were blacklisted on the mere suspicion that they were communist sympathizers, a very sorry chapter in American history. My position was that people's political views were not material unless they advocated the violent overthrow of the government.

I explained my displeasure to Eddie Goldenberg, senior adviser to the prime minister, who had been helpful to me on previous occasions and with whom I enjoyed good relations. He seemed sympathetic to my position. I told him that I was going ahead with the appointment, hoping that he would use his access to the prime minister to smooth things over for me.

What about the threat that all doors would be closed to me in government if I went ahead with the appointment? It never materialized. I had full access to federal cabinet ministers, senior deputy ministers and other government officials, senators and provincial premiers throughout my time as CBC president. I concluded that some ministers had been overzealous in their well-intentioned effort to promote Canadian unity, but that cooler heads had prevailed, recognizing that they had gone too far. At any rate, the matter never came up again.

The first six months of 1994 had been busy and productive. I had filled vacancies for the two key television vice-presidencies and implemented a new streamlined organization structure. The controversy over the scheduling of the CBC's evening national newscast had been resolved[86]. A popular decision to restore late-night local newscasts had been made. We had successfully renewed the television rights for hockey and secured the Canadian broadcasting rights for the 1996 Atlanta Olympics. In addition to the awarding of a new television licence for our French language 24 hour news channel RDI (Reseau de l'Information), the CRTC had also renewed our French and English Television network licenses for five years. The broad elements of a multi-year strategy were in place and, with the "Windsor Enterprise" and other positive union-management initiatives underway, we could look forward to productive times ahead.

At the same time as all this was happening, the parliamentary Standing Committee on Canadian Heritage had been asked by Minister Dupuy to assess and to make recommendations on:

"The role of the CBC in the multichannel universe, including success criteria appropriate to Canada's public broadcaster;

How the CBC planned to provide its mandated services within its projected financial situation; and:

The impact of advertising as a means of funding the CBC and the feasibility of alternative revenue-generating mechanisms that could reduce the corporation's dependence on advertising revenues."

We were scheduled to appear before the Committee in November of 1994 and the summer was to be spent planning our presentation and continuing the bridge-building process. The radio and television vice presidents, together with their programming staff, were concentrating on developing bold and exciting ideas. The parliamentary presentation was to combine all the elements of our thinking about the future in one strategic plan, which would reflect a broad cross-section of input and serve as a blueprint for the next four years.

Patrick Watson resigned as CBC chair in June 1994. In accordance with the Broadcasting Act, I became acting chair, a role that I did not want, but which I performed for the next nine months. On June 16, the Globe and Mail referred to Watson's tenure as "an unrelieved disappointment". This was followed by the characterization of Patrick Watson, Gérard Veilleux and Ivan Fecan as "the triumvirate that ran the country's broadcaster as its excellence eroded, its audience declined and its vision dimmed". The editorial went on to say about Watson that "The Saviour of the CBC was soon seen as its undertaker; no wonder the poor man leaves tired and dispirited". These were strong words and I lost no time rebutting the Globe and Mail's editorial with my own op ed published on June 25, 1994. Not only did I take exception to the cheap shots levelled against Watson, Veilleux and Fecan; I also corrected many of the misconceptions and contradictions printed by the Globe without any of their reporters having interviewed me or any member of my senior staff.

I defended Watson publicly because the attacks on him were unfair. First of all, as board chair, he did not have any executive authority. He chaired board meetings, but his vote counted no more and no less than that of any other director.

Unfortunately, Watson also came to the job of CBC board chair with a set of prejudices from which he never escaped. As he tells it in his autobiography "This Hour Has Seven Decades", he saw the people at head office as a bunch of "manipulators" who stood in the way of the kind of exciting change that he had in mind to revitalize the CBC. Anyone who has seen the brilliant British TV sitcom "Yes Minister", followed by its sequel "Yes, Prime Minister" will recognize the plot. The often indecisive minister Jim Hacker is full of good intentions, but his every move is thwarted by the supreme manipulator Sir Humphrey Appleby, who uses every trick in the book to prevent any initiative that might threaten the status quo.

According to Watson, each new CBC president was quickly "seduced" by sinister head office vice presidents, who were "very adept at taking control of these fly-by-night prime ministerial appointees who were nominally president and CEO of the Corporation, but seen by the entrenched bureaucrats as a bit of a nuisance, slightly politically tainted, outsiders who could, during their fixed term, be managed in such a way that the relatively tranquil long term tenure of those VPs on the sixth floor at 1500 Bronson Avenue[87] would be undisturbed".

Watson's take on how CBC head office operated is difficult to reconcile with reality. When Pierre Juneau became president, he recruited several vice presidents, including those working at the head office, from outside the corporation. He also made several substantive organizational changes throughout the corporation, not all of them popular. Veilleux brought in a new executive vice president, Michael McEwen, who was then vice president for English Radio, not a head office position. In fact, throughout the Juneau, Veilleux and Manera presidencies, there were many changes at the vice presidential level, including the appointment of several individuals from outside the CBC.

Again in his memoirs, Watson tells the reader that "if I were to achieve any of the strategic thrust I had hoped for I was going to have to start a more Machiavellian process of building alliances and destroying enemies". How sad that people dedicated to the cause of public broadcasting would be seen by Watson as "enemies". At any rate, I think that he is being too hard on himself. He was Machiavellian enough for me.

On June 29, 1994, Heritage Minister Dupuy ominously advised me of the possibility there would be further cuts to the CBC's parliamentary appropriation. The scenario described by the minister involved 5% cuts in each of three years beginning in 1995; these cuts would be in addition to the two $50 million cuts we were already expected to absorb. The minister explained that the federal government's deficit had been higher than anticipated, necessitating further cuts across the board. He stressed that CBC was not being singled out and that no final decision had been made.

I was taken aback by this threat, which was to hang like a sword of Damocles over the CBC for several months. Only days earlier, Dupuy had restated the government's commitment of no new cuts to the CBC in a speech he had delivered in Victoria.

Over the next several months I dedicated a great deal of my energy to lobbying against such draconian cuts, which could result in a potential loss of up to 4500 positions and have a catastrophic impact on all the services offered by the CBC.

With the board's concurrence I delivered speeches across the country, met with leaders from the broadcasting, education, business, union and arts sectors, to ensure they all understood what was at stake. I also spoke with several provincial premiers, city mayors, cabinet ministers, senators, senior officials in the federal government and just about anybody else who was prepared to listen.

I was fortunate to be able to rely on the advice of Bill Neville, a member of the CBC board of directors (who had served as special adviser to Prime Ministers Joe Clark and Brian Mulroney). For example, when I contemplated meeting with the caucus of the Liberal party, Neville suggested that I ask for a similar meeting with the caucuses of all other political parties in the House of Commons. I had not considered this because the Liberal party was in power and, thus, were the only party that could make a difference in funding decisions affecting the CBC. But optics are important and I am glad I listened to Bill's advice, as my meeting with the caucus of the Liberal party generated some controversy when Jacques Parizeau, then premier of Québec, called for my resignation! He claimed that, by meeting with the caucus of the

Liberal party, I had compromised the CBC's independence. It was a cheap shot, but it helped me when I pointed out that I had made the same request for a meeting with the caucuses of all political parties represented in Parliament, including the Bloc Québecois. Bill Neville also accompanied me to a meeting with the Hon. Paul Martin, who was then the Minister of Finance. His participation in this crucial meeting added substantial value to my message, even though, in the end, we did not obtain the results we had sought.

One of the cabinet ministers with whom I spoke was André Ouellet. We had a very cordial meeting in his office in the Lester Pearson Building. The discussion was wide ranging, but my object was to get as many cabinet ministers as possible to understand that any further budget cuts to the CBC would cause serious damage to the institution. Ouellet heard me out, but made no commitments. This was appropriate, of course. Final decisions would be made by the entire cabinet at a later date. Before I left his office, he asked me whether the CBC might be prepared to assume the costs of Radio Canada International. This service cost about $15 million per year and had traditionally been funded by the Foreign Affairs department, since it was aimed at an international audience. I thought he was joking. Here I was, trying to make Ouellet aware of how precarious the CBC's situation was, and he wants me to absorb another $15 million? His department, like all other government departments, was being asked to cut back its budget and he was looking for a way to dump the Radio Canada International costs to the CBC. How convenient to be able to reduce his department's budget by transferring a $15 million expenditure to another agency!

In addition to lobbying against further cuts to the CBC budget, I oversaw preparations for the CBC's appearance before the Heritage committee, which took place on November 1, 1994. On

247

that day, my colleagues and I appeared before this committee, armed with a strategic plan called "A New Commitment". This plan embodied three distinct but mutually supportive elements: a program strategy, an accountability strategy and a financial strategy.

My presentation was passionate and sometimes hard-hitting, with a strong personal touch. Briefly, here is what I proposed for the following four years:

"An English TV schedule that would have been 95% Canadian in prime time and 80% Canadian throughout the day;

Expanded regional, national and international coverage in French Television information services; increased opportunities for drama, mini-series and movies;

More emphasis on regional programming and reflecting local concerns as exemplified by additional French radio news bureaux in Prince Edward Island, the Eastern townships and the St. Maurice area;

A new English radio station in Victoria and the development of new services for specialized audiences;

Annual accountability sessions on each of our four networks during which the president and senior managers would hear directly from listeners and viewers and account for the performance of the CBC;

Further efficiencies of $120 million per year with a consequent staff reduction of about 1000; and

Reduced dependence on commercial advertising."

In return, the CBC was asking Parliament to act on the government's commitment: stable funding and an alternative source of funds. We were not seeking more funding, but rather stable funding, dependable and diverse.

In a multi-channel universe, Canada simply had no other medium than the CBC to provide the nation-enriching and nation-building service that we needed to survive as an independent country in spirit as well as in name.

During this Parliamentary Committee hearing, which was broadcast on the parliamentary cable channel, my colleagues and I answered a multitude of questions posed by members of the committee. Afterwards, the national press grilled me on various aspects of the presentation, including whether I would be prepared to implement further budget cuts should they materialize. In response, I did not explicitly threaten to resign, but I made it clear that I would not "preside over the dismantling of the CBC".[88]

National coverage of the committee hearing and subsequent press conference was extensive on radio, television and in print, both English and French. Most of the coverage was either neutral or favourable to the CBC. The Calgary Herald, for example, had this to say: "The rehearsals and Manera's confident manner paid off. Although the committee had heard weeks of complaints about the CBC from other witnesses, none of the parliamentarians, including its most outspoken public broadcasting critics, seriously challenged the presentation". Even Minister Dupuy told me that my presentation had been well received.

In January 1995, Québec Premier Jacques Parizeau launched several commissions that would travel to different parts of Québec to seek citizen input on the issue of sovereignty for Québec. Parizeau was obviously attempting to sell his separatist idea, and he would be using these commissions as a means to help him achieve his objective. In fact, their mandate included the drafting of "A declaration of sovereignty." Hence, there was no question that these so called public consultations were stacked in favour of the sovereignty option.

There were strong concerns by some members of the federal government about the planned coverage of these travelling commissions by RDI (Reseau de l'Information), CBC's French language TV news channel. There was a feeling that, through this coverage, the CBC would be giving Québec Premier Parizeau a platform to deliver his sovereignty propaganda. No cabinet minister ever suggested that CBC coverage should be biased in favour of federalism. But there was a belief that coverage of these commissions by RDI represented a bias in favour of sovereignty. I did not share his view.

I was told that the government would be finalizing budget decisions in the near future, and that I should bear this in mind. Could such remarks be construed as a threat of deeper budget cuts if I didn't comply with the government's wishes? Reading between the lines had been a vital component of my listening skills. In this instance, however, no matter what message I might have perceived, it was quite irrelevant in terms of what measures I should be taking.

What mattered to me was whether there was any credible basis for the argument that my journalists were skewing news coverage in favour of the sovereigntist agenda. I made appropriate enquiries with my people in Montreal and familiarized myself with their planned coverage of these commissions.

The hearings were certainly newsworthy. Not to cover them would have been unthinkable for a journalistic organization. The plan was to provide one hour of coverage each day to the work of these commissions. For a twenty-four news channel, I did not find the one hour time allotment excessive. In the event that any viewer were to perceive our coverage to be biased, the appropriate review processes would come into play.

Had I issued instructions to curtail or eliminate coverage of these commissions, it would have raised legitimate suspicions of political interference. To use my authority in such a fashion could only be justified if I was convinced that a very grave error was being committed, and I would have had to explain and defend such action publicly. I had no evidence on which to base such an action on my part. In all likelihood it would have been counter-productive, giving a boost to the sovereigntist movement. My conclusion was that the coverage of the work of these commissions was appropriate and justified by their news value. I issued no directive nor made any suggestion to alter the planned coverage.

Of course, I understood very well that the stakes for Canada were high. The separatist threat was real, with a referendum on Québec sovereignty looming ahead. So I tried to see things from the federal government's perspective. The prime minister and his cabinet colleagues carried a heavy responsibility. They were trying to keep the country from breaking up. Measures that would be deemed highly improper under normal circumstances might be justified by the extraordinary events then taking place. In fact, there was never any doubt in my mind that ministers in the federal government were acting in what they felt were the best interests of Canada. Having given me the mandate to steer the CBC through these troubled times, I had to demonstrate that I was up to the challenge. No matter how hard I tried to find a way out of my dilemma, however, I couldn't help but feel that the government's strategy was wrong headed on several grounds.

I had been quite direct during my first meeting with Minister Dupuy, on November 11, 1993, when I told him: "You know, Mr. Minister, a free press is an essential ingredient of democracy. This means that, from time to time, the CBC's reporting is bound to displease some ministers, and that is why Parliament has passed laws to guarantee the independence of the CBC". Dupuy's response had been unequivocal. He said he understood fully the need for journalistic independence and the "arm's length" principle of management, and he accepted gladly that from time to time he would have to defend the CBC against criticisms from his colleagues in cabinet and caucus. Now, I began to wonder whether I could still rely on that earlier assurance.

It was my view that the government was missing the boat by not making use of the fact that the French language services of the CBC, commonly referred to as Radio-Canada, were highly popular in Québec. One of the arguments advanced by the sovereigntists was that only an independent Québec could ensure the survival of the French language and culture. It would have been relatively easy to challenge such a notion by pointing out the key role played by Radio-Canada over the previous sixty years or so in fostering the use of French and in the development of the Québécois culture. Radio-Canada was a federal institution, created by the Parliament of Canada, funded more generously than its English language counterpart (on a per capita basis), managed by a federally appointed board of directors and president. A positive message along these lines could have been very effective in countering one of the most powerful motivators underpinning the Québec sovereignty movement.

My personal views on how Canada should approach the Québec sovereignty issue were published in an opinion article in the Ottawa Citizen several years later.[89]

In that article, I was critical of the leadership of all three federal political parties for their failure to adopt a united position on the issue of Québec sovereignty. They seemed more interested in scoring political points than in addressing the issues.

As the sovereignty movement evolved from its sometimes violent beginnings, to its blaming of Canada for every problem facing Québec, to an acknowledgement that Canada was not such a bad country after all but that Québec could do better on its own, to an acceptance (at least by Jacques Parizeau) that any future referendum should have a clear question, the federalist position has oscillated between demonization of separatists to panic to complacency. This incoherence has not helped the federalist cause.

It was my view then, and remains so now that federalist leaders should adopt a strategy along the following lines:

1. Stop demonizing the sovereignty movement. After all, the sovereigntists have pledged to reach their goal through democratic means. You can't win hearts and minds by attacking millions of Quebeckers who support sovereignty. It's wrong and bad political strategy to attack such a large part of the population.
2. Remind Quebeckers that a "Yes" vote to a clear question in favour of Quebec separation will not authorize Québec to declare itself a sovereign country. It will still be a part of Canada until negotiations with the rest of Canada have been concluded. Of course, in accordance with the Supreme Court decision, both parties will have an obligation to negotiate the terms of Québec's separation in good faith. No one should be under any illusion that these negotiations will be easy, but at the same time, we should

253

not be telling Quebeckers that a vote for separation will necessarily result in catastrophic consequences. It isn't true, and Quebeckers won't buy it anyway.

3. Québec and the rest of Canada can achieve more by remaining together than by splitting up. What would a sovereign Québec do to preserve the French language and culture that being part of Canada prevents it from doing?

4. What kind of example would we set for the rest of the world if an advanced, civilized, democratic, and modern industrial society like Canada is unable to accommodate differences in language and culture?

A positive message, delivered consistently by all federalist parties, could go a long way to achieve winning conditions for a strong and unique Québec identity within a strong and united Canada.

The federal government's discomfort with separatists within the CBC's French language services was not new. In 1969 then Prime Minister Pierre Elliott Trudeau had threatened to put the CBC's French network under some form of trusteeship if "separatist propaganda" was allowed to continue. He had condemned what he saw as "the use of public funds by the CBC to destroy the country."

I do not know whether Trudeau's views in 1969 were supported by the facts. It is possible that he had valid grounds for his concerns. I can only speak with knowledge about events that took place during my watch and can state without reservation that I saw no evidence, nor was any evidence brought to my attention, that anyone was abusing his/her position for politically partisan purposes. As far as Trudeau's public outburst in 1969, there is an interesting account of how then CBC President George Davidson handled it in Knowlton Nash's book."[90] Davidson responded by saying: "Mr. Trudeau is a taxpayer and he's got the same right to express his opinion about the CBC as any other taxpayer. And we'll pay the same amount of attention to his comments as to any comment we get." Upon learning of Davidson's response, Trudeau telephoned to congratulate him!

In November 1994, my wife and I attended a reception at Rideau Hall in connection with the annual Governor General Performing Arts Awards. There we met and chatted with the former prime minister. As soon as I introduced myself as President of the CBC, Trudeau, without any prompting, told me that his minister of communications, Gérard Pelletier, who was responsible for the CBC, had been quite forceful in admonishing him never to interfere in the operations of the CBC! This is entirely consistent with Knowlton Nash's account. Perhaps it's a stretch to read between the lines of Pierre Trudeau's comments to me, but I like to think that it was his way to express regret for his 1969 remarks.

By the fall of 1994, several CBC board members had reached the conclusion that the government was unlikely to spare the CBC from the deep budget cuts that were forthcoming. There was a general feeling within the board that we needed to plan for the worst case scenario. It took me a bit longer to reach a similar conclusion and I eventually organized a working group to develop various options that would have to be considered if the government failed to honour its earlier financial commitments to the CBC. It's fair to say that, although I set up the process, my heart wasn't in it.

Meanwhile, Minister Dupuy kept telling me that no final decisions had been taken and that he was still fighting on behalf of the CBC to ensure that it would enjoy a "privileged position". The signals we were getting from all other sources, however, were not at all encouraging. On November 25, 1994 I requested a meeting with the prime minister, pointing out that my ability to do my job depended not only on my management skills, but also on my credibility with the public and with my staff if the commitments made by the government on which I had relied, were not honoured.

Staff morale at the CBC concerned me deeply. I had always told my employees the truth. I wanted very much to sound optimistic, but could I do that and still feel I was being honest with them? It was a difficult balancing act.

The pressure at work was bad enough, but I was also coping with the fact that my father was dying. There was a strong likelihood that the government would break its promise on stable funding for the CBC, in which case I saw no choice but to resign.

I discussed my request for a meeting with the prime minister with Eddie Goldenberg, his senior adviser. I continued to have good relations with Eddie. He indicated that such a meeting could take place, but only after budget details had been finalized. I had heard rumours that "Manera is not putting anything on the table," suggesting that I should offer to make cuts. That would have let the government off the hook, something that I was not prepared to do. It caused me to recall something that US President Teddy Roosevelt had said: *"The importance of a promise lies not in making it, but in keeping it."*

Towards the end of January 1995, I received a late-night phone call at home from David Dodge, the deputy minister of finance. He confirmed budget cuts of 5 percent to the CBC appropriation in each of the next three years, in addition to the $100 million cuts that had been announced by the previous government. He saw no possibility of additional revenue sources materializing. He also told me that there was no reason to keep this information confidential. Various government departments had already announced their cuts and he thought it made sense for the CBC to do the same.

On February 9, 1995, I told Eddie Goldenberg that I would be resigning. Eddie tried his best to talk me out of resigning, as did Privy Council Clerk Jocelyne Bourgon when I met with her on February 13. Both conveyed the prime minister's wish that I stay. Just a few days earlier (February 7), in response to Parizeau's call for my resignation, the prime minister had said in the House of Commons: "I have every confidence in Mr. Manera. He is an experienced man, he's been working at the CBC for a long time. He of course must defend the CBC." Notwithstanding his expressed confidence in me, the prime minister never replied to my request for a meeting with him.

Goldenberg asked me to hold my resignation until Chretien was ready to announce my successor. I agreed, even though I was very uncomfortable with not being able to tell my board of directors. However, I made it clear that I would not stay beyond March 31. I also felt that my board should have at least one month's notice. This meant that I would have to make my resignation public not later than the end of February.

At 3 p.m. on February 27, 1995, I met with Canadian Heritage Deputy Minister Marc Rochon, who handed me a written document outlining the budget levels for the CBC over the next three years.[91] The cuts were identical to the "hypothetical" scenario that Dupuy had described during our meeting of June 29, 1994, when he first advised me of the program review exercise. The only surprise for me was the further elimination of the annual $15 million appropriation for Radio Canada International. This is what Minister Ouellet had suggested a few months earlier when I had met with him. Upon leaving Marc Rochon's office, I personally delivered my letter of resignation to the prime minister's office.

My resignation was the leading item in most major national Canadian newspapers, newsmagazines, TV and radio networks. Naturally, Dupuy, Martin and Chretien were questioned by the media about the CBC cuts.[92] In response, there was evasion, obfuscation and denial. I have never been able to understand how the government's communication strategy could have been so amateurish. What was wrong with saying something to the effect that the government would be unable to honour its budget commitments to the CBC because the country's finances were in such bad shape that drastic measures were necessary? It would have been a more credible explanation than the nonsense that was being spouted in Parliament and elsewhere. I think that more damage is done when politicians deny that a particular promise has been broken than the actual failure to keep that promise. I expanded more fully on my decision in a French language television interview on Radio Canada.[93]

After ten years with the CBC, my gut wrenching decision to resign as its president was more painful than any other in my professional career. I wanted very much to build on the foundation laid by my immediate predecessors, Veilleux and Juneau, a CBC that was an instrument of nation building that would allow all Canadians to share experiences and perspectives in an increasingly inter-dependent world. From the beginning of my tenure as president, I was confident that a climate where creativity would thrive could be created and sustained. The "Windsor Enterprise" had demonstrated that it was indeed possible to "build bridges" between management, employees and their unions. This singular achievement had prepared the ground for further collaborative and exciting projects with other partners from private and public sectors. The key ingredient was a shared commitment to inform, enlighten and entertain audiences from a Canadian perspective.

Despite the inner turmoil that tormented me, it felt good to know that, at no time during my watch, had the independence of the CBC been breached. On a personal level, there was great sadness at not having been able to realize all that could have been achieved. But there was also a certain sense of serenity in the knowledge that I had given all the energy and commitment to the cause of public broadcasting that I could muster.

About a week after the announcement of my resignation[94], I told my dad about it. He was then hospitalized and close to the end of his life. He thought that was a good thing since, from now on, I wouldn't have to get up early every morning. I had not shared with him the details of what was happening with my job, in order not to add to his suffering. However, he saw a copy of MACLEAN'S magazine in one of the hospital's waiting rooms. It carried a full page article on my resignation, with my picture in the centre. The article's title was "And now, bad news." It was good that my father didn't ask me to explain what that meant.

CHAPTER FOURTEEN

I became officially retired on April 1, 1995. A few days later, I gave a speech at the prestigious Canadian Club in Toronto.[95] While many of the details in this speech are now dated, the central points in it continue to be relevant.

After the speech, I walked over to the CBC building where a reception was held for me by the Toronto staff. The reception, which was attended by many of the CBC's on air personalities, as well as managers and other staff, was very touching, as each member wrote a brief message in a book that was later presented to me. I will always treasure that book, as well as the hundreds of messages that I received not only from CBC employees, but also from many Canadians from all walks of life.

One such a message was from Ontario Premier Bob Rae. He called to express his dismay at the federal government's decision to dramatically cut the CBC's budget, despite earlier commitments not to do so. He invited me to meet with him at Queen's Park, which I did shortly after. He was nearing the end of his term and indicated that this prevented him from offering me some type of appointment. I appreciated his gesture, but it was not my intention to seek any appointment at that time. Parenthetically, I have always felt that Rae has gotten a bum rap for his handling of the worst recession since the Great Depression that hit Ontario during his time as premier. His social contract, and resulting "Rae days" saved many jobs, as did his rescue of Algoma Steel from bankruptcy. But life is not always fair, and despite his good intentions, Rae suffered politically from circumstances over which he had little or no control.

Over the years after my departure from the CBC, I have continued to advocate on its behalf. Usually, after leaving an organization, most people move on and don`t give much thought to what happens to their former employer. For some reason, although I have certainly moved on, I haven`t been able to let go. I have remained involved through speeches and press interviews, writing opinion articles and letters to the editor, giving guest lectures at Carleton University and making presentations to Parliamentary committees. Here are a few highlights:

In January 1997, I joined forces with three of my predecessors (Pierre Juneau, Al Johnson and Laurent Picard), in writing an opinion article "To save the CBC", published by the Globe and Mail and a French language version "Crise sans précédent à Radio-Canada", published by La Presse.

At least one of my interventions (supported by Pierre Juneau) seems to have had a positive impact. In 1998 the Liberal government   introduced Bill C-44, which would have given it the power to fire the president and directors of the CBC without cause. Had such a bill been enacted into law, it would have dealt a serious blow to the independence of the CBC. Through our strong opposition to these measures, Juneau and I were able to mobilize sufficient media and public support to cause the government to withdraw its proposed legislation.

After the successful battle against Bill C-44, I decided that I would no longer speak about the CBC. I had been gone for three years and felt that it was time for someone else to take up the cause of public broadcasting. But my pledge was short lived, because in 2005 there was a lockout by the CBC of its unionized employees. I was quite concerned about this development and tried to be helpful behind the scenes, without taking sides. Eventually, the impasse was resolved and I urged, through opinion articles and media interviews, employees and managers to set aside their differences and focus all their energy on delivering the best possible programs.

In 2006, a new Conservative government was in power. I wrote and the Ottawa Citizen published an opinion article arguing for changes to the CBC's governance that would enable the board to appoint the CBC president. I also recommended that board appointments be depoliticized and that two employees be added, in order to contribute their knowledge and expertise to the development of board policies and strategies. I have continued to advocate these measures on several subsequent occasions. Later the same year, in another opinion article, also published by the Ottawa Citizen, I suggested that the CBC should no longer bid on hockey rights, allowing the private sector to take over. This was a major departure from my earlier position that the CBC should continue to carry Hockey Night in Canada. I realized that it was only a matter of time before private interests, with much deeper pockets than the CBC, would outbid it for the hockey rights. I felt that it was much better if the CBC were to accept this reality before it came to pass. It eventually happened, of course, at a time and under circumstances which were not favourable to the CBC.

In 2007, former CBC board member Bill Neville and I collaborated in a presentation to the Parliamentary Committee on Canadian Heritage that was studying the role of the CBC. We worked hard for several weeks on this presentation, with valuable assistance from Paul Gaffney and Dr. Abraham Tarasofsky[96]. Our presentation was well received. We made specific recommendations on programming, funding and governance.

Many of those recommendations are still pertinent, but the rapid expansion of Internet based platforms provides new challenges as well as new opportunities for the CBC. It is now possible, for example, to think in terms of subscriber paid premium services streamed to a properly equipped television set to supplement the basic CBC services. We are in a transition stage, where some experimentation with different digital delivery models is taking place. Nevertheless, it's important to keep in mind that content is what matters. Production methods and delivery models are means to an end, not ends in themselves.

I was not alone in pointing out government attempts to breach the CBC's independence. In 2010, Tim Casgrain, appointed chair of the CBC board by Prime Minister Stephen Harper, wrote a sharply worded letter to the prime minister in which he slammed Tory attacks, saying that the Conservatives had disparaged the public broadcaster and that such attacks on the CBC had been wilfully destructive, undermining its independence. Casgrain warned the party and government MPs against intruding on the broadcaster's independence as they sought to influence the content of programming. He went on to point out that the government came dangerously close to intruding on the independence of the broadcaster when it sought to influence the content of programming or determine whose views would or would not be represented on its airwaves.

Casgrain's term on the CBC board, which ended in 2012, was not renewed. That same year, the CBC's budget was cut by $115 million over three years, resulting in the loss of another 600 jobs.

In 2013, the federal government introduced Bill C-60, which gave Treasury Board the power to interfere in the CBC's union negotiations. Once more, I felt compelled to publicly intervene, pointing out that such a measure represented a breach of the arm's length relationship between the CBC and the government of the day. Sadly, the bill passed and remains in place. It was one of several issues that I raised with the Senate Committee on Transportation and Communications during a hearing in June 2014. The Committee's report, which came out in 2015, was a huge disappointment. I called it a "Blueprint for Marginalizing the CBC" in an opinion article published by the Ottawa Citizen.

On May 17, 2016, in yet another opinion article published by the Ottawa Citizen, I took the CBC board to task for what I considered poor leadership during its time in office. The highly politicized board had failed the CBC and, by extension, the Canadian people. It had not spoken out publicly on behalf of the CBC. Its 2020 strategic plan was woefully inadequate in terms of the CBC's information programming goals.

As this is being written, there is a new government in Ottawa. It has restored some of the funding cut from the CBC in prior years and appears open to the revitalization of this important institution. I hope that it follows through and that I will no longer feel compelled to speak out on behalf of the CBC.

CHAPTER FIFTEEN

In keeping with Benjamin Franklin's philosophy that *"There is nothing wrong with retirement, as long as it doesn't interfere with work,"* I created a consulting corporation in 1995, called Manera Consulting Inc. and proceeded to seek consulting work. My first contract was with the National Arts Centre, on whose board I had previously served. Over the next seven years, I was fortunate to land several other interesting assignments in the fields of broadcasting, education and human resources.

Three projects were particularly significant. One was for the Telelatino Television Network in Toronto. At the request of the proprietors, I reviewed their entire operation and advised them on organization, staffing and negotiations with the Italian public radio and television network (RAI), which supplied a lot of their Italian language programming, as well as with the Shaw Cable Company, which was interested in acquiring a share of this business. My report was well received by the partners and they invited me to serve on their board. Over the next several months I made numerous trips to Toronto and continued to advise them until Shaw bought a share of the company. This project gave me an opportunity to be involved with a group of Italian speaking individuals (all our board meetings, which I chaired, were conducted in Italian,) and to re-connect with the Italian-Canadian community.

Another project involved advising the Polish National Broadcasting Council in Warsaw. Poland was still in the process of freeing itself from the shackles of communism. I gave several seminars on journalistic practices (making extensive use of the CBC journalistic policies) and the potential challenges and benefits of the new digital technology that would soon be coming on stream.

My entire experience on this assignment was very positive, constructive and quite enjoyable. The Polish people, who suffered under the tyranny of communism for many years, were eager to make the transition to a free society. I was amazed at their love of music, which I shared. Every evening I was taken to a concert or opera! I even got to visit the house where Chopin was born!

While in Poland, I also visited Krakow and the nearby former German concentration camp at Auschwitz-Birkenau. It is impossible to describe the feeling one gets when walking through the camp, the many remaining structures, the gas chambers and the walls against which prisoners were shot. Over one million people, mostly Jews, were killed here by the Nazis. For several years, thousands of people were murdered here every day. When the camp was finally liberated by the Allies, only 7000 people remained alive, most of them looking like walking skeletons. Slave labour, starvation, torture and murder represent the legacy of one of the most cruel and inhumane regimes in world history. One cannot remain indifferent to such barbarism and the incomprehensible human suffering that it caused. There are many exhibits of old shoes, clothing, eyeglasses, suitcases and other meagre possessions of the people who died here. There are also a number of memorials, the most touching for me being that created by the Italian government (perhaps because it was written in my mother tongue). It speaks to the incomprehensible horror of what took place here, with great eloquence and sensitivity, exhorting all who see it to ensure that no such horror is ever repeated. Unfortunately, many similar horrors have continued to take place throughout the world during the time since Auschwitz-Birkenau was in operation, and continue to this day. As I completed my tour and walked out back to the car, I knew that this experience would have a lasting impact on me.

My third major assignment was for the Public Service Commission of the Canadian federal government. It involved interviewing promising candidates for future promotion to the assistant deputy minister level. Many retirements were expected, and the government wanted to create a pool of pre-qualified individuals who might be called upon to assume greater responsibilities. I conducted a three to four hour interview with each candidate and then wrote a lengthy report on their strengths and weaknesses. This was immensely interesting work. I carried out over one hundred such interviews and got to meet many very talented individuals. I also developed a greater knowledge and appreciation for the many important functions of the Canadian federal government.

On a personal note, my father died on April 18, 1995. It was a very sad occasion, as are all deaths of close family members. But he had lived to the age of 80, and had not suffered excessive pain during his last days. His life had been simple, devoted to God and to his family. He had worked hard and honestly. He was loved and respected not only by his family, but also by the many people who had known him. Many visitors came to pay their respects at the funeral home, including several of my former colleagues from the CBC and old friends from our Montreal days. Deborah wrote a very moving obituary for the local newspaper.

My mother, who was 82 at the time, continued to live in the apartment she had shared with my father. Although Lella and Deborah helped her out in many ways, she was still relatively independent and did her own shopping and cooking.

Deborah had bought her own apartment a few years earlier and was making excellent progress in her chosen career of human resources. Andrew was still at home, working part time at a grocery store while attending Carleton University. He received his Bachelor's degree in Economics and Law in 1995.

In May 1995, Lella and I made a short trip to Naples, Florida, where we had previously re-established contact with our friend Pasquale Siravo from our California days and his partner Jane. Knowlton Nash, former CBC anchor and his wife Lorraine had a home in Naples and they had recommended the area to us. And so we bought a condominium in Naples, where we spent most of the winter over the next seven years. A photo of Lella and me in our Florida condo is shown below.

As I have already mentioned, my mother had a half-brother, Basilio Galluccio, who had emigrated to the US in 1913. For many years he had written to his mother and other family members back in Sicily, but at some point, they had lost track of each other. When I visited New York in the early 70's, I tried to track him down without success. But in 1996 we had a new tool, the Internet, which enabled me to discover that he had died in 1980 in Poughkeepsie, NY. Soon I was talking by telephone with one of his daughters, Virginia Francese, who was excited to learn that she had an aunt (my mother) living only a few hundred miles from her. She made arrangements to come to Canada where she was able to meet my mother and the rest of our family. The two of them embraced and couldn't stop crying. It was truly a joyous occasion. Virginia was a wonderful person and my mother couldn't have been happier to meet her. Eventually she came back for a second visit with her sister Mary. The dream of a lifetime had been realized. Had the Internet existed in the early 70's, I might have been able to locate my mother's half-brother while he was still alive. Apparently he was, like me, an opera fan and I am sure that we would have had a great time together.

During the late nineties mom began to experience a number of health problems and had to be hospitalized a few times. We made an attempt to have her stay with us in our home since she was obviously no longer able to live alone. But despite Lella's devoted care and support, it was clear that mom, who could be quite stubborn, needed an environment where professional care would be available around the clock. Meanwhile, an Italian Canadian community group had been raising funds to build a nursing home for elderly Italian-Canadians and mom became one of the first residents at Villa Marconi. Her spacious room had a large window sill where she could have many plants in containers, facing the garden below.

The staff at Villa Marconi had many dedicated individuals, including several who spoke Italian, and who took very good care of mom. Of course, we visited often, bringing her to our home for lunch every Sunday and generally making sure that all her needs were met.

Mom celebrated her ninetieth birthday on October 4, 2002. The event was attended by many of her friends, including some who travelled from Montreal, and all of our family. While she had some bad days, most of the time she was quite cheerful and full of spunk. Her short term memory had declined but she remembered past events reasonably well, although she would sometimes get the details mixed up. Her reasoning capacity and sharp wit remained relatively good for quite some time. She passed away peacefully at the age of 96 in November 2008.

The year 2002 involved several transitions, including the termination of my consulting practice. I had been working for nearly fifty years and decided that I should dedicate my remaining time to family and as a volunteer on several community boards. I had previously served on the board of Algonquin College and the Education Quality and Accountability Office for the Province of Ontario.

I now became a member of the board of governors of the Ottawa Hospital, a large teaching and research hospital. This enabled me to work with several outstanding individuals in senior management and at the board level, all dedicated to providing high quality health care to the community. My life-long love of books and music provided the impetus for serving on the board of directors of the Ottawa Public Library and Opera Lyra.

That same year, Lella and I sold our Florida condo. Although we enjoyed spending our winters there, we wanted to travel to other places. The Florida condo tied us down somewhat. We also had to fly back several times during the winter, in order to spend time with my mother. We sold our big house in Nepean. Our children had places of their own, hence the house was too big for Lella and me. The heater in my greenhouse had failed during the time when we were in Florida and I had lost all my prized plants. Although I got the heater repaired, I didn't have the stamina to start all over again. Maintaining the yard also became more of a challenge, as I began to experience more problems with my back and knees.

We found a very nice condo overlooking a golf course in Kanata. It was large enough for our needs but not so large as to be a burden. We had great neighbours and enjoyed the surroundings.

Although living in a condo had its advantages, I missed the pleasures (yes, even the back aches) of gardening. So it was that, during a sunny winter day in 2008, Lella and I ventured into an open house not far from where we lived and discovered a beautiful bungalow for sale. We bought it on the spot! We have never regretted this decision. Our bungalow has sufficient yard space for me to indulge in my love of gardening. In fact, with an attached sunroom and grow lights in the basement, I am able to garden year round! There is nothing more relaxing than to be sitting in my sunroom on a sunny winter day, sipping a martini, surrounded by flowering hibiscus and agave plants, while listening to my favourite music, against the backdrop of the snow covered woods outside.

Our daughter Deborah and son Andrew have continued to make us proud not only in terms of their career successes, but also in terms of the truly caring and wonderful persons that they both are. Andrew and Lena were married in 2005, which was a truly joyous occasion for all of us; we are very fond of Lena, who is like a daughter to us. Both children of my sister Ester and her husband Bill also married, and we were delighted to be a part of their celebrations.

Lella and I have taken several trips to Italy, Florida, California, Peterborough, Montreal, and the Niagara peninsula, where we still have family and friends. We celebrated our 50th wedding anniversary with a Caribbean cruise, and later enjoyed a Mediterrenean cruise, accompanied by our daughter Deborah.

In January 2010, we were blessed by the arrival of our grand-daughter Brianna Grace. She has enriched our life immeasurably and we are most grateful to see her develop as a bright, happy and affectionate child. This was followed by the arrival of our second grand-daughter Brittany in April 2013, who promises to be just as wonderful as her sister.

I don't know what the future holds, but I look back with gratitude and happiness at the interesting and rewarding life that my family and I have been privileged to enjoy. Now in my 77th year, I can honestly say that I did what I could, with what I had, wherever I was.

FOOTNOTES

[1] Either the English language name (CANADIAN BROADCASTING CORPORATION) or the French language name (SOCIÉTÉ RADIO-CANADA) may be used to describe the entire corporation. Since these memoirs are being written in English, I will generally use CBC as the name of Canada's public broadcaster. There will be occasions, however, when I use Radio-Canada to stress that I am talking exclusively about the French language services of the CBC.

[2] One of his sons (brother to my father) had his picture taken sitting down in the town square while holding a newspaper, pretending to be reading it. One of his friends poked fun at him: "Who are you trying to impress? We all know you can't read – you're even holding the newspaper upside down". Without missing a beat, he replied: "Those of us who can read can do so right side up or upside down – it doesn't matter"!

[3] It was considered a sign of respect to name one's first-born after one's father if male. My father had wanted to name me Sebastiano as well, but the municipal government would not allow it. One of his other brothers had already named his first-born Sebastiano. Years after I was born, however, another one of his brothers succeeded in naming his first male child Sebastiano!

[4] He had learned how to read during his military draft period.

[5] We assumed these English language speakers were American, but there were probably some Canadian and British visitors as well.

[6] At the time, I had no way of knowing that a few blocks from where we were staying there lived a fourteen year old girl named Raffaella Marchesini who seven years later would become my wife.

[7] Many years later I would learn about anti-Semitism during the Fascist regime in Italy. Mussolini initially favoured discrimination against Jews, but not persecution (these were his own words). During the latter part of WWII, however, Mussolini, who had been Hitler's mentor, had now become his junior and unreliable partner. As Hitler's control of Mussolini became nearly absolute, Italian Jews suffered real persecution, and many ended up in Nazi concentration camps, where they lost their lives.

[8] The whole issue of multiculturalism and reasonable accommodation has generated a great deal of controversy in recent times. My own view is that immigrants need support, either from their own community or from government (or both) during their early years after arriving in the new country, but that they should be encouraged to integrate in the mainstream society as soon as possible.

[9] I could not imagine at the time that many years later, I would not only understand how television worked, but also become president of the CBC, Canada`s national public broadcaster.

[10] I still have a copy of this book, signed by the author.

[11] I had the pleasure of meeting Pierre Berton when he was on "Front Page Challenge" at the CBC.

[12] This is how this shift worked. On Sundays one had to be on duty from 5 p.m. to 1 a.m.; on Mondays from 8 a.m. to 5 p.m.; on Tuesdays from 12 a.m. to 8 a.m. There were only seven hours between the end of one shift and the beginning of the next. After allowing for travel time, eating, showering, etc. there would be less than five hours left for sleeping. By Tuesday morning, having had insufficient sleep on two consecutive nights, one would be extremely fatigued.

[13] My days off were Wednesday and Thursday; the other clerk was off on Tuesday and Wednesday. A simple exchange of days off enabled me to get at least eight hours sleep on Monday night, without any negative impact on the other clerk.

[14] The room cost $6 per night.

[15] I had acquired the barbells in an unsuccessful attempt to develop a more muscular body.

[16] The Immigration authorities had granted me permission to work part time.

[17] My Canadian driver's licence was acceptable in California for a limited time only.

[18] By now, I knew that getting fired did not mean getting shot!

[19] Had I worked in an establishment with a liquor licence, which I did for a brief time when business at Nina's Little Italy had temporarily declined, I could have earned a lot more money. I knew several waiters who were lucky enough to land such jobs; they drove Cadillacs and owned large homes.

[20] That's what "flight attendants" were called in 1958.

[21] The term "African-American" was not used at the time.

[22] This was not a deliberate strategy on my part. It just worked out this way.

[23] I scored in the top 25% in the engineering part, top 10% in the verbal aptitude part and top 5% in the quantitative aptitude part.

[24] Lella has never shared my passion for opera!

[25] The Canadian Atomic Energy Commission also was interested in hiring me to design transistor circuits at Chalk River, but I decided that teaching was what I really wanted to do.

[26] I never did get a high school diploma!

[27] It was eventually removed.

[28] The federal government had a special grant for buyers who purchased winter built houses. This program was put in place to encourage winter construction, and it helped us with our down payment.

[29] This college would later change its name to "Fleming College".

[30] Nearly thirty years later, I would be appointed a member of the same Council of Regents.

[31] I paid for my own!

[32] Twenty-seven years later, he heard me on a radio interview in Alberta, where he was working. He called me and identified himself, expressing his appreciation for the interest I had taken in his progress at Sir Sandford. That call made my day!

[33] The most useful analogies are those based on money, something that almost everybody understands. Unfortunately, this is not always possible.

[34] I made extensive use of a little known service provided by the US government. The American military produced training manuals, including laboratory experiments in a wide range of technical disciplines. I was able to find a catalogue, and ordered dozens of such manuals that I then passed on to my faculty, to help them develop their own lesson plans and lab experiments. There was no charge by the US government for these materials, not even for the shipping costs!

[35] Twenty-seven years later, I was invited to give a speech to launch the college's new fundraising foundation and Ram was there, still teaching at the college. We gave each other a big bear hug, both very happy to meet again. I had given him a chance to prove himself, and he had not disappointed me. But I never did find out what the "P" stood for!

[36]Ironically, twenty-eight years later I would become chair of Algonquin College's board of governors.

[37] I can think of no greater honour than to be considered "one of us" by other teachers and sometimes wonder whether I would have been happier remaining one!

[38] At Niagara, as had been the case at Confederation, I taught a course in electronics. This created a heavier workload for me, but it also enabled me to speak with credibility about educational issues, and demonstrated that as president, I was not isolated from the challenges faced by faculty and students.

[39] This was not uncommon at the time. Such threats had been received at Confederation College while I worked there. Other colleges were similarly affected.

[40] During the time when I was chairman of the collective bargaining committee for the COP, I expressed the opinion publicly that it would make more sense for each college to bargain individually with its union. This led to a formal complaint by the union to the effect that I had improperly interfered with the collective bargaining process. This was nonsense, of course, and had the complaint proceeded, it would have been found groundless. Instead of allowing this distraction to proceed, the colleges' chief negotiator told the union that there would be no further meetings with them until they withdrew their spurious complaint. The union folded, and things got back on track.

[41] The book sold about 20,000 copies worldwide over fourteen years. I earned substantial royalties which paid for several vacations, a new car and a few items of furniture which we still enjoy. The most satisfying part was the many letters I received from all over the world (the US, Asia, Europe, South America). In 2005, thirty-two years after its first printing, it could still be found in the libraries of hundreds of the most prestigious universities, colleges, corporate and military research facilities, and public libraries in the USA, the UK, Canada, and at least sixteen other countries.

[42] These radio stations must bear some responsibility for the fiasco, for failing to confirm such a serious matter before going on the air with the story.

[43] Until now, I had followed a firm rule that, once someone resigns, and the resignation is accepted, it cannot be revoked. This was based on the belief that it was improper for someone to use the threat of resignation to get their way. This experience, however, taught me that sometimes exceptions may be justified by unusual and compelling circumstances.

[44] While this project was not immediately realized, the college was eventually successful in building a campus in Niagara on the Lake.

45 Over 400 community leaders served on the college's advisory committees.

46 Later renamed president.

47 These are full time equivalent (FTE) numbers.

48 If Langara ever separated, Jock Denholm could reasonably expect to be named as its CEO. Whatever his private feelings on the matter, he was always scrupulously correct in his behaviour, supporting the board's decision to have a single college.

49 Dr. Kennedy was head of the computer department at the University of British Columbia (UBC). An exceptionally talented individual, he was also a person of impeccable integrity, widely admired and respected. He had played a crucial role in the period leading up to the departure of Dr. Gilligan and the management of several difficult issues afterward.

50 Dr. McGeer was on leave from UBC, where he was employed as a professor and medical researcher. He was regarded as a leading authority on Alzheimer disease.

51 In 1994, nine years after I left VCC, the provincial government formally designated Langara College as a separate institution from VCC.

52 I drove Minister McCarthy in my Chevy Vega, which had developed serious rust problems, including a leaky roof. It was raining quite heavily at the time (when does it not rain in Vancouver?) and the Minister, who was sitting in the passenger seat, got wet. I apologized profusely, but she was quite understanding. Soon after, I bought a new car.

53 The real estate agent who showed me this parcel of land was Gordon Campbell, who would later become Vancouver Mayor and eventually Premier of British Columbia.

54 Nathan Divinsky at the time was married to Kim Campbell, who later entered politics and sat in both the BC legislature and the Canadian Parliament. She also served briefly as Canada's first female Prime Minister. Unfortunately for her, in 1993 she led her party to the worst defeat in Canadian political history, winning only two seats (and losing her own) in the election. She had done some part time teaching at VCC, but I got to know her during the time that she served as a trustee on the Vancouver School Board. Our paths crossed on several occasions, including the time when she was a cabinet minister in the Mulroney government.

55 NDP refers to the New Democratic Party.

[56] The amount of $50 million in the early eighties would be equivalent to something well in excess of $150 million as this account is being written, some thirty-five years later.

[57] Bill Vander Zalm went on to serve as Premier of British Columbia from 1986 to 1991.

[58] Also attending the KEC official opening was Vancouver Mayor Mike Harcourt. After the ceremony was over, Minister Smith, Mayor Harcourt and I were chatting together about the coming provincial election. Smith was a minister in the conservative Social Credit (Socred) government, while Harcourt was a member of the left leaning New Democratic Party. The two of them decided to bet $5 each on the outcome of the election. They trusted me enough to hold their combined $10, which I dutifully delivered to the victorious Smith after the election. In a letter thanking me, Smith had this to say: "Delighted as I was at the government's impressive majority, doubling my money at the same time served to sweeten the victory". Years later, Harcourt led the NDP to form the government in BC. And he served as Premier from 1991 to 1996. I enjoyed good relations with both Smith and Harcourt.

[59] I actually preferred teaching night school classes, in part because there was less risk of interference with my "day job", but also because the students were more mature and took their studies much more seriously than the typical day student. At BCIT, virtually every one of my students was already employed in the electronics industry and all were highly motivated. BCIT was also located near my home, which involved very little travel time.

[60] There are times and circumstances in publicly funded organizations when secrecy in the development of various controversial options may be justified for a variety of reasons. Ultimately, it is a judgement call, to be made after due consideration of the risks and benefits.

[61] In the year 2011 the Dutch government formally apologized for this massacre, claiming that the number of people killed was 150. The number of 431 killed came from the local community in Indonesia's Java island.

[62] Aside from attending various college related conferences in Québec, the only opportunities for my speaking French in Vancouver were interviews I gave to the French language CBC radio or television stations.

[63] Ten years later, I would resign as president of the CBC over budget cuts, but the circumstances were altogether different. At the CBC, I had a written commitment by the federal government that no budget cuts would be applied to the CBC beyond those previously announced. At VCC, the provincial government had never made a similar commitment.

[64] Jock was principal of the Langara Campus and had also served as acting CEO of VCC during the period preceding my appointment.

[65] Knowlton Nash – Speech to the Empire Club – April 14, 1994

[66] Anyone who thought that I was leaving the presidency of Vancouver Community College because I was looking for a job where I wouldn't have to cope any longer with the implementation of budget cuts was quickly disabused of this notion.

[67] For readers who are technically inclined, the random number generator that I designed involved a 5 MHz pulse generator. Each pulse was fed to a counter that reset itself automatically after reaching the number 49, which was the largest number that could be picked in the lottery. The count was shown on a numeric display similar to what is found in digital clocks. The "randomness" was achieved by pushing a button that froze the display at whatever number was then being "counted". Since 5 million pulses were being generated and counted each second, this arrangement guaranteed that the number being displayed was random.

[68] His decision in October 1982 to grant Trudeau 15 minutes of air time on three occasions to address the nation on the economic challenges of the time was condemned by both opposition party leaders (Joe Clark of the Progressive Conservative Party and Ed Broadbent of the New Democratic Party), who accused Juneau of political favouritism. When the Progressive Conservative party came to power in 1984 under Prime Minister Brian Mulroney, Juneau was seen as too closely connected to the previous Liberal government. This proved to be a serious handicap during his remaining term at the CBC.

[69] Knowlton Nash. *The Microphone Wars.* McClelland & Stewart Inc., 1994

[70] All vice presidents, including me, supported the final decisions.

[71] The Canadian Revolution by Peter C. Newman; page 358

[72] Marie Poulin was Pierre Racicot's successor.

[73] "Direct CBC fee called unrealistic" – July 25, 1991 – Report on Business

[74] I published a short book "The Greenhouse Effect" in which I describe my experiences building and operating this greenhouse.

[75] Plus $1 million letter of credit which we were able to cash.

[76] Digital technology permits "compression" of a broadcast signal into a narrower slice of the available frequency spectrum.

[77] The earlier legislation provided for an executive vice president selected by the president and board, but subject to approval by the federal cabinet through an order-in-council.

[78] Kim Campbell, although she had lost the election and been defeated in her own riding, was still prime minister on this date. Several CBC board members had been active in her election campaign. Jean Chretien became prime minister on November 4, 1993.

[79] The CBC reported to Parliament through the Minister of Canadian Heritage.

[80] There were three vacancies at the highest vice presidential level: French Television, English Television and my own position, Resources and Administration. I eventually filled all three, two of them with women.

[81] "permanent" in this context meant a full five year term, the maximum period allowed by the Broadcasting Act.

[82] In deference to Canada's constitutional monarchy, the actual order-in-council states that I was appointed president of the CBC by Queen Elizabeth the Second, on the recommendation of Ramon John Hnatyshyn, Governor General of Canada.

[83] A notable exception was J. Alphonse Ouimet (1958-1967), an electrical engineer who was named "Father of Canadian Television" for his leadership role in building the CBC's TV system, then the largest in the world.

[84] "A Dream Betrayed – the battle for the CBC", published by Stoddart Publishing Company in Toronto in 1996.

[85] Several years earlier, the CBC had foreseen the need for multiple outlets and had applied for licences to operate second English and French television services. Unfortunately, the CRTC had turned down those applications amidst concerns that there wouldn't be sufficient production or financial resources to do the job.

[86] During the Veilleux presidency, the national evening television newscast, then called "Prime Time News", had been rescheduled from 10 p.m. to 9 p.m. This change was part of a broader programming strategy that had been supported by all members of CBC senior management, including me. But TV program scheduling is an art, not a science, and sometimes the best planned decisions turn out not to work. This was certainly the case with the scheduling of this TV newscast, which suffered significant audience loss after the change. I came under intense pressure to reverse this decision as soon as I was appointed president. I asked Jim Byrd, English TV vice president, to perform a thorough examination of audience reaction and agreed with his recommendation to return "The National" to its earlier 10 p.m. slot. The Board of Directors approved this change, which also provided for the program to be available on cable at 9 p.m.

[87] This is where head office was located.

[88] A video clip of this hearing is available at
https://www.youtube.com/watch?v=NPYzv0iqhdE

[89] "A Rational Approach to Sovereignty – Jan. 2, 2006

[90] The Microphone Wars, page 392; McClelland & Stewart Inc., 1994

[91] The CBC's parliamentary appropriation of $1,091 million for 1994-95 would be cut to $1,065 million in 1995-96, to $957 million in 1996-97, and $839 million in 1997-98.

[92] Clip available at https://www.youtube.com/watch?v=m0HfQeoOzKM

[93] Clip available at https://www.youtube.com/watch?v=ohsD1v_8q6k

[94] A video of my announcement to CBC staff is available at:

https://www.youtube.com/watch?v=16-uauNaJDw

[95] Audio available at https://www.youtube.com/watch?v=JPj7BmbNhtc

[96] Paul Gaffney was a long time broadcaster and strategic planner with the CBC, while Dr. Abraham Tarasofsky had a long career as an economist in academia and the federal government.

283

65213450R00159

Made in the USA
Charleston, SC
23 December 2016